THE SIGNIFICANCE OF PARALLELS
BETWEEN 2 PETER AND OTHER
EARLY CHRISTIAN LITERATURE

Society of Biblical Literature

Academia Biblica

Saul M. Olyan,
Old Testament Editor

Mark Allan Powell,
New Testament Editor

Number 10

The Significance of Parallels
between 2 Peter and Other
Early Christian Literature

THE SIGNIFICANCE OF PARALLELS BETWEEN 2 PETER AND OTHER EARLY CHRISTIAN LITERATURE

Michael J. Gilmour

Society of Biblical Literature
Atlanta

THE SIGNIFICANCE OF PARALLELS BETWEEN 2 PETER AND OTHER EARLY CHRISTIAN LITERATURE

Library of Congress Cataloging-in-Publication Data

Gilmour, Michael J.
   The significance of parallels between 2 Peter and other early Christian literature / by Michael J. Gilmour.
      p. cm. — (Society of Biblical Literature Academia Biblica ; 10)
   Includes bibliographical references and index.
   ISBN 1-58983-049-0 (pbk. : alk. paper)
   1. Bible. N.T. Peter, 2nd—Criticism, Textual. I. Title. II. Academia Biblica (Series) ; 10.
   BS2795.52 G55 2002b
   227'.93066—dc21

                                                   2002011760

07 06 05 04 03 02   5 4 3 2 1

Printed in the United States of America
on acid-free paper

For Kyla

to whom I would gladly and gallantly
hand my very last piece of gum . . .

CONTENTS

ACKNOWLEDGMENTS

I count myself fortunate to have had such tremendous support from family and friends during my studies. At every step of the way my mother, my brothers and their families, in–laws, and close friends have offered their encouraging words and kind assistance. To them all I express heartfelt thanks.

The editors of *ARC*, *Didaskalia*, and *The Evangelical Quarterly* kindly gave permission to reprint material previously found in those journals. Among my teachers I would like to express my thanks to Dr. Dennis Stoutenburg who taught me that laughter can make any task lighter (a true jokerman!). If I could emulate his commitment to scholarship and his spirituality to even a small degree, I would be satisfied. בתורת יהוה חפצו. Professor Ian Henderson of McGill University offered many helpful suggestions when he read an earlier version of what is now Appendix 1 of this book, originally submitted to him for his seminar on the historical Jesus. And in particular I thank my advisor Professor Frederik Wisse of McGill University whose influence on this project is extensive. Like Prufrock, I am "a bit obtuse." He did much to help sharpen my thoughts along the way and traces of his ideas are found throughout this study well beyond what footnotes indicate.

Finally, none of this would have happened without the constant support, assistance, and friendship of my wife Kyla. This book—originally my dissertation—represents the culmination of a long tradition. If it were not for her help with my school work, I would still be floundering in grade 11 math! This project is gratefully dedicated to her.

CHAPTER 1
INTRODUCTION

Great abilities . . . are not requisite for an Historian; for in historical composition, all the greatest powers of the human mind are quiescent. He has facts ready to his hand; so there is no exercise of invention. Imagination is not required in any high degree; only about as much as is used in the lower kinds of poetry. Some penetration, accuracy, and colouring will fit a man for the task, if he can give the application which is necessary.
> —Samuel Johnson, James Boswell's *Life of Johnson*

1.1 THE TASK OF LOCATING TEXTS

Dr. Johnson is both right and wrong. He is right to downplay the role of invention; the historian's task is not to create history, but to present it. However, he seems to be describing an ideal historical project for which all the necessary data is scattered across the scholar's desk. His or her task is merely to organize these into a coherent presentation without resorting to fanciful reconstruction. Rarely however does such an ideal situation occur. He is wrong therefore to assume that the historical task is a simple one. Because history is not the mere gathering of facts, historians must at times venture into the realm of informed speculation. Beginning with what is known, there must be an attempt to account for the evidence. This thesis is primarily a study of historical method and will examine the situation facing historians when the facts are limited. In particular, it will focus on the possibilities and limitations of determining a context or locating an ancient document in history, on the basis of similarities with and differences from other texts.

For a document to be well understood and appreciated, it must be placed against a larger backdrop: when was it written? why was written? if possible, who wrote it? and so on. Of course this is not to say that reading is meaningless without such information. A piece of poetry of unknown origin may be recognized as a beautiful work of art. A religious, devotional work may inspire the reader, even if it is not known from whence it came. But such reading does not involve an analysis seeking to fill in all that can be known about the text in question or an attempt to extract from that same text all that can be known about the time and place in which it was written.[1] Such is the task of the historian who also reads that poem or religious writing. The document is then approached as evidence for the historical context in which it was written.

At this point historians often face a problem: a context may be needed to illuminate the text though the only access to that historical setting is the writing itself, which does not directly disclose it. Circular reasoning is therefore a real danger: one ends up inferring a context from a text while at the same time explaining the text on the basis of this inferred context. Such a scenario is quite possible in the situation pertaining to early Christianity, for here the data is limited.[2] Historians of this period are often forced into speculative reconstructions of the wider historical contexts, working on the basis of texts, while at the same time hoping to better understand them. Consensus is not easy to achieve and so, to paraphrase Qoheleth, 'To the making of *history* books there is no end.'

The search for contexts in which to place texts is necessarily a search for a larger framework or model that allows the available bits of evidence to be placed in relation to one another.[3] In reading 1 Corinthians and *1 Clement*, for example, one might say that different stages in the church's development can be readily

---

[1]Of course ancient authors were not concerned to answer the questions brought to their work by later historians. On some occasions authors assumed a certain amount of knowledge in their intended audience and this may be relevant for understanding the text (e.g., information about specific issues being addressed as in Paul's letters). This is generally only the case with non–literary texts. Such documentary writings are usually written with a specific readership in view.

[2]"The interplay between dating and development [is] especially problematic. History lives off chronology but is never content with chronology. It seeks causality, which is to say, development. The historical model is not satisfied with a rich but disjointed collection of vignettes of the NT [New Testament] period. It reaches insatiably for sequence, for the possibility of a narrative. In fact, however, the NT canon offers, and will always offer, only scattered vignettes of the earliest Christian period. Worse, Christianity was at first so unnoticed by outsiders that there is little external framework for dating the writings so that they could securely be used as sources for a developmental picture" (Johnson 1999, 8).

[3]Helpful at this point is Jeffrey Carter's distinction of *descriptive comparison* (by which he means "the practice of discerning the particularity of a phenomenon by comparing it to features of its environment" [1998, 136]) and *explanatory comparison*. The latter is the opposite of description because "instead of specifying differences, explanation connects and combines phenomena by positing correspondences. . . . it makes claims of useful generality by overlapping selected parts (a collection of perhaps incomprehensible descriptive facts) and fabricating meaningful whole. Explanation gathers distinguishable features and characteristics and then stipulates their participation in an understandable system, in a necessarily generalized superstructure" (136–37).

recognized.[4] Certainly this is an asset in understanding these letters, and it allows historians to draw from them information about their contexts with a certain degree of confidence. But how is it that historians of the early church often assume that the *Gospel of Thomas* is later than, say, Matthew? In these cases much less is known about the specific historical contexts than is known for 1 Corinthians and *1 Clement*[5] and yet by and large there is wide agreement that *Thomas* is later than Matthew.[6] Since little (if anything) is known about the background of these writings, the conclusion may be, at least in part, impressionistic. Ideas about the general development of the church allow scholars to suggest that Matthew reflects an earlier stage of development.[7] Only when there is some general understanding of where Matthew or *Thomas* belongs can students proceed to extract from them clues about historical context. Again, texts often provide the only window into the context in which they were produced. Authors, however, were not attempting to supply the needed data for historical reconstruction and, as a result, it may be that the context (date, occasion, provenance, authorship, intended readers) cannot be determined.

1.2 The Difficulty of Locating 2 Peter

Second Peter illustrates well the type of ambiguities facing historians of early Christianity outlined in section 1.1. In the present section, both the date of this letter and the historical situation behind it are briefly considered in order to make this point. This section will also introduce the scholarly analysis of 2 Peter, which is used in this book as a test case. By appealing to parallels between texts, are historians able to overcome the obstacles presented to their enquiry resulting from

---

[4]A later date for *1 Clement* is inferred, for example, by the more developed church hierarchy. It should be noted however that this assumes a developmental mode—namely that the church moved away from simple, charismatic leadership (suggested by Paul in his letters) to a more hierarchical, structured leadership (as in *1 Clement*). Developmental models present difficulties that will be discussed further in ch. 2. First Corinthians and *1 Clement* are documentary writings with specific audiences addressed (Christians in Corinth in both cases as stated in the texts).

[5]As documentary writings 1 Corinthians and *1 Clement* address a specific situation whereas Matthew and the *Gospel of Thomas*, as literary writings, are more general in scope.

[6]Because they are literary writings, developmental theories are not relevant as they do not deal with the early church directly. More useful for dating purposes is attestation. Use of Matthew by Ignatius rules out a date after 100 C.E. The example of the *Gospel of Thomas* is used here because of the range of dates assigned to it. Helmut Koester allows that "[i]n its most original form, it may well date from the first century" (in Robinson 1988, 125). More often a second–century date is assumed, again on the basis of attestation—a *terminus ad quem* of 200 C.E. is provided by a Greek fragment of this gospel.

[7]For example, if it is assumed that the *Gospel of Thomas* is derivative from the canonical Gospels, then obviously it is later. If this view is not assumed (e.g., Crossan 1991, 427) then there is greater flexibility for dating this apocryphal text.

a lack of data? Or, in other words, is the simple observation that texts of unknown historical location (date, occasion, provenance, authorship, intended readers) resemble other texts of known location a reliable tool for placing documents in history?[8]

According to one survey of the literature, 2 Peter has been assigned to almost every decade from 60 C.E. to the end of the second century (Bauckham 1988a, 3740; see also idem 1983, 157), but most scholars try to be more precise in their efforts to date it. One summary of the evidence for dating 2 Peter is found in a 1992 doctoral dissertation by Robert Bouchat. He observed a number of features in the letter that led to inferring a late first–century date for the epistle. Among the clues found, it was observed that unlike 1 Peter, 2 Peter reflects a concern with the delayed Parousia (the imminent eschatology of 1 Pet 4:7 is compared with the anxiety suggested by 2 Pet 3:8). Furthermore, dependence on Jude was thought to indicate a date later in the first century (meaning after Peter's death, usually thought to be in the 60s). Together these point to a *terminus a quo* of no earlier than 70 C.E.

However, as Bouchat notes, determining a *terminus ad quem* is not as easy. It is possible that the *Apocalypse of Peter*, which is usually dated to the first half of the second century, makes use of 2 Peter (cf. 4.5). Similarities between the opponents described in 2 Peter and first–century proto–gnosticism do not shed much light given that the developmental history of Gnosticism is not without ambiguity. More helpful, argues Bouchat, is the observation that no other NT writing defends so explicitly the hope of the Parousia in a context when its delay has created tension (2 Pet 3:4). Here a window is opened on the time of this letter's composition: it is after the time when other NT documents were written and before the second century, when the delayed Parousia was no longer a concern (223–27). Bouchat concludes that a date before 100 C.E. is thus indicated by the evidence, though there is no proof that excludes a later date (esp. 254–57). He admits that this is an argument from silence (256) and so states his conclusion cautiously, admitting that "it is not possible to preclude a second–century setting for 2 Peter" (257). This admission illustrates the frustration facing historians about absolute dating of some early Christian writings. It also illustrates the problem addressed by the present study. After all the evidence has been gathered, firm conclusions remain elusive. For a number of reasons, 2 Peter presents a challenge to those seeking firm conclusions about historical placement (a situation true of other texts as well).

1.2.1 SECOND PETER LACKS EXPLICIT CLUES ABOUT ITS ORIGIN AND ADDRESS

Like various other writings in the NT, 2 Peter is a general or catholic writing. It is addressed simply to "those who have received a faith as precious as ours"

---

[8]Framed negatively, do differences between texts also allow for such approximate location? Cf. the comments on 1 Corinthians and *1 Clement* above.

(1:1).[9] If it were certain that the earlier letter implied by 3:1 was 1 Peter, this would provide some support for the view that 2 Peter derived from Rome, but this is debatable for various reasons. First, it is questioned whether 1 Peter is meant in 2 Pet 3:1 at all. "The first letter" has also been understood to indicate: (1) an earlier part of 2 Peter (McNamara 1960, 13–19); (2) Jude (Robinson 1976, 195; Smith 1985, 74–78); (3) a lost letter by Peter (Zahn 1953, 2:197–98; Green 1987, 134–35; Lenski 1945, 237–38, 336); and (4) traditional Petrine teachings generally, out of which 2 Peter itself was built (Barker, Lane, and Michaels 1969, 351–52). The majority of scholars see 1 Peter as the intended letter implied by 3:1.

Second, it is true that there is wide agreement that 1 Peter derives from Rome. Among other things, the cryptic reference to Babylon (5:13) seems to function as a cipher for Rome (cf. Rev 14:8; 16:19; 17:5; 18:2, 10, 21). Yet even if 2 Pet 3:1 does refer to 1 Peter, it is possible that while the author may have known 1 Peter, his own letter was written from a different location.

1.2.2 SECOND PETER IS USUALLY THOUGHT TO BE PSEUDONYMOUS[10]

Typical are statements like that of Andreas Lindemann who finds "die Kennzeichen der Pseudonymität sind besonders deutlich" (1979, 91, supported by reference to 1:16–18 and 3:1). If 2 Peter is indeed a pseudonymous letter, as the great majority of scholars maintains, then historical placement of this document is greatly complicated. Some reasons for questioning apostolic authorship can be briefly summarized.[11]

For one thing, (1) 2 Peter's relation to Jude needs to be considered. It is beyond dispute that some literary relationship exists between Jude and 2 Peter, and most commentators have found Peter to be the borrower. The specific reasons for determining this are presented and evaluated in 4.1. A date for Jude is as difficult to determine as it is for 2 Peter though generally it is thought to have been written after 70 C.E.[12] which, if true, would put 2 Peter to a period after Peter's death (which was, according to tradition, in the mid 60s C.E.; cf. *1 Clem.* 5). It may also be important to ask whether a pillar in the early church would make use of Jude, who was not an apostle. Next, (2) connections to 1 Peter may or may not be relevant. Differences in style when compared to 1 Peter suggest that these two documents

---

[9]Unless otherwise stated, all biblical citations are taken from the NRSV.

[10]The adjectives pseudonymous (falsely named) and pseudepigraphal (falsely attributed) are used interchangeably in this book. The latter is preferred to pseudepigraphic as suggested by the *SBL Handbook of Style* (Alexander et al. 1999, 162) because it appears to be used more often in the literature on the subject (e.g., Meade 1986; Dunn 1997). Otherwise, the *SBL Handbook of Style* is followed for all spellings and abbreviations, as well as notes (author–date citations), bibliography, and other formatting details.

[11]This summary was included in Gilmour 2001, 294–96.

[12]One indication of this later date is found in vv.17–18, where the author speaks of the apostles in the past tense.

were written by different authors (discussed in 4.2).[13] Furthermore, (3) reference to Paul's letters as Scripture (3:15–16) is thought to point to a later period of the church's history as also the reference to the time of the apostles as in the past (3:2, 4). This speaks against a time of writing when many of them were still living. (4) There is a conspicuous emphasis on Peter–as–author which, it has been argued, suggests in–authenticity. (5) The author seems at home in a Hellenistic religious and philosophical context; this is far removed from the Peter known from the Gospels. (6) There was a wide tradition of pseudonymous writings using Peter's name and so it would not be unusual to understand 2 Peter as another example of this (even if it is earlier in date than the others; cf. discussion of the *Apocalypse of Peter* in 4.5). (7) A concern with proper interpretation of Scripture and a high regard for apostolic tradition suggest greater similarity with the emerging catholicism of the second century than with the young faith evidenced by the earliest NT writings (cf. 2.2.2). This type of reasoning involves assumptions about the development of the church that need to be supported (discussed in ch. 2). (8) Second Peter is poorly attested in the second century and, related to this, (9) the church was reluctant to accept this document into its canon—a fact that speaks against apostolic authorship. (10) And perhaps the most significant argument is that of genre. Second Peter has been identified as a testament, a farewell discourse. In many instances such literature is clearly pseudepigraphal in nature.[14]

These arguments are not all of equal weight, and it will be seen that none of them is decisive by itself. One's final conclusion often rests on an evaluation of the scruples involved in pseudepigraphy and whether it is compatible with canonical literature (i.e., would the church have knowingly accepted pseudonymous literature into its canon and could such forgeries have gone unnoticed).[15] As this is a book dealing with historical methodology, a decision on this issue is not the objective. Rather, it is concerned to evaluate the extent to which conclusions about the historical location of 2 Peter are based on parallels of language and thought and to consider how reliable such a procedure is. The immediate point here is simply to state that uncertainty about authorship greatly heightens uncertainty about historical location.

---

[13]Though this does not indicate very much if, as is often the case, 1 Peter is also assumed to be pseudepigraphal. On the other hand, even if Petrine authorship is accepted for these letters, variety in style may be explained by the use of a different amanuensis (see 1 Pet 5:12). See further comments in 4.2.

[14]E.g., *The Testament of the Twelve Patriarchs*. Chester and Martin suggest that the genre of 2 Peter is among the clearest indications of a post–Petrine setting (1994, 139). Cf. appendix 2, p.152 above.

[15]For discussion about the relationship of pseudepigraphy and canon, see Ellis (1992) and Porter (1995). A response to the latter is provided by Wall (1995).

1.2.3 IF PSEUDEPIGRAPHAL, 2 PETER IS POTENTIALLY DECEPTIVE WHEN MINED FOR CLUES ABOUT HISTORICAL CONTEXT

The situation would be something like the following. The early readers would have assumed the letter to be an authentic writing from the Apostle Peter who, writing long ago, prophetically described their situation (i.e., when they were reading). This description of later events, coming from the pen of Peter (as it was believed), presented only vague, symbolic descriptions of events that he did not see first hand.[16] As a result, the readers would not expect the description of their opponents to be too precise. Not surprisingly, this makes any attempt to identify a specific crisis facing the readers very difficult, yet there is a tendency in many studies of 2 Peter to do just that. Were the errorists gnostics or proto–gnostics? Christians influenced by Epicureanism or Stoicism? There is no consensus (cf. further discussion in 5.1.1).

Since an exact fit of the letter's polemic with any known group in the early church is not possible, another model is needed to make sense of the language of 2 Peter. In an article by Frederik Wisse on the epistle of Jude, a case is made for viewing the portrait of the false teachers found in that text as a general description and not a reference to a historically specific crisis facing the readers (1972). Heresiologists of the first five centuries tended to caricature sectarians, assuming that all heretics were essentially alike. Such procedures point to a heresiological tradition in which later writers built on the work of their predecessors. Do NT writings stand within, or at the beginning of, this heresiological tradition? Almost without exception, commentators view Jude as a response to specific heretical dangers facing the church.[17] The alternative offered in Wisse's article is that "the letter could be a tract to the church at large . . . dealing with the eschatological false prophets" (136). While this position has not found unanimous agreement,[18] it has

---

[16]Some theories of authorship suggest that the fiction was well known to the readers. This view is hard to defend however because of the lack of concrete evidence to support it.

[17]Many suspect some form of libertine gnostic (e.g., Werdermann 1913) or proto–gnostic (e.g., Rowston 1974–75, 555–56; Sidebottom 1967, 71, 74–76) opponents, but this has been questioned (Bauckham 1983, 12–13). For instance, it has been pointed out that the cosmological dualism which characterizes Gnosticism is absent in both Jude and 2 Peter (e.g., Knight 1995, 81–83; cf. Neyrey 1980a, 506 n.12). While not as frequent as it once was, examples of scholarly writings that assume without qualification that 2 Peter and Jude responded to gnostic opponents can still be found. One popular university textbook reads: "Apparently, the false teachers Second Peter is concerned about, like those condemned in Jude, are Gnostics who claim to be purified from the world but are in fact entrapped in it through their immoral behavior. . . . Peter has had a mystical experience of true divinity every bit as powerful as the Gnostics claim to have had . . . . The Gnostics would also have disputed the parousia" (Hauer and Young 2001, 352).

[18]It has been questioned by Bauckham (1983, 3, 39) but viewed more favourably by Neyrey (1993, 52). A recent article by Lauri Thurén (1997) attempts to "lay bare [Jude's] first setting" (451) and in so doing calls attention to the problems of drawing historical information from a text which lacks explicit historical references and engages in polemics. As Jude is a

much to commend itself. To begin with, it is consistent with the nature of apocalyptic literature[19] more widely to say, as Wisse does in relation to Jude's opponents, "we look in vain for veiled historical references to the rebellious nature of the errorists" (140). Apocalyptic symbolism may have its genesis in earthly events or persons but it is expanded to become universal in scope (Albertz 1994, 589–91). As a consequence, it is not surprising that the event generating the literature—if in fact there was an event behind it—can at times be lost.[20] Even if specific opponents are pictured here, it is certain that little can be gleaned from polemical language regarding their identity. But is it sufficient to state simply that their identity is lost? Wisse's recognition of the "eschatological false prophets" and the use of Old Testament (OT) types more accurately represents the broader world view of apocalyptic writing (1972, 135 [cf. Jude 4, 18]; 140 [cf. Jude 11]). Given the general references to the coming of false teachers elsewhere in the NT (Matt 7:15; Mark 13:22), Jude's opponents are correctly understood to be non–specific.

Wisse illustrates the dangers of appealing to subtlety on the part of the author, an assumption present in many commentaries.

> . . . it is most improbable that we suddenly get here a historical reference among otherwise prophetic and symbolic statements. . . . It would be completely out of character with the total letter if he were to use subtle allusions in some isolated instances (139).

> To assume that . . . the author is turning the Gnostics' own language against themselves attributes too much subtlety to the author. . . . The reader has in no way been prepared for clever puns (141).

---

carefully crafted piece of rhetorical literature, it is precarious to take statements at face value, especially in the absence of the opponents' case (455). Thurén's approach to Jude pays attention to characteristics of rhetoric, particularly the technique of *vituperatio* (457–59). By applying the principle of dissimilarity, he looks for "indicators which deviate from standard rhetorical procedures and stereotypical criticism" (462) in order to gain clues about the opponents' identity. These are few: the interest in the opponents' speech may point to internal problems, discontent, and criticism within the community itself; and the denial of Christ may be a theological accusation, though also possibly an ethical challenge (463). These are modest conclusions. Yet while Thurén agrees with Wisse (1972, 131) that early Christian letters could lack a specific situation, it is maintained that the "tone of Jude suggests that it was originally written for a particular (although not necessarily acute) situation" (464). Correctly, it is said that "such a situation remains inaccessible . . . since additions to the general characterization would require uncontrollable hypotheses" (464–65).

[19]Jude has been classified as Jewish Christian apocalyptic (Rowston 1974–75, 561), more specifically an epistolary sermon or midrash which employs apocalyptic.

[20]One example of this is the Isaiah apocalypse (Isa 24–27). Efforts to place the destruction of the unnamed city in history have resulted in random speculation. More productive is the suggestion that "the thought is not of the annihilation of a particular city but of urban life generally" (Albertz 1994, 570). With respect to Jude, "The very generality of his attack on these interlopers dissuades us from trying to identify their specific ideology" (Neyrey 1993, 52).

Again, no identifiable historical references seem to be imbedded in such language (142).

It is suggested here that these insights into the nature of Jude are also pertinent to 2 Peter, since so much of Jude is incorporated into it (cf. discussion of Jude's priority 4.1). Furthermore, the lack of a fixed address may be relevant. If 2 Pet 3:1 indicates knowledge of 1 Peter, this letter may also have been circular (cf. 1 Pet 1:1). In this case the author would be concerned with a description of God's opponents *in whatever form they may appear in your particular church*. If this is correct, then great care is necessary as details in the text may not necessarily correspond to the circumstances of author and audience.[21]

Though it does not supply the information needed to determine its date, occasion, provenance, authorship, and intended readers, there remains a strong interest in attempting to locate 2 Peter within the history of earliest Christianity.[22] This has led scholars to attempt locating 2 Peter on the basis of more general developments in Christian thought, observing both similarities and differences between 2 Peter and other early Christian literature. Various attempts at locating 2 Peter will be examined in chapter 2. What is of particular interest for this study is the use of parallels between texts (verbal, thematic, and so on) as a tool for assisting in this process.

1.3 THE USE OF PARALLELS

Discussion about the use of parallels in biblical studies has occurred largely in the history of religions school of research. With an interest to observe how earlier phenomena were incorporated into later belief systems, it is natural to place great importance on parallels between religious movements. Yet the dangers involved in this type of work have been recognized for a long time. Earlier in this century Adolf Deissmann pointed to methodological issues involved when exploring points of contact between religious and cultural traditions:

> Some kind of an understanding as to methods of work would certainly be desirable at the outset . . . . I will only remark that in the case of each single observation made I find the questions resolve themselves for me into the alternative: is it analogy or is it genealogy? That is to say, we have to ask: Are the similarities or points of agreement that we discover between two different religions to be regarded

---

[21]This is not to say that 2 Peter and Jude derive from the same situation, a view often found in older commentaries. One of the gains of more recent work on these epistles is the recognition that these two writings, despite their clear literary relationship, have unique settings. For example, Cavallin's redaction–critical study of 2 Peter and Jude (1979, 263–70) concludes that the former places more stress on "the teaching activity of the adversaries" (270). See the contributions by Fornberg (1977), Neyrey (esp. 1993), and Bauckham (esp. 1983).

[22]There are still many scholars seeking to defend the traditional view of authorship for 2 Peter as well. This too involves locating the text to a specific context (see p.15 n.1 and p.33 n.30 for examples).

as parallelisms of more or less equal religious experience, due to equality of psychic pitch and equality of outward conditions, or are they dependent one on the other, demonstrable borrowings? ([1927] 1995, 265).

Recognizing the potential for misuse of parallels (apparently having in mind especially those who would want to dismiss them),[23] Deissmann offers certain guidelines for consideration. Among them, he suggests: (a) in cases of inward emotion and religious experience and naïve expression of these emotions and experiences in word, symbol, and act, one should always try to regard the particular fact as analogical; and (b) in cases of formulae used in worship, professional liturgical usage, or the formulation of certain doctrines, one should try first to regard the particular fact as genealogical (265–66).

In more recent literature the concern to explore the similarities and differences between different religious and cultural traditions rightly continues to be sensitive about proper methodology. Currently in NT studies, great attention is given to parallels between the early canonical Christian literature and the Dead Sea Scrolls, as well as the rabbinic, Hellenistic, and gnostic literatures.[24] Naturally unique methodological concerns must be addressed in each area of study, including the role of parallels in research.

Another helpful study in this regard is Jeffrey Carter's treatment of methodology, which has already been referred to in an earlier note. Observing parallels is one thing, but what do they mean? How are they to be used in scholarly analysis? Carter's study is an examination of methodology used in comparative religious studies, and he begins with the observation that there is a distinction between academic description and explanation. Comparative religious study involves an interest in both particularity (historical and cultural detail) and generality (similarity, relationship, and the like). A meaningful comparison must take both into consideration, and this involves the application of two forms of comparison which Carter calls "descriptive comparison" and "explanatory comparison" (1998, 133–34; see p.2 n.3 above).

Descriptive comparison can be defined as "the academic process that

---

[23]Deissmann's first edition was published in 1908. It is interesting to note that just over fifty years later (during his presidential address to the annual meeting of the Society of Biblical Literature on December 27, 1961), Samuel Sandmel was decrying the dangers of an *over–use* and *over–estimation* of parallels in biblical scholarship: "I am not seeking to discourage the study of these parallels . . . . However, I am speaking words of caution about exaggerations about the parallels and about source and derivation" (1962, 1). Donaldson wrote, more than 20 years after Sandmel's address, that "the problem to which he [Sandmel] drew attention continues to be a pressing one for NT scholarship" (1983, 193).

[24]E.g., Evans, Webb, and Wiebe 1993, esp. xviii–xxii; Metzger 1968; Boring, Berger, and Colpe 1995, esp. 11–32; and Ferguson 1993, 1–3. Further assistance in clarifying the role of parallels in exploring the relationship between texts has been provided by Dennis Stoutenburg. In a study of the complicated dynamics involved in comparing the NT with rabbinic literature, he has given attention to the matter of defining parallels (1996, esp. 81–87).

accentuates particularity by marking and perceiving differences" (134). When this process occurs, it is then possible to distinguish objects, ideas and events from one another:

> An adequate description, in this way, succeeds in separating, contextualizing, and narrating the individuality of phenomena; it provides enough detail to determine exactly how something can be discriminated or differentiated from its environment and from other things (134).

Explanatory comparison, on the other hand, is largely concerned with placing the particulars in a meaningful relationship to one another (full discussion, 136–39). If descriptive comparison is concerned with details, explanatory comparison is concerned with generalities. He defines explanatory comparison as "the practice of designating the generality of a phenomenon by stating its similarity, relationship, or connection to another phenomenon. It is an operation of abstraction, a process of mapping a theory onto descriptive facts" (138). There can be problems in such comparison:

> . . . when unchecked, this form of comparison can slide into trivialities. It can lead to sweeping and ungrounded claims of generality divorced from the particularities of culture and history. Though this sort of slippage is rare nowadays, it is also an unsatisfactory form of comparison because it fails, by itself, to balance the particular and the general (138).

At this stage of comparison, scholars are concerned to take selected parallel parts of the phenomena that are being compared and fabricate, in Carter's words, a meaningful whole.

One final area where there has been a concern to recognize lender–borrower, precursor–successor text relationships is in studies concentrating on intertextuality. Here the focus is largely on how texts (and other sources) have been incorporated into later writings that contain deliberate, but often subtle reinterpretation. Once again scholars have seen in this type of research a potential danger, the possibility of discovering parallels that are not really there. Some have therefore proposed guidelines to guard against what Robert Brawley has called "whimsical correlations" between texts.[25]

Though the use of parallels in the present study can be distinguished from history of religions research and intertextual studies, many methodological concerns are still relevant. The focus here is not so much on the impulses of earlier linguistic or conceptual sources behind the NT, or in how these may have been incorporated and reinterpreted in the NT, or in how the NT writers influenced later religious

---

[25]An important outline of criteria is provided by Hays (1989, 29–32). For a summary of these, see appendix 8 below. For comments on Hays' criteria and suggested modifications, see Brawley 1995.

thought (though these phenomena will be considered). Rather, the interest is in whether and to what extent those parallels, both analogical and genealogical relationships between texts, can assist the historical placement of individual writings by providing such clues as when and where texts were produced. With respect to 2 Peter then, the issue in this thesis is not so much what it says as when (approximate chronology) and where (context) it said it. The focus here is on methodology and the place of parallels in assisting such historical research.

More than other early Christian texts, 2 Peter holds out promise that parallels will assist in locating it. The author may have known a number of other writings. Parallels with Jude appear to involve literary dependence one way or the other. Paul's letters are referred to (3:15–16), and the author even knows something about them (some things are "hard to understand"). At one point, Paul's teachings are connected with a concern in the letter ("[as] Paul wrote to you"), but the apostle is not explicitly quoted. In calling the text a "second letter" (3:1), the author appears to indicate knowledge of 1 Peter. The Gospels may have been known (e.g., the transfiguration, 1:16–18). Other literary relationships have been proposed, most significantly with the *Apocalypse of Peter*. Others are less likely (e.g., Josephus, Philo).

Second Peter provides a suitable test case then to consider the use of parallels for locating texts. It will allow some general observations on this matter, and both the strengths and weaknesses of this use of parallels will be further clarified. An analysis of some of those parallels thought to indicate 2 Peter's dependence on earlier texts, as well as the use of 2 Peter in second–century writings, specifically the Apostolic Fathers and the *Apocalypse of Peter*,[26] will be addressed in chapter 4 below.

1.4 PROCEDURE

The remainder of the book is outlined as follows. Chapter 2 contains an evaluation of various attempts by NT scholars to locate 2 Peter. This survey will serve two purposes. First, since locating 2 Peter to a specific context has proved difficult (1.1), scholarship has attempted to provide an approximate location for this document on the basis of various developmental models. A few examples of this strategy will be presented, and some strengths and weaknesses of each will be observed. Second, attention will be given to how these models rely on parallels for supporting evidence. This will provide a foundation for chapter 3, where more specific comments on the place of parallels in the study of ancient texts will be offered. A presentation of various criteria needed to avoid an inappropriate use of parallels is offered. For the convenience of the reader, it is suggested that reference be made to appendices 3–7 (pp.154–58) to assist with cross–referencing these

---

[26]The choice to focus on these writings rests on the assumption that this literature is most germane to the issue of locating 2 Peter.

criteria. With these guidelines in place, attention is then given to specific parallels between 2 Peter and other texts often thought to indicate (a) sources behind 2 Peter, (b) the milieu in which 2 Peter was written, and (c) texts that have made use of 2 Peter (ch. 4). Here the suggestions made in chapter 3 are applied to specific examples of parallels between 2 Peter and other early Christian literature.

Finally, some general comments on the scholarly analysis of 2 Peter are offered in chapter 5. Appendices 1–2 develop particular themes introduced throughout.

CHAPTER 2
THE LOCATION OF 2 PETER

> Let us begin by leaving on one side for the time being the questions of authorship and literary dependence [of II Peter and Jude] and look at the documents for the clues they afford which are relevant to placing them in 'period'. I deliberately put it that way, because neither II Peter nor Jude contains any positive indication of absolute dating. It is a question of where they belong in relation to other comparable literature, and more than usually therefore the arguments are in danger of being circular. If this other literature itself is dated late, then these epistles will follow; if early, then the same will be true.
>
> —John A. T. Robinson, *Redating the New Testament*

Where does 2 Peter fit in the history of the early church? It gives no date, it may well be that its stated setting, namely that it is the last will and testament of the Apostle Peter (1:12–15; cf. 3:1), is fictitious,[1] and there are few clues which betray

---

[1] A significant number of conservative scholars maintains that 2 Peter belongs in the mid–first century and constitutes a genuine letter from the Apostle Peter himself (e.g., Bigg 1901; Lias 1913; Blum 1981; Mounce 1982; Caffin 1983; Green 1987 [assumed "provisionally" (39)]; Kistemaker 1987; Hiebert 1989; and most recently Kruger 1999). Also relevant here are Ellis (1992) and Charles (1997; 1999 [in Walters and Charles]) who raise questions about the use of pseudepigraphy in early Christianity that are not often addressed. In his forthcoming commentary on 2 Peter in the NIGTC series, Scott Hafemann will offer a defense of the Petrine authorship of this epistle (mentioned in personal correspondence and noted here with permission). Under the heading of traditional authorship, views resembling J. Ramsey Michael's thesis can be mentioned. Noticing a "double time perspective" in 2 Peter, by which is meant the contrast between the lifetime of Peter ("as long as I am in this body," 1:13) and future provision ("after my departure," "at any time," 1:15), he proposes that a follower of the apostle composed this document. "This seeming paradox could be explained if Second Peter were regarded as a compendium or anthology of genuine Petrine material put together in testamentary form by one or more of the apostle's followers after his death. The relation of Second Peter to the historical Peter would then be somewhat analogous to the relation between the Gospel writers and Jesus, who promised that after his death the Holy Spirit would bring to their remembrance the things

unambiguously a specific geographical or historical environment. As a result of this lack of direct evidence about its origin, the best NT scholars can do is one or both of the following closely related options: they can attempt to determine a relative date and location for this document on the basis of developmental hypotheses about early Christianity, or they can attempt to determine an approximate date and location for this document relative to other early Christian literature (parallels) with which it appears to share certain features.[2]

Since the evidence for early Christianity is fragmentary, owing in part to the accidents of history and to the fact that the first generations of the church were not interested in recording their story for posterity,[3] scholars must resort to hypothetical developmental schemes in order to organize the scattered bits of information that are available to them. The better they fit, it is argued, the more probable the developmental scheme becomes. Historians face a puzzle that is missing some essential pieces. Or, to think in more linear terms, the progress from vague origins to the more developed (and historically verifiable) forms of Christianity in the later centuries needs to be accounted for. *There exists an end result but no complete understanding of the causes that led to it.* How did the catholic church of later centuries emerge from the small Jewish sect that followed Jesus' teachings?

There are different ways of imagining the development of Christianity

---

he had taught them (John 14:26 [cf. 2 Pet 1:15]). Such an approach would recognize some truth in the critical assertion that Second Peter brings the apostle's authority to bear upon certain problems that became more acute after his death" (Barker, Lane, and Michaels 1969, 352). In making this proposal, Ramsey is careful to remove any guilt from the later author arguing that there was no intent to deceive. On the contrary, by placing Peter's name to what was in fact Petrine material, this writer showed integrity by giving proper credit to the apostle.

The traditional view of authorship provides a clear historical location for the author, namely Rome, (usually) during the reign of Nero in the years just preceding Peter's martyrdom, and, for the audience, Asia Minor (see 1 Pet 1:1). As this study is primarily concerned with methodology, it is appropriate to consider what role parallels play in the arguments of those defending an early, apostolic authorship of this document. In particular, this often occurs in the negative; by noting the absence of features expected in later (i.e., second–century) Christian literature, especially pseudepigraphal texts, some argue that evidence is found supporting traditional authorship for 2 Peter. This is discussed further in 3.3.9. On the presuppositions involved in conservative scholarship, see p.33 n.30 and p.86 n.14.

[2]Meaning here early Christian texts for which a location is known. For example: (a) a historical setting for 2 Peter is unknown; (b) there are parallels between 2 Peter and *1 Clement* and other literature associated with the Roman church in the late first and second centuries; (c) 2 Peter therefore must also belong to that context.

[3]Some qualification is needed here. While it is true that the Book of Acts is a historical account resembling other ancient histories in some respects, it is also clear that Luke was very selective in his choice of subject matter. His interests were also theological, meaning that he was concerned to explain the works of God as much as to record the activities of the church. As for the accidents of history, not everything written by the earliest Christians has survived (1 Cor 5:9; Col 4:16). Along with that, not all topics of interest to early believers would have been written down and so the picture that emerges from these few writings is far from complete.

(examples follow), and theories put forward are often closely related to the individual scholar's ideological viewpoint. Such preconceived notions can potentially illuminate as well as cloud an already vague picture. By this it is suggested that preconceived ideas about development have a snowball effect: what traces the early church left of itself for modern historians (almost exclusively writings) are forced into service to answer questions they were never intended to answer. This leads to distortion, as these writings are made to speak on behalf of the modern scholarly developmental model, not on behalf of the original author. The ancient authors can thus be misrepresented as their work is viewed through a lens that is anachronistic. The very nature of the literature itself also stands in tension with the goals of historians. Theological documents were not concerned to create windows that open beyond the purview of the author into the wider society.

To illustrate, what are Paul's writings evidence for? He left behind more first–century Christian writings than anyone else, but this does not mean he is representative of what *all* Christians, or even a majority of Christians, believed. Paul's writings were occasional letters, addressed to particular communities in response to specific issues. It does not follow then that he has left behind a somewhat complete presentation of his own theological views, something like Thomas Aquinas' *Summa Theologica*, John Calvin's *Institutes of the Christian Religion*, or Karl Barth's *Church Dogmatics*. Historians need to place reasonable expectations on the early Christian writings. To what extent do preconceived developmental schemes illuminate or distort the evidence?[4]

These and related questions are asked in this chapter. Section 2.1 contains a description of two attempts to place early Christian writings in a general historical framework (with special attention to 2 Peter). In these cases, confidence in the available data leads scholars to argue that 2 Peter's location in history can be determined. Such confidence implies that no appeal to a developmental model is necessary. Following this, 2.2 contains a description of three developmental models. As seen there, when the historical data proves to be insufficient to locate a text to a specific location, scholars attempt to provide a relative location of texts based on theories. Then, in 2.3, follows an evaluation of these developmental models. Finally, an evaluation of the place of developmental theories for locating texts is offered.

2.1 SOME ATTEMPTS AT LOCATION: HISTORICAL RECONSTRUCTIONS

Scholars turn to developmental models to locate texts when the data proves to be insufficient for historical reconstruction. However, not all are convinced that the

---

[4]Of course, it is easier to accuse an author of bias than it is to eliminate it from one's own work. The great challenge facing historians is to recognize those presuppositions that exist and to keep them in view while proceeding cautiously in the historical task.

historical evidence is too limited to allow specific conclusions about the location of 2 Peter. In the two examples that follow, 2 Peter is located without any type of developmental scheme.[5]

2.1.1 BO REICKE'S MODEL: LOCATION IN A POLITICAL CONTEXT

Bo Reicke's Anchor Bible commentary on 2 Peter (1964) has been replaced by Jerome Neyrey's (very different) work in that series (1993), yet this older volume deserves attention in relation to the present topic. Reicke's study is distinctive in that he approaches James, Jude and the canonical Petrine writings as sharing a similar environment; he thus treats the category Catholic Epistles/General Writings as a more cohesive unit than is often the case. Reicke's thesis is significant for the present study because his attempt to locate 2 Peter in a very specific historical context is not based on a developmental theory but on internal and external clues about political realities addressed by the text.

The reigns of Nero (54–68 C.E.) and Domitian (81–96 C.E.) presented the Christian communities with severe challenges, and it is in these times of crisis that Reicke situates James, 1 and 2 Peter, and Jude. As he reads them, each of these writings advocates respect for and obedience to the political authorities or warns against social unrest, in a way similar to Paul's admonitions. The fact that Paul needed to teach such things likely indicates that at least some Christians did not view the political authorities of the day in a positive light. Their views resembled those of John the Seer, who demonized Rome in his Apocalypse.[6] What reason would Paul and the authors of these epistles have for advocating harmony within society?

The rise of Jewish zealotism may be the key to explaining this. Jewish zealots represented a threat that needed to be addressed by the Romans as well as a crisis that needed to be endured by the early church. Despite the original desire of the church to remain close to Judaism, relations gradually became strained. By the time 1 Thessalonians was written (ca. 51 C.E.), the Judean church was experiencing persecution at the hands of the Jewish community (1 Thess 2:14); and despite concessions by some Christians to Jewish points of view—perhaps for fear of Jewish zealots who threatened the church—there was eventually a clear break. The

---

[5]Those who maintain that the Apostle Peter wrote this letter would also fall in this category (see n.1). In the examples that follow, Petrine authorship is not assumed.

[6]Reicke raises an interesting question when he asks why Nero indicted Christians as an enemy and accused them of Rome's disastrous fire (cf. Tacitus *Ann.* 15.44): "how could Nero and his people fail to see that the disciples of Christ were innocent believers in a kingdom that was not of this world? The answer is that some Christians may have preached against Rome, as later John the Revelationist did in Asia Minor" (1964, xxi). Paul, he notes, was concerned when he found inclinations to social unrest in the congregation (Rom 12:18–13:14; 16:17–20). This may be reading a little too much into the Tacitus passage. By all appearances it appears that Christians were simply a convenient scapegoat.

Christian congregation in Jerusalem may have migrated East (Pella in the Transjordan, if Eusebius is reliable) because of the disorder caused by zealotry, which culminated in the Jewish War. James was killed by nationalistic Jews (Josephus, *Ant.* 20.9.197–203), perhaps because he challenged zeal for the law that led to extreme political actions. This may be indicated if James' praise for this zeal as recorded in Acts (21:20; ca. 58 C.E.) is compared to the anti–zealotic position found in the book of James (this assumes there is a link between the leader of the Jerusalem church and this document). If so, such teachings would resemble Paul's admonitions to avoid social unrest (Rom 12:18–13:14; 16:17–20). They also resemble 1 Peter, which also contains a call for obedience to the state. Ironically, both Paul and Peter are said to have been martyred because of zeal and strife (*1 Clem.* 5:2–7).

Though the Jewish nationalism leading up to the War contributed to the separation of Christians from the Jewish community, early indications suggest that the church recognized a need to give up one–sided Jewish traditions in the interest of converting the Greco–Roman world (e.g., zeal for Jerusalem, external observances of the law). Paul and Peter (i.e., 1 Peter) can be numbered among those placing an emphasis on the evangelization of Gentiles. "In both cases," Reicke writes with reference to Paul and Peter, "it is not a question of political opportunism but of an honest concern for the success of the gospel and the salvation of mankind" (xx). Excessive devotion to the law, which encouraged a challenge to the state, would result in disaster; and it did not take a prophet to recognize the dangers of zealotry.[7] In the years after the Jewish defeat, Christian teachers would look back to those same zealotic tendencies (excessive opposition to Roman rule) and see them as dangerous and so again, during the Domitian era, Christian writings encouraged civil obedience during a time when there was every reason to forsake it. Persecution of Christians occurred in the final two years of Domitian's reign, and, after this time, Reicke reasons, it would be impossible for Christians to speak so favourably of government officials,[8] because of the extent of the state's cruelty towards them (as suggested by Revelation). And so, the writings dated to the nineties prior to those final years of Domitian's reign (James, 2 Peter, Jude), again reflect a positive attitude toward government, an attitude

---

[7]Jesus recognized the inevitable confrontation of Jewish zealots with Rome during his lifetime (Matt 24; Mark 13; Luke 21) and this is historically plausible (cf. Wright 1996, 340).

[8]Reicke bases these comments on his interpretation of 2 Pet 2:10 which speaks of the false teachers who despise authority and "are shameless enough to defame dignitaries" (his translation [in loc.]; cf. "they revile angelic majesties," NASB). These are understood to refer to the same dignitaries spoken of elsewhere in the NT in contexts where obedience to civil authorities is urged (e.g., Rom 13:1–7; Titus 3:1–2; 1 Pet 2:13–4:6; see discussion, 167). A more natural way of understanding δόξας in this context is to see angelic glories described (cf. Jude 8).

inconceivable in the years following his reign.[9]

Such is Reicke's reconstruction of the setting of 2 Peter and the other epistles addressed. This reconstruction does not commend itself for various reasons, not least its portrayal of Christians as always innocent victims of the Jewish community. It is hard to imagine that Christians themselves did not provoke Jewish ire, as reflected in Acts and elsewhere. But the interest here is not in Reicke's specific conclusions but in his methodology. He has moved from a reconstruction of first–century religious and political history—which themselves are not stable entities providing a reliable foundation on which to build—to the location of 2 Peter and other literature. In the step from reconstruction to location of texts, he reaches the following rather specific conclusions: 1 Peter is dated to the Neronian context (71); James (4, 6–7) and Jude (192) to ca. 90 C.E.[10] Finally, he dates 2 Peter to about 90 C.E. with the suggestion that "if one takes into consideration the positive attitude toward the magistrates and society expressed in Second Peter as well as Jude (II Pet ii 10; Jude 8), then a suitable background for both of these epistles is to be found some years before the end of the reign of Domitian (A.D. 81–96)" (144). This understanding of the context helps shape exegesis of the text. Instead of Jude's "things they do not know" (10a), 2 Peter speaks of "those whom they do not recognize" (2:12) in the parallel passage.[11] Each has a different shade of meaning; one is concerned with legal order in general (Jude), the other with the Roman authorities specifically (2 Peter; 203).

Again, Reicke's conclusions and the details of his exegesis are not the main concern here. What is instructive for the present purpose is his methodology. First, it does not build on a preconceived idea about the development of Christian thought or the Christian movement as a whole. Secondly, Reicke's cautious use of literary parallels is noteworthy, as they are not determinative in reaching his conclusions.

---

[9]Reicke's volume includes a general introduction to this group of writings which provides an overview of the experience of Christians under Nero and Domitian (xv–xxxviii). See also the introductions to each individual writing and his exegesis of key passages throughout.

[10]His evidence for this rests largely on his exegesis of Jude 8–10a and 16 which he translates as follows. "In like manner these also, hypnotized as they are, defile flesh, reject authority, and defame dignitaries. The archangel Michael, when he contended with the devil in a dispute over the body of Moses, did not presume to impose a defamatory judgment on him but said: 'May the Lord punish you.' But these defame what they do not know" (Jude 8–10a; Reicke's translation [in loc.]). "They are grumblers and complainers who pursue their own lusts. And their mouth [sic] utters bombast while they adulate certain individuals for the sake of advantage" (Jude 16; Reicke's translation [in loc.]). The thrust of the examples used by Jude in these verses is that "slander or reviling spiritual or social dignitaries is contrary to God's will," a theme that Reicke suggests is linked to the need to respect the social order. The false teachers, therefore, were guilty of attacking the existing government (202). By defaming things they do not know, Jude's opponents challenge the existing authority structures in a way analogous to Koran's sons who challenged the holy order of God's people (203).

[11]Reicke does not see a direct literary dependence between Jude and 2 Peter, rather, he argues that "the best assumption is that both epistles derive from a common tradition" (190).

This is most visible in his refusal to assume that Jude and 2 Peter are directly related, opting instead for a Q–type hypothesis. The author's reserve here is commendable. Any theory about the location of 2 Peter or Jude is automatically tentative, because the direction of dependence is beyond absolute confirmation. Theories based on parallels supported by less evidence are even more suspect. Also, literary parallels are recognized as valuable when they play *a supporting role* in reaching conclusions about historical location. Reicke appeals to them to lend further support for a position based on other evidence: e.g., "similarity between Second Peter and First Clement strengthens the case for dating Second Peter during the years preceding Domitian's persecution of the church, or about A.D. 90" (145). He calls in the similarities between *1 Clement* and 2 Peter only after his reconstruction of events was in place (namely, historical–political realities).

2.1.2 SPECIFIC GEOGRAPHICAL CONTEXTS

A second example of scholarly location of 2 Peter that exhibits confidence in the available data is found in attempts to isolate a specific geographical provenance and destination for the text (for convenience, these topics are treated together). There is general agreement that both author and audience were at home in a culturally pluralistic, Hellenistic environment.[12] The readers have escaped the world's corruptions (1:4; 2:20), a description perhaps more suitable for describing Gentile converts than Jewish (cf. 1 Pet 1:14; 2:9–10; 4:3–4 where similar reasoning can be employed). Also pertinent is the audience's familiarity with Pauline writings (3:15–16), which may locate them generally to the territories of his mission. Beyond this, a wide range of theories about origin and destination has been put forward.

David Henry Schmidt proposed that one way of explaining the presence of both Jewish and Greek influences on 2 Peter may be found in a comparison of similar characteristics in the writings of Philo, who used Hellenistic philosophical language to communicate Jewish beliefs (1972, 105). This would suggest that 2 Peter came from Egypt. Also supporting this idea is the claimed influence of 2 Peter on the *Apocalypse of Peter*, believed by some to have originated in Egypt owing to the fact that it was known to Clement of Alexandria (e.g., Kelly 1969, 237). This latter connection is not helpful however, as the origin of the *Apocalypse* is not certain, and, even if it did originate in Egypt, it was circulated widely

---

[12]The case for this has been made most strongly by Fornberg (1977) who paid attention to various social indicators in 2 Peter and used these to further understand the first readers (esp. ch. 6). His views have been taken up, among others, by Charles (1997, throughout, though see esp. 44–49).

It has been argued that 1:1 ("those who have received a faith as precious as ours") suggests that the intended first readers were Gentiles in contrast with Jews. This verse could, however, be understood to mean the readers in contrast to the apostles (cf. 2 Pet 3:2). Some older commentators argued that a Jewish readership was intended (see below).

(Moffatt 1911, 368).[13] Also in favour of the Egyptian context are the relatively early manuscript attestation afforded by P[72] and the fact that Origen was the first to refer to 2 Peter by name (Eusebius, *Hist. eccl.* 6.25.7–8).

An audience in Palestine (or possibly Syria) has been suggested.[14] Zahn reached this conclusion partly on the basis of 1:16, which connects the author to other witnesses of the transfiguration (and 3:2, "your apostles"; 1953, 2:194–221).

> Those to whom 2 Peter is directed must be persons among whom Peter laboured as a missionary, *i.e.* persons belonging to the circumcision. The language used to describe the gospel in i.16 is applicable to it as it was preached in Israel—in other words, among the contemporaries and countrymen of the Lord and His apostles, who were more or less familiar with the facts of the gospel history (Acts ii.22, x.37). . . . the readers were, for the most part, if not altogether, Jewish Christians, and . . . are to be sought in Palestine and the regions adjoining (1953, 2:202, 208).

On the other hand, Jerzy Klinger has argued against a Jewish audience by noting the striking omission of any reference to the Caesarea Philippi episode (Matt 16:13–20)—so important an event in Peter's career—to establish the apostle's authority. Rather, the author bases this claim to authority on the transfiguration narrative. Klinger points out that the Caesarea Philippi episode (as it is recorded in Matthew) has a Jewish–Christian character (e.g., the identification of Jesus by disciples as one of the Hebrew prophets, terms like Bar–Jona, bind and loose, keys of the kingdom, and ἐκκλησία [i.e., the Hebrew *qāhāl*]). All together, these indicate that "this passage, as well as the entire Gospel according to Matthew, was intended for Christians from among the Jews. The addressees of *2 Peter* did not belong to that category at all" (1973, 160–61). This line of argument is problematic at different levels. For one thing, this is an argument from silence that cannot support such a significant claim. For another, it is not certain that 2 Peter is dependent on the written Gospels (4.3), and even if it were, an assumption is implied here that the author could not/would not translate relevant material into the language and culture of the intended readers. It is not even certain that Matthew was addressed to a Jewish–Christian community (cf. Pettem 1987), though this is the usual view.

Connections between 2 Peter and Asia Minor have been observed by numerous scholars (e.g., Elliott 1992, 5:287; idem [with R. A. Martin] 1982, 129–30; and Charles 1997, 137, 146–48 [and throughout]; idem 1998, 63 n.33). A traditional reading of the text would make this connection based on the address of 1 Peter coupled with the view that 2 Pet 3:1 refers back to those same readers. At the same time, for those assuming 2 Peter is pseudonymous, it is equally plausible that in order to gain a hearing for his own letter the author deliberately

---

[13]Furthermore, as will be seen in ch. 4, the dependence of the *Apocalypse of Peter* on 2 Peter is debatable.

[14]Samaria has also been proposed (see Falconer 1902).

referred back to a letter that was previously accepted by the intended readership. Association with Asia Minor is further supported by parallels with inscriptions found in that area (see discussion under 3.2.4).

Second Peter is commonly associated with Rome. In 3:15 the author speaks of Paul writing "to you," and if Romans is the referent here (as Mayor, for one, believes), locating the readership to Rome is an obvious step. Bauckham's formulation of the Roman provenance hypothesis is the most comprehensive. In its favour are the many points of contact between literature associated with Rome (*1* and *2 Clement*, the Shepherd of Hermas) and 2 Peter (see 4.6). To say that 2 Peter resembles the Roman literature of the late first and early second centuries may be accurate, but this does not necessarily allow for location of the epistle in the Roman Christian community. Second Peter could just as easily have been an influence in shaping this environment as a product of it (cf. this same line of argument below with respect to the category early catholic as a location for early Christian literature).[15] Determining which Pauline letter or letters may have been intended by the reference in 2 Pet 3:15–16 is also inconclusive (4.4), so this cannot be cited as evidence in support of provenance or readership, though because the readers had received correspondence from the apostle it is reasonable to suggest broadly a location within Paul's missionary territory.[16]

One needs to allow for travel—whether of documents or authors—as a possible complicating factor with any geographical theory. In the end, it must be admitted that there is insufficient evidence to determine a specific geographical setting for the provenance and destination of this letter.[17]

---

[15]Lenski is skeptical about a Roman provenance, arguing that the first letter of warning (implied by 3:1) must have been lost (i.e., 3:1 does not refer back to 1 Peter). He does not think it is plausible to suggest that this document could have been lost if it too derived from Rome: "if he wrote from Rome, it is difficult to determine how his first letter of warning became lost, and how his second letter of warning [2 Peter] needed so long a period of time before it became generally known and accepted as coming from his pen. The probabilities are in favor of the assumption that these two letters were written long before Peter reached Rome, perhaps while he was still on his journeys" (1945, 238).

[16]If the reference to Babylon in 1 Pet 5:13 is understood to be literally Babylon, this suggests yet another possible provenance for 2 Peter. As a point of interest, this position is held by the Jehovah's Witnesses in their literature. With respect to 1 Peter, it is argued that the term Babylon should be taken literally, because the address of 1 Pet 1:1 is certainly intended to be literal (The Watch Tower Bible and Tract Society 1990, 252). Given that Peter was the apostle to the circumcision, it is reasonable to suppose he traveled to Babylon as there was a large Jewish population there—so the argument goes. Further support is found in the omission of any reference to Peter in Paul's letter to the Romans. "[W]hy does he fail to mention Peter? Simply because Peter was not there at the time!" (252).

[17]Klaus Berger has presented a history of the theology of the NT organized largely around geographical lines (1994). A major concern signalled by at least one reviewer is that "This geographical principle does . . . have its consequences. The geographical *space* maintained by [Berger] forces him to make a striking reordering within NT *time*" such as, for example, the early dating of John's Gospel (Hübner 1999, 38). See also the reviews by Légasse (1996) and

2.2 DEVELOPMENTAL MODELS

When there are reasons to doubt the sufficiency of the available data for locating a text in a precise time and place, the next best thing is a relative location based on presuppositions about the development of early Christianity and/or similarities with and differences from other texts. In this section three attempts to locate texts are briefly summarized.

2.2.1 FERDINAND CHRISTIAN BAUR (1792–1860)

In an effort to present a strictly historical interpretation of the early church, F. C. Baur reached radical conclusions which are largely dismissed by contemporary scholarship. Baur observed an ideological conflict in the pages of the NT between Pauline and Petrine forms of Christianity that gave way to a synthesis in the mediating position of the emerging catholic church. This Hegelian model of human history provided the needed criteria for him as writings could be placed in this developmental framework according to their ideological orientation.[18] For Baur, 2 Peter clearly illustrated the movement toward mediation.

Various NT documents reflect this tendency of mediation and settlement, among them James and both Petrine letters (1831, 205). By praising Paul and the wisdom given to him, by appealing to his letters and warning against the misunderstandings his letters can occasion, the author of 2 Peter expresses his interest in mediation (206). And since Peter is approaching death (2 Pet 1:13–15), putting such words in his mouth takes the form of a last will and testament, making the message all the more worthy of consideration (206).

In Baur's reconstruction, 2 Peter is thus located within a party, namely that concerned with mediating the conflict between these variant forms of early Christian expression. In Baur's terms, this was a wider tendency in later Christian texts that reflects the emerging consensus position of the catholic church.

Oberforcher (1995).

      With respect to 2 Peter, Berger takes the interesting step of tracing the theological roots of this epistle to distinct strands of early Christian thought. Berger perceives similarities with Antiochene theology (e.g., "Die Autorität des Petrus und das Stichwort 'Weg der Gerechtigkeit' lassen den Einfluß Antiochiens erkennen" [1994, 520]) and notes especially how the author of 2 Peter preserves proto–Markan theology. Second Peter's interest in the transfiguration and omission of reference to the death and resurrection of Jesus is an indication that 2 Peter continues to represent the error exemplified in Mark's disciples, specifically Peter, who favoured a glory–theology (i.e., transfiguration) over a suffering–theology (see Mark 8:32).

      The discussion about Paul points to the post–Pauline period in Ephesus. According to Berger "2 Petr gehört zu den Schriften in der Diskussion um das paulinische Erbe" and in this respect its position resembles the "paulinischen Schultradition" (520).

      [18]Baur seems to be correct in his identification of conflict in the early decades of the church (see esp. Gal 2:11–14). He may be going too far however to assume that all early Christian literature either takes sides in the debate or reflects a later synthesis.

2.2.2 EARLY CATHOLICISM: ERNST KÄSEMANN (1906–1998)

One of the major themes in twentieth–century NT scholarship involves the discussion of whether and to what extent characteristics of late second–century catholicism can be found in the NT itself (see discussion in Dunn 1990, ch. 14). Among characteristics of this later stage of Christian history often said to appear in the NT, even if in an incipient form, are a declining expectation of Christ's imminent return, increasing institutionalization of the church, and the reduction of the Christian message into established forms. The issue resembles Baur's developmental model in certain respects. Both Baur and proponents of an early catholic (usually lower case) developmental model would agree that such features as those just listed are typical of the later second century and that the presence of such features in the NT must indicate a late composition of those texts. What Baur calls catholicism of the late second century represents the synthesis of warring factions in the church. However, the term *Frühkatholizismus* (early catholicism) suggests that the process leading to these developments is different. It is either understood as a falling away from the earliest gospel or, more positively, as the coming to light of what was implicit in the NT itself (Dunn 1990, 341).

This treatment of early catholicism will focus largely on the writings of Ernst Käsemann.[19] Though he is not the earliest proponent of this approach to Christian texts,[20] his work is often introduced in discussion of this developmental model, especially with respect to 2 Peter.

For Käsemann, the term early catholicism generally means those writings which antedate the emergence of the great church but still show features fully expressed in that institution (such as hierarchy and a formulated rule of faith). Käsemann saw in 2 Peter an example of this phenomenon. Faith, once a Spirit–motivated response of individuals to the self–revelation of God in Christ, had become an object which is obtained (2 Pet 1:1; 2:21). Revelation "is now a piece of property which is at the community's disposal," and since this contradicts other NT writings (1982a, 174), he can argue, "we are compelled to admit the existence not merely of significant tensions, but, not infrequently, of irreconcilable theological contradictions" (1982b, 100). He speaks of the distinction between letter and Spirit (2 Cor 3), which describes an abuse of God's revealed will, namely, that men do not let God's claim upon them remain his. They imagine God as prisoner of his own ordinance and therefore begin to venerate the law as a self–existent reality rather than as a proclamation of the divine will. This sheds light on his views of 2 Peter:

---

[19]A recent tribute to Käsemann in the pages of the *Anglican Theological Review* provides a fascinating introduction to the life and thought of this important NT theologian (see Zahl 1998).

[20]Use of the term early catholicism (*Frühkatholizismus*) goes back to F. C. Baur (R. P. Martin 1993a, 223) though some suggest it was first used by W. Heitmüller or E. Troeltsch (Neufeld 1972 [this reference taken from Martin]).

...we cannot keep God imprisoned even within the canon of the New Testament. Because the Jews held this view of the Old Testament, Paul speaks of the Old Testament canon as 'the letter that killeth'. The same is true of the New Testament if it is approached in the same way. The canon is not the word of God *tout simple*. It can only become and be the Word of God so long as we do not seek to imprison God within it; for this would be to make it a substitute for the God who addresses us and makes claims upon us (1982b, 105–06).

He finds in the phrase "the truth that has come to you" (2 Pet 1:12) an example of the church's tendency of doing this very thing.

According to Käsemann, the following catholic traits are found in 2 Peter. First, an issue confronting Christians early on in the church's history was the delay of the Parousia. The original readers of 2 Peter "were embarrassed and disturbed by the fact of the delay of the parousia, a fact naturally used by the adversaries to bolster up their argument" (1982a, 170), and, in fact, this letter was intended to provide a defense of the primitive hope.

Second, Käsemann argues that revelation had become an object only to be interpreted by ecclesiastical authority (1:12; 2:21; 3:2). A key passage in his thesis at this point is 1:19–21:

So we have the prophetic message more fully confirmed. You will do well to be attentive to this as to a lamp shining in a dark place, until the day dawns and the morning star rises in your hearts. First of all you must understand this, that no prophecy of scripture is a matter of one's own interpretation, because no prophecy ever came by human will, but men and women moved by the Holy Spirit spoke from God.

Käsemann's reading of this passage is approximately as follows. Presented here is the ministerial's strategy for opposing gnostic enthusiasts and the reason why primitive Christian prophecy has disappeared. The latter was too dangerous to be allowed, and so the church adopted a hierarchy with ordination, which was a natural opponent to both gnosis and Christian prophecy. Since the interpretation of Scripture could be manipulated by opponents, it too had to be regulated. In 2 Pet 1:21 the Scriptures are said to be inspired, and since only Spirit can interpret Spirit, the interpreter must have the Spirit of God. But it can no longer be assumed that every Christian has the Spirit (as Paul taught, Rom 8:9), and so Spirit is viewed as bound to official ministry. This all points to a transformation which has occurred by the time 2 Peter was written; in contrast with the pristine gospel, this early catholic framework pictures faith "transformed unmistakably into *fides implicita*: I believe what the Church believes" (191; full discussion, 187–91).

Third, the Christology of 2 Peter is "[t]he real theological problem of the epistle" (178). Allusions to the Parousia of Christ (1:16), his kingdom (1:11), the Day of the Lord (3:10, 12) and judgment (2:3–4, 9; 3:7) are not indicative of the character of the letter. Reference to entering the eternal kingdom as a goal (1:11 cf. 1:5–10) and the hope of "participating in the divine nature" (1:4; i.e., Hellenism) indicate a "purely man–centred" Christology. Only the portrayal of the Lord as future judge (2:9, 12; 3:10–13) links eschatology and Christology. Regarding allusions to the Parousia, "It is true that formal allusions are made [to the Parousia but] conventional turns of phrase have little meaning unless their object of reference is clearly identified" (178).

Käsemann's essay on 2 Peter is among the most influential studies of this epistle to emerge in the last fifty years. And while many scholars have subsequently challenged his conclusions, and indeed the early catholic model as a whole (see below), this essay remains a significant attempt to locate 2 Peter (namely, in post–Pauline catholic Christianity of the second century).

2.2.3 TRAJECTORIES

James M. Robinson and Helmut Koester have suggested a model for locating texts that is based on the recognition of movement in early Christianity. Rather than imagining the context of the NT and the early church as monolithic, it needs to be viewed as a moving, evolving reality.

> The Jewish, Greek, or gnostic background or environment cannot be mastered by reducing it to a mass of disorganized parallels to the New Testament but must be reconceptualized in terms of movements, "trajectories" through the Hellenistic world (Robinson and Koester 1971, 13).

According to this model,[21] ideas/concepts/tendencies evolve over time and, as the process of development is recognized, it is possible to locate texts along the proper point of the trajectory.[22] Progress in early Christian thought is easily recognized;

---

[21]These ideas are not entirely new: "Koester and Robinson have made an important suggestion about new ways of thinking, and they have, perhaps inadvertently, reactivated some insights of the church fathers. They have recognized, as Tertullian did, that contexts are the key to meaning, that 'orthodoxy' and 'heresy' are directions of movement, not fixed positions. They have recognized, as Origen knew, that Christianity moved through a series of language worlds, not just languages, and that with each 'translation' it underwent subtle but pervasive changes" (Henry 1979, 110).

[22]"Helmut Koester and James Robinson have suggested that we shift the images we use for thinking about the relationships of apostolic Christianity and Gnosticism from 'backgrounds' to 'trajectories.' According to these scholars, ideological tendencies and psychological states have a kind of independent life which can be plotted along historical graphs. A particular text is then located not against some particular background, but rather by its points on the trajectory. Its place is defined as much in terms of what comes after it as in terms of what comes before it. The imagery of trajectories also permits the interpreter, using a great deal of caution, to trace a curve back beyond the point at which the earliest documentary evidence begins, and hence to speculate about the state of a particular tendency where the evidence is lacking but the questions are insistent" (Henry 1979, 109–10).

"La catégorie fondamentale est celle de «trajectory», qui, en «reconceptualisant» les concepts de «background» et d' «environment», renouvelle la problématique entière. En effet, elle

changes can be observed from Jesus to Paul, Paul to Mark or Ignatius, from Ignatius to Irenaeus or Origen, and then to Augustine or Athanasius (10). One way this model can be understood specifically in relation to the Apostle Peter is in the suggestion that a school of followers who held to his teachings was formed in the years after his death. Robinson and Koester do not speak of a Petrine school, but at times they do refer to a Pauline school and the role it played in the transmission and development of the apostle's teachings. Referring to the progression of Christian thought described above (Jesus to Athanasius), Robinson writes:

> This is not simply a case of random variety, of pluralism. A more penetrating analysis reveals individual items to be exponents of intelligible movements. Thus one can trace a course from the subphilosophical cultural level of primitive Christianity, via the philosophical pretenses of the apologetes, to the philosophical ability of the Alexandrian theologians; or from Paul's theology to that of the gradually bifurcating Pauline school, with one stream moving via Ephesians to 1 Peter, Luke–Acts, the Pastorals, and on to orthodoxy, the other via Colossians to Valentinus, Basilides, Marcion, and on to heresy . . . . (10).

The idea of theological trajectories is illustrated later, during Robinson's consideration of developing views of the resurrection. Tracing the "fanatical or mystical form of belief in the resurrection" combated in the Pastorals (see 2 Tim 2:18), Robinson points out that this error was already addressed in Paul's first letter to the Corinthians (see 1 Cor 15:23 [understood as Paul correcting an error]). What was imagined in Corinth was an already consummated eschaton for the initiated. The development of this error can be observed in later writings.

> One can to some extent trace the missing links in such a development (missing largely because writings from the opposing side have not survived) by noting how such views gradually worked their way into the part of the Pauline school that gained admission into the canon (34–35).

Robinson follows a trail of realized eschatology in Col 2:12–13 and Eph 2:5–6 (deuteropauline texts written after Paul's death but consciously developing his thought) and in later gnostic literature. In this example, one is able to trace the progress of an idea from its source (Paul), through interpretation of that idea by Paul's followers (Colossians, Ephesians; a Pauline school), to later writings (gnostic literature among the Nag Hammadi Library) that could still connect their

---

permet de considérer les positions successives qu'adopte un phénomène donné dans le champ du Christianisme primitif et de son environnement comme formant une ou plusieurs séries de lignes évolutives: leur diversification s'expliquerait par un certain nombre de facteurs historiques qu'il s'agit de déceler et de décrire (cf. *Sitz im Leben*)" (Haulotte 1974, 113; see also the helpful reviews by Wilson [1972, 475–77] and Kistemaker [1973, 338–40] for brief summaries and evaluation).

views with the Apostle Paul.[23] As a model of development, the study of trajectories represents a way of locating texts lacking explicit information for placing them in a specific historical context.

A subset of this trajectories model would contain the identification of ancient schools. Proposals suggesting a school around a prominent teacher represent another way of locating ancient texts. In NT studies, the Johannine literature especially has been treated in this way, but it has been applied to the Petrine writings as well. Various scholars have expressed approval for this explanation of their relationship to one another (though with little evidence in support). For example:

> . . . the epistle [1 Peter] was pseudonymous but emerged from a Petrine school (Best 1971, 63).

> Are the two documents [2 Peter and the *Apocalypse of Peter*] the work of two writers who belonged to the same school, whose thoughts moved in the same directions, and to whom the same expressions and words had grown familiar?. . . The fact that there is a similarity between the two writings, not only in words or in definitely marked ideas, but also in general conceptions . . . seems to be an argument of some strength in favour of the view that the two documents are the product of the same school (Chase 1898–1904, 3:816).

> 2 Peter carries marks of having been composed by members of the 'school of Peter' . . . at a time when Peter's memory was cherished and his aegis claimed for teaching required to repel rival teachers . . . . [t]he author of 2 Peter was a devoted member of the Petrine school (Chester and Martin 1994, 145, 139; cf. 90–94).

> Rome is . . . at least a plausible candidate for the composition of II Peter within a Petrine "school" (Brown 1997, 768).

More extensively, Marion Soards has explored this thesis in his "1 & 2 Peter, Jude: Evidence for a Petrine School" (1988; cf. Vanessa Ward's addenda to the *ANRW* articles on 1 Peter, 2 Peter, and Jude in the light of Soards' thesis, 1988). Among his observations, he points to literary similarities and dissimilarities in the documents which, he argues, are best explained if these texts were all written in

---

[23]"In view of this direction of Pauline interpretation in the Deutero–Pauline period it is not too surprising when the same Paul who had opposed baptismal resurrection in Corinth came to be claimed as theirs by precisely those gnostic movements that held to this heresy, such as the Valentinians; indeed Paul was hailed by them as 'apostle of resurrection' [Tertullian, *Praescr.* 33.7]. The Coptic gnostic library from near Nag Hammadi has filled in one missing link, by turning up a gnostic document 'On the Resurrection' that affirms explicitly (49:15–16), 'Already you have the resurrection,' and quotes Paul (42:24–28) in support of precisely the same left–wing Deutero–Pauline development once opposed by Paul himself that was moving toward that heresy. . . . Thus we have fairly early in the second century a clean split in the understanding of Paul: gnostics appeal to him for support of baptismal resurrection, while the pastorals reject that view as heresy (2 Tim. 2:18)" (35–36).

and/or used by different people in one community. Along with liturgical features found in 1 Peter, 2 Peter and Jude, and similarities in theology and use of the OT, he notes the shared use of pseudepigraphy and source material (among other things).[24]

2.3 DEVELOPMENTAL MODELS, PRESUPPOSITIONS, AND THE LOCATION OF TEXTS

2.3.1 LOCATING TEXTS: A GENERAL SUMMARY OF APPROACHES USED

Each of the models described above testifies to scholarship's limited knowledge of the early church and represents an attempt to fill in the blanks by creating a larger picture which explains the available data and locates that data in a broad scheme. However, as will be shown, sketching the big picture involves assumptions about the church, which, though perhaps correct, cannot be verified to the satisfaction of scholarship as a whole (cf. 3.2.9 [the importance of scholarly consensus]). While each of these models offers certain insights into the developing church and the place of literature within it, they cannot offer a completely satisfactory reconstruction.

Evidence usually cited as the basis for locating 2 Peter can be outlined generally under one of the following headings. In what way is 2 Peter (a) properly located within a recognizable religious or geographical milieu, (b) the product of (therefore dependent on) an earlier religious milieu, or (c) an influence on (therefore a source for) a later, recognizable religious milieu? In each case the evidence is found in texts. Ideally all three are considered together.

Attempts to locate 2 Peter *within* a recognizable religious, cultural,[25] or

---

[24]Cf. his summary statement (3828). He also points to P[72] as "a kind of physical evidence that this interpretation is not merely a cleverly devised myth" (3840). This papyrus codex from the third century includes only 1 Peter, 2 Peter, and Jude from the NT as well as two Psalms and six noncanonical documents. "Thus, one sees concrete proof that the three letters which are viewed together in this study were held together, apart from other NT writings, by some early Christian(s)" (3840).

[25]Some attempts to identify the religious or cultural milieu remain too general to distinguish the world of a specific text from the wider contemporary world around it. For example, while reconstructions of the social location of the author offered by socio–rhetorical studies are valuable, especially for modern readers concerned to understand a culture removed by two thousand years, they do not narrow the ancient environment sufficiently to distinguish a specific text from the broader backdrop (with respect to 2 Peter, see especially Neyrey 1993). There is also an implied assumption in such studies that an author necessarily reflects the context in which he or she is writing (cf. 3.3.5 below). The same could be said of those studies reading texts through a specific hermeneutical lens. For example, little has been done in reading 2 Peter from a feminist perspective (but see Dowd 1992; Selvidge 1999, 399 [briefly]; and more thoroughly, Rosenblatt 1994). Though some light may be shed on the possible place of women in the specific congregation(s) addressed, and perhaps also on the biases or prejudices shaping

geographical milieu take a variety of forms as has already been seen. Whether 2 Peter is situated within a school (e.g., Soards), region (e.g., Bauckham), or theological perspective (e.g., Käsemann), it is believed that parallels in vocabulary or ideas assist in locating it on the basis of similarities with other texts.

At other times, a location for 2 Peter is determined by its *dependence on* earlier traditions or texts.[26] At issue here is the possibility of determining a *terminus a quo* for 2 Peter. When Jude is viewed as a source, the date of Jude becomes a basis for dating 2 Peter. If it is maintained that 2 Pet 3:15–16 implies a late stage in the developing Pauline corpus, then again the location of 2 Peter is based on dependence of this document on an earlier phenomenon.

Some are concerned to find evidence of 2 Peter's *influence on* later traditions. Here there is an interest to discover traces of 2 Peter in later Christian writings. If 2 Peter's priority over Jude is maintained, the NT itself provides the earliest attestation (so Bigg 1901, 210; cf. Moo 1996, 18; this position is not widely held). Second Peter is not actually quoted in the second century, though its influence on various texts has been suggested (see 4.5 and 4.6). In this case, the hope is to find a *terminus ad quem* by which the date of 2 Peter can be narrowed.[27]

---

the author, this is still evidence for the broader context of the text, not a specific milieu discernable within it.

[26]Here, the idea of development *away from* earlier traditions would also fit (so again, Käsemann).

[27]Generally not much has been said about 2 Peter's influence on later theology. One tantalizing example of this is found in a study by the Russian theologian Jerzy Klinger, who has explored a few ways this letter helped shape later Christian thought. For one thing, he suggests 2 Peter is "the first document reflecting, in a rudimentary form, the idea of the primacy of the two leading Apostles Peter and Paul [a statement which assumes 2 Peter is earlier than *1 Clement*], which was accepted by the Universal Church from the second century, and which the Church of Rome has lost in her theology since the fourth century by limiting herself to the primacy of Peter, although she preserved the older form in her liturgical awareness (the common feast of the two leading Apostles)" (1973, 159). In the letter's response to the liberalism of false disciples of Paul, under the name of another authority equal to Paul, Klinger finds that 2 Peter represents "an important step in the development of Christian thought" (159). At another point, he suggests that 2 Peter "opens a new road which leads to Christian gnosis" (161). Most intriguing is his observation that in its response to erroneous disciples of Paul, 2 Peter represents a return to a law–based morality that is combined with the 'by faith alone salvation' emphasis found in Paul. The ethical model put forward by 2 Peter is influenced by Stoicism. Here again Klinger discovers in 2 Peter a theme that influenced subsequent Christian theological thought: "In this respect, *2 Peter* appears to me as the first document which furnishes a Christian basis for such an argument [i.e., putting pagan philosophy on equal footing with OT ethical law], even if it does not make the argument explicit. . . . it seems to me that *2 Peter* is the most ancient attempt at a specifically theological synthesis on the border between the end of the New Testament revelation and the beginning of the development of Church tradition" (168).

What is of interest here is Klinger's approach, namely that he is consciously looking for ways 2 Peter left its mark on subsequent theological developments. Unfortunately certain questions are not addressed. For one thing, he never demonstrates whether it was 2 Peter specifically or ideas available from other sources that was the influencing agent. Even if

2.3.2 LOCATING TEXTS AND DEVELOPMENTAL THEORIES

Reaching specific conclusions about where certain Christian writings belong involves prior decisions about how early Christianity developed. Once this framework is in place, it is only a short step to locating a document on the basis of features which the writing has or does not have. The following models illustrate a few possible patterns (there are overlaps in some cases).

a) One model understands the church to have emerged from early competing parties (Baur). Over time, a mediating position brought about a harmony that eventually culminated in catholic Christianity. Philosophically undergirded by Hegel's thesis–antithesis–synthesis developmental model, Baur constructed a framework that allowed for the location of early Christian documents, including 2 Peter.

b) The church represents a process of decay from an early ideal (Käsemann). Unlike 'e' below, there is not a complete break with a golden past, but there is a gradual slipping away from the ideals demonstrated by the earliest Christian writings (i.e., Paul). Second–century Christianity (usually thought to include 2 Peter) is *qualitatively* unlike first–century Christianity, though it reflects attempts to imitate the past.

c) The church represents a process of development from immaturity towards maturity. Some writers have understood the post–apostolic developments leading toward institutional, catholic Christianity as a positive step in the growth of the gospel into its fullest expression. In view of this model of development, even if 2 Peter is understood to be a late text, a negative stigma is not necessarily attached to it. Roman Catholicism would fit here.[28]

d) The first century was the church's golden age, which should be imitated in the present. Most conservative communities of faith that hold Scripture to be an authority in some sense (even if the Bible is supplemented with other revelation; cf. 'e' below) will recognize in all the NT writings authoritative texts that are of equal value. Unlike 'a' or 'b,' one cannot set one text over against another as being qualitatively different in terms of its authority for matters of faith or historical

---

Klinger's observations are correct, the *terminus ad quem* suggested by such history of ideas is too general to assist in the task of locating 2 Peter to a specific context.

[28]With respect to 'b' and 'c', see Elliott's study of early catholicism which states that certain Protestant and Catholic scholars betray presuppositions in their research influenced by their ecclesiastical backgrounds (1969). His own model represents an attempt to avoid the polemics charged against those described in his study. Elliott argues that the gospel involves change. "The gospel is *change* because this dynamic relating of God to man through Jesus in history constitutes a change from alienation and incompleteness to integration and integrity. The gospel is good news. . . . It is recognized and described and manifested as good news because it changes and ameliorates a 'bad' situation. As the historical characteristics of the 'bad' situation change, so the explication of the gospel will accordingly change" (222 [his italics]).

reconstruction.[29]   Most who adhere to such a model would assume Petrine authorship of 2 Peter, because the idea of pseudepigraphy is morally inconsistent with the ethical thrust of the NT and at odds with the concept of canon.[30]

e) The first century of the church's existence was a golden age brought quickly to a close by an absolute and destructive apostasy that resulted in a complete loss of the truth. Only at a later time, with the arrival of new revelation or correct interpretation of the earlier revelation (i.e., the Bible), was an understanding of the gospel message restored. To illustrate, the official commentary on Revelation published by The Watch Tower Bible and Tract Society argues that a great apostasy began shortly after John's death and involved such things as the substitution of the term Lord for the name Jehovah, and the doctrine of the Trinity (1988, 30). Similarly, the Church of Jesus Christ of Latter Day Saints speaks of a break in continuity with apostolic times (Palmer, Keller, Choi, and Toronto 1997, 271). In this case, rather than recovering proper doctrine from the Bible as in the case of the Jehovah's Witnesses, an additional authoritative Scripture was introduced that provided further revelation (i.e., the *Book of Mormon*). Such a model contains a clear distinction between the past and the later time of renewal, when the gospel is rediscovered. Latter–day Saints speak of a restoration of the truth which involved, among other things, a land prepared for the purpose of this revelation, where religious freedom and pluralism could exist. Since most religions were tied to governments, America was uniquely qualified to meet this need.[31] For this reason, the restoration would begin there (i.e., the discovery of further revelation by Joseph Smith in 1823).[32]

---

[29]There may be some distance between acceptance of this presupposition as a tenet of faith (e.g., 2 Tim 3:16 applied to the NT itself along with the OT) and the religious use of all NT writings by believers in a religious community. Sermons and perhaps personal reading of Scripture may tend to favour some writings over others (e.g., some may find the Gospels more edifying than the Apocalypse; or perhaps Paul's letter to the Philippians more comprehensible than Hebrews).

[30]Consider the following comments: "if the Pastorals are Scripture, their claim to authorship, like all other assertions, should be received as truth from God; and one who rejects this claim ought also to deny that they are Scripture, for what he is saying is that they have not the nature of Scripture, since they make false statements. . . . [and] if we are to regard 2 Peter as canonical we must regard it as apostolic also" (Packer 1958, 184–85).

[31]The importance of religious freedom for the restoration is implied in the *Book of Mormon*: e.g., "And men are instructed sufficiently that they know good from evil"; "Wherefore, how great the importance to make these things known unto the inhabitants of the earth" (*2 Nephi* 2:5, 8).

[32]Elsewhere in Latter–day Saints literature the following description is found: "After the death of Jesus' Apostles, the power of the priesthood and many truths of the gospel were taken from the earth, beginning a long period of spiritual darkness called the great Apostasy. . . . During the long centuries of the Apostasy, many honest men and women sought the fulness of gospel truth but were unable to find it. . . . the Lord in his mercy had promised that his gospel and priesthood power would one day be restored to the earth, never to be taken away again. As the nineteenth century dawned, his promise was about to be fulfilled and the long night of

f) A more general category, similar in some respects to 'a,' recognizes diversity in early Christianity, with different communities holding to distinctive theological teachings. Here the terms orthodoxy and heresy prove to be misleading, as there was no pristine gospel from which later distortions emerged (i.e., in some cases heresy preceded orthodoxy). Rather, Christianity was from the beginning a diverse religion with a variety of expressions. What remains today as the voices of orthodoxy (2 Peter, as part of the canon, represents this orthodoxy as it was eventually selected as an authoritative and apostolic voice over many other texts that were rejected by the church) simply represents the party that won out in the end (cf. Bauer 1971, xxi–xxv).

There are other models,[33] but these illustrate sufficiently how prior assumptions about development guide in the location of texts.

2.3.3 EVALUATION OF DEVELOPMENTAL THEORIES

It needs to be recognized that, in each of these examples, presuppositions favour one model over the others. In one case, philosophical assumptions are quite obvious (a); in four others (b, c, d, e) it could be argued that the religious convictions of the scholar make a particular developmental theory more attractive than others.[34] Some Protestants may have a bias against catholic tendencies that

---

apostasy was about to end" (The Church of Jesus Christ of Latter–day Saints 1996, 1).

[33]For example, according to a history of religions model, Christianity is a syncretistic religion (classically, Gunkel 1903, 95). In this view, a variety of currents flowed into evolving Christianity including mystery religions and Gnosticism. In opposition to the history of religions model is the view proposed by Adolph von Harnack. For him the Christian message was superior to the environment in which it was proclaimed: "in the course of [the apostolic age] the Gospel was detached from the mother–soil of Judaism and placed upon the broad field of the Graeco–Roman empire. The apostle Paul was the chief agent in accomplishing this work, and in thereby giving Christianity its place in the history of the world. . . . The Gospel did not come into the world as a statutory religion, and therefore none of the forms in which it assumed intellectual and social expression—not even the earliest—can be regarded as possessing a classical and permanent character. The historian must always keep this guiding idea before him when he undertakes to trace the course of the Christian religion through the centuries from the apostolic age downwards" (1958, 139). Jesus' message was understood correctly by Paul who disseminated that message into the Greco–Roman world. But unlike the history of religions model, the true essence of Christianity is not the product of syncretism (though it is time–bound and so reflects the context in which it is presented). On the contrary, the Christian message is superior to its environment. White writes in his description of Harnack's view that for him "the essence of Christianity remained constant through the shifting sands of the ages, even though it was all too often covered over by drifts and dunes of institutional and social expression" (1985/86, 99). The Christian message was, in terms of its content, virtually isolated from its historical environment (Kümmel 1972, 313–14).

[34]Or perhaps, as some would no doubt argue, it is the reverse: conclusions about historical development in the early church came first and these resulted in, or contributed to, a particular decision in matters of faith (?).

appeared in the second century. If hints of these tendencies are found in the NT (and they have been observed in 2 Peter), they may lead to a negative assessment of the text (so 'b'). On the other hand, Roman Catholic scholars would naturally be more comfortable with so–called catholic elements in the NT (so 'c').

Conservative Bible readers recognize in the Scriptures a unique authority— the church is built on the foundation of the apostles and prophets (i.e., the whole Bible [cf. Eph 2:20]). With this starting point, all NT texts by definition are apostolic in origin or have apostolic authority, and this requires early dating of the NT writings. Among the presuppositions involved here is the belief that the decisions made by the early church in its selection of authoritative texts were in some sense inspired.

The models that posit an early apostasy with recovery of spiritual truth at a later time are the most vivid examples of an apparent link between a faith stance and historical reconstruction ('e'). The very nature of such traditions requires that most if not all developments in the history of Christianity and Christian thought apart from the apostolic testimony be rejected. The latter is interpreted in the light of the group's distinctive insights.

A further example of religious presuppositions guiding scholarly constructs is found in theories about the development of Christianity that involve a denigration of Judaism. An example of this is found in the idea of a distant God among some history of religions theorists. Here too religious biases and presuppositions are involved.[35]

---

[35]It has been suggested that a sense of God's distance from his people provides an explanation for the increased presence of angels in postexilic literature (on the need for theological interpretation of Israel's political catastrophe generally, see Albertz 1994, 375–99). Accordingly angels became mediators between a distant holy God and his fallen creation: "The belief in angels—already familiar and well established in the Hebrew tradition—formed a vital bridge between God and his universe which otherwise would have been difficult to construct" (Russell 1964, 237). Such an approach was thoroughly applied by Wilhelm Bousset in his widely influential *Die Religion des Judentums im späthellenistischen Zeitalter* (3d ed. 1926). His main thesis was that there was an erosion of monotheism in postexilic Judaism, partly demonstrated by the angelology of the period. Since God no longer spoke directly to the prophets but rather to angels, God was perceived to be more distant (329). Furthermore, the intercessory role of angels meant that he was no longer of central importance (329–30). Prohibitions against the worship of angels (e.g., Rev 19:10) and accusations by early Christian writers of Jewish angel worship (e.g., Origen, *Comm. Jo.* 13:17; *Cels.* 1:26; 5:6) were conclusive evidence for Bousset of the decay of Jewish monotheism.

The full implications of such an approach are alarming. Earlier in this century G. F. Moore demonstrated that the notion of a distant God in ancient Judaism does not exist. It is rather a modern Protestant polemic being read back into ancient texts (Moore 1921). More recently Hurtado has presented a careful challenge to Bousset (1988, esp. 24–35). He points out that far from showing a sense of distance between God and his people, the organization of angels and their presence throughout the world can be understood as an attempt to emphasize the power of Israel's God. Israel's position was small among the contending world powers, and since their God was closely tied to the nation, a need may have been perceived to assert his power and

2.3.4 FURTHER EVALUATION OF DEVELOPMENTAL MODELS

At this point, a more detailed analysis of some of the models introduced earlier in this chapter is offered,[36] particularly, the presuppositions involved in these theories and the extent to which literary parallels are cited as evidence in support of them.

A few responses to Käsemann's thesis (Käsemann being the writer who best illustrates the major themes of the early catholicism model in relation to 2 Peter) and the early catholicism model more generally can be given.

First, it was seen that Käsemann found in 2 Peter a shift from early Christian eschatological beliefs: there was embarrassment over the delay of the Parousia and the epistle no longer showed evidence of the primitive view that the end had already dawned with the coming of Jesus. Instead, the last days follow the coming of Jesus and the apostolic proclamation, meaning that eschatology is now orientating itself "along the line of the current secular conception of time" (1982a, 170). This assessment of 2 Peter is somewhat puzzling. Far from suggesting that the author of 2 Peter downplayed eschatological expectation, the reverse seems to be true. Second Peter speaks of the Parousia in relation to its readers (1:19; 3:14) and its opponents (2:1, 12). Even though he addresses the problem raised by the delay of the Parousia (i.e., the mockers, 3:4, 9), the arguments do not postpone Christ's coming to the distant future, rather "they are traditional Jewish apocalyptic arguments which belong in the context of Jewish apocalyptic's characteristic tension between the sense of eschatological imminence and a wrestling with the problem of delay" (Bauckham 1983, 151). It is simply not true that the epistle

---

significance. "Over against the apparent earthly insignificance of Israel, . . . God is shown to be the true king of all in the sphere of ultimate reality—the heavenlies. God's might and awesomeness are portrayed by means of the most impressive model of earthly power known to the writers of these texts, the imperial court and its hierarchy. . . . In other words, the image of the angelic hierarchy was intended as a way of relativizing the earthly structures of authority and power with which Israel had to contend in this period. This is not evidence of a distant God at the center of Jewish religion but the opposite!" (26). Bousset's study points to an attempt to magnify Christianity by presenting a bleak portrayal of Judaism (27; cf. Moore 1921, 252–54; Charlesworth 1985, 29–31).

[36]Many of the comments on early catholicism are relevant to Baur's reconstruction as well. There is no further discussion on arguments of geographical provenance and destination because the variety of theories suggests that certainty is not possible. Connections to Rome and Asia Minor are indeed strong though the qualifications mentioned about the movement of authors and texts should be remembered. There is also no further critique of Reicke's thesis. As noted in the discussion above, his ideas have not been taken up by subsequent commentators. His idiosyncratic exegesis of specific passages and his tendency to move quickly from historical setting to specific details of texts assumes a correspondence between the two that cannot be proven. This is a common tendency in NT scholarship but one that is problematic, mainly because reconstructions are always speculative and open to question. Therefore, the move from reconstruction to text can be inaccurate due to the conclusions reached regarding the former.

downplays eschatological hope.

Second, Käsemann argues that revelation had become an object only to be interpreted by ecclesiastical authority (1:12; 2:21; 3:2). In addition to the fact that such authorities are nowhere mentioned in the epistle, a key passage on which this thesis rests (1:19–21 [cited on p.26]) is quite possibly misinterpreted.[37] In his understanding, this passage explains first how the official ministerial opposed gnostic enthusiasts. At the same time, it represents the cause for the decline in primitive Christian prophecy. By adopting a hierarchy with ordination, the church silenced both. Since the interpretation of Scripture could be manipulated by opponents, it had to be regulated. This all points to a transformation that occurred by the time 2 Peter was written. In contrast with the early (Pauline) gospel, (later) early catholic literature pictures faith reduced to faith in the church's teaching (1982a, 191; full discussion, 187–91).[38] This thesis involves serious difficulties.

---

[37]There is ambiguity in 2 Pet 1:19–21 and interpretation has gone in two directions: it either sees orthodox versus private interpretation at issue, or, a question of whether or not the prophets knew what was contained in their oracles (Neyrey 1980a, 516). Käsemann introduces a specific question with respect to the OT prophecies mentioned in 2 Pet 1:19–20: "We might well wonder why all mention of primitive Christian prophecy has disappeared" (1982a, 187). However, it needs to be recognized that what "the prophetic message" (2 Pet 1:19) refers to is ambiguous as the various suggestions indicate. It has been understood to refer to (a) OT messianic prophecy (Käsemann; Bigg; Mayor); (b) the whole OT understood as messianic prophecy (Schelkle; Kelly; Bauckham); (c) a specific prophecy (Fornberg); (d) OT and NT prophecies (Plumptre; Sidebottom); (e) 2 Pet 1:20–2:19 (Robson); and (f) the transfiguration as prophecy of the Parousia (Neyrey). By asking this question (quoted above) of 2 Pet 1:19–21, *Käsemann introduces a question that does not obviously present itself in reading the first chapter of 2 Peter*. As a result he is able to make various assertions: prophecy was dangerous in the hands of gnostics; a monarchical episcopate was formed to provide protection; 2 Peter had no knowledge of Christian prophecy (1982a, 187–88). He is selective when exegetical options exist. A further example is found in his exegesis of 1:20. Does the phrase ἰδίας ἐπιλύσις mean "one's own" ("no one can interpret any prophecy of Scripture by himself," NEB) or does it imply "the prophet's own" ("no prophecy of Scripture came about by the prophet's own interpretation," NIV)? Most frequently the first alternative is followed (Käsemann included) and in its favour is Peter's interest in combating false teachers in the following chapter; the emphasis would then be that interpretation is not man's business but the Holy Spirit's (cf. 3:16). However, it has been argued that this reading overlooks a likely connection between vv.20–21 and the preceding verses where the issue is not interpretation but authentication, namely the origin and reliability of Christian teaching concerning grace, holiness, and heaven (Neyrey 1980a, 518; Bauckham 1983, 232; Green 1987, 101). The point here is that although an alternative reading exists, it is only mentioned in passing in Käsemann's exegesis. This raises some suspicion about his theory which rests heavily here on ambiguous language (cf. comments in 3.5.4 below). At best it is a possibility. It does not acknowledge the other major option—that "one's own" is a reference to the prophet's own interpretation (so NIV). He acknowledges that ἰδία ἐπιλύσις "is a matter of dispute among Protestant exegetes" but he attributes this to a failure to take account of the antithesis, i.e., they miss "the polemical point of the passage" (1982a, 189).

[38]Statements in 1:12 ("the truth which is present with you") and 2:21 ("the holy commandment delivered to them") are cited as evidence that revelation is now a piece of

Green for one writes of it: "Of all this, needless to say, there is no hint in the passage itself" (1987, 101 n.1).

Third, for Käsemann the Christology of 2 Peter is the real theological problem of this letter (1982a, 178). References to the eschatological hope do not accurately describe the character of 2 Peter. Rather, references to entering the eternal kingdom as a goal (1:11 cf. 1:5–10) and the hope of participating in the divine nature (1:4) indicate a man–centred Christology (178). Second Peter is pictured here as an extreme form of doctrine quite distant from more typical expressions of NT faith; it attempts to accommodate Christianity to Hellenistic culture. This is based on observations about the fading Parousia hope, the christological orientation of the writer (cf. above), and further specific comparisons with Paul (e.g., no reference to the cross; doctrine of justification replaced with a works/rewards/punishment formula [183–85]). In each of these instances, Käsemann is found building on a significant pre–understanding of the nature of early Christian development: he assumes that Paul's teachings represent the norm. As a result, by the time 2 Peter was written (he believes mid–second century) there was a moving away from Paul's standard.[39]

Some final reflections on early catholicism are more general in scope. James Dunn's revised *Unity and Diversity of the New Testament* (first ed. 1977; second ed. 1990) helps illustrate some tendencies in the current scholarly discussion of early catholicism. In his foreword to the new edition, Dunn summarizes and responds to concerns expressed after the initial publication of this book.

> With chapter XIV, 'Early Catholicism', the principal problem was the title itself. 'Early Catholicism' is becoming an outmoded term, the product of Lutheran confessionalism, and it has a distinctly pejorative ring (1990, xxix).

Apparently such a ring was heard in the first edition of *Unity and Diversity*, provoking the censure of some Roman Catholic reviewers (examples are given). While Dunn denies that this was the intention, he admits that avoiding the negative association with the term early catholicism is difficult. Still, he chose to retain it in the new edition (except lower case letters are used to avoid confusing catholicism as he sees it with Roman Catholicism) for two primary reasons. First, because some proposed alternatives would not necessarily be an improvement (e.g., early orthodoxy would face the same problem with Eastern Christianity as catholicism

---

property. However, there is no reason to see here anything but the passing on of tradition, something not unique to 2 Peter (cf. 1 Cor 15:3).

[39]Cf. Schulz whose definition of early catholicism is very broad. Among features he includes are a misunderstanding of Paul's message of justification and an un–Pauline understanding of the law (1976, 80). On the basis of his definition all NT writings apart from Paul are early catholic. His definition as been criticized for being too broad (e.g., Dunn 1990, 422 n.11) as it incorporates whatever is not in accord with the Paulinism of the principal Pauline letters. Early catholic tendencies and characteristics are found in 20 of the 27 NT writings.

does with Western), and second, the term does plug in with "an important strand of discussion running through most of the twentieth century" (xxx).

On the whole, however, there remains no consensus on how appropriate the early catholicism model is for the categorization of early Christian texts. Some authors appear to avoid the term altogether in favour of other designations.[40] In addition to the pejorative ring mentioned above, several specific weaknesses with the term are often repeated and likely account for a decline in its use in recent scholarship. One concern is the lack of an accepted definition of what the expression means. Sometimes it has been defined too broadly (e.g., Schulz). At other times, definitions may be too narrow and therefore exclude texts which should in fact belong. One introduction to the NT makes the comment that *Frühkatholizismus* "is not always defined, and there is no agreement as to exactly what the term connotes" and "'early catholicism' is an expression of uncertain meaning (each interpreter seems to have his or her own understanding of what it signifies)" (Carson, Moo, and Morris 1992, 124 and 462).[41]

There is also a tendency to make too sharp a break between earlier and later texts. As a result, the continuities that exist are not given adequate attention. For example, Tord Fornberg notes that several features generally regarded to be early catholic can be documented in earlier writings (e.g., faith as assent to a collection of tenets [Rom 6:17] and inspiration of the Scriptures [1 Pet 1:10–12], 1977, 3–6). At the same time, other features said to characterize these writings were not clearly formulated until a later period (e.g., a fixed canon). Fornberg finds only the inspiration of Scripture and the struggle with heresy in 2 Peter and he concludes that the label early catholicism is "an artificial category which cannot do justice to a document such as 2 Peter" (1977, 5).[42]

Also to be considered is whether Paul—usually held to be the standard of earliest Christian thinking from which early catholic texts depart—is correctly represented in the supposed contrasts between his writings and ministry and the activity of the later church. With respect to Paul, Tom Robinson has discussed the tendency to overstate Paul's ties to charismatic forms of ministry, with the result

---

[40]E.g., Bart Ehrman's use of "proto–orthodox" seems to be functioning as a substitute in his introduction to the NT (1997, e.g., 332–39, 393–96; cf. his definition, 6–7).

[41]This is illustrated in relation to Jude, a letter often said to be early catholic. Three common features in definitions—the fading of parousia hope, an interest in the church as an institution, and the use of credal forms to summarize the faith—are all lacking in Jude (462).

[42]There have been occasions when the designation of texts as early catholic has relied on overstatement and understatement. Käsemann illustrates the former in comments about the omission of Pauline concepts (1982a, 183–85) and the latter in his habit of down–playing aspects of 2 Peter's theology (e.g., eschatology; 178). Critiques of Käsemann's essay are often marked by a certain ambivalence: e.g., "There is in Käsemann's estimate, both truth and exaggeration. He has overstated the case in several ways, chiefly in ignoring the fact that the denial of imminence in the parousia hope is the sectarian's position, not the author's. The latter has a strongly held belief in Christ's coming to judgement in apocalyptic glory (1.19; 2.12; 3.10–14)" (Chester and Martin 1994, 149–50).

that an understanding of the apostle is distorted.[43] It is often assumed that Paul represents the centre of NT thought, and so any movement away from his writings (or whatever, or whoever else is taken to be the standard) is understood as a departure from the original form of the gospel. But this runs into problems. Is it not possible that Paul was exceptional or unique in his formulation of the gospel message (cf. 3.3.5; 3.5.3)?[44] Furthermore, it is not impossible that other texts which differed from Paul's may have been closer than Paul to the experience of everyday Christians (perhaps even 2 Peter).

As noted above, some have argued that 2 Peter was the product of a school associated with the Apostle Peter. Notably, Marion Soards has presented this hypothesis in some detail. Soards supported his case for a school by looking at the Petrine–Jude writings in relation to Alan Culpepper's characteristics of ancient schools (1975, esp. 258–60).[45] Soards acknowledges that characteristics 6, 7, and 9 are common to all early Christian congregations and therefore do not distinguish one from another, yet "the criteria established in the remaining points are sufficiently specific to provide adequate testing of the hypothesis that the Petrine community was a Petrine school" (1988, 3842). There is special pleading at points in his argument.[46] Furthermore, Jude and perhaps also 1 Peter were direct

---

[43]While Paul does appear to favour a charismatic view of office to the extent that he reflects on the matter, it is also possible that he had a somewhat ambiguous view of the issue. "Certainly it is an incautious reconstruction that contends that Paul, had he been alive, would have strenuously resisted the kind of re–definition of office that makes it more institutionalized" (1990, 241). There is a danger in reconstructions of early Christianity of imposing a logic or order to developments which did not exist among early Christians.

[44]Paul's unique thinking on the matter of the law in relation to the Gentile mission illustrates the point. Here his views were not widely taken up: "He was honored yet pushed aside; he was the egg–head among the operators, unique rather than universal" (Stendahl 1976, 71, full discussion 67–77). Cf. Crossan: "I do not think Paul was as important theologically or historically in the first Christian century as he was in the sixteenth Christian century, and that later importance often blocks our ability to assess his original significance" (1998, xxi).

[45]Culpepper finds: "the greatest similarities among the schools [nine examples are examined] lie in the following areas: 1) they were groups of disciples which usually emphasized φιλία and κοινωνία; 2) they gathered around, and traced their origins to a founder whom they regarded as an exemplary wise, or good man; 3) they valued the teachings of their founder and the traditions about him; 4) members of the schools were disciples or students of the founder; 5) teaching, learning, studying, and writing were common activities; 6) most schools observed communal meals, often in memory of their founders; 7) they had rules or practices regarding admission, retention of membership, and advancement within the membership; 8) they often maintained some degree of distance or withdrawal from the rest of society; and 9) they developed organizational means of insuring their perpetuity" (258–59).

[46]E.g., when commenting on point 4: "It is *safe to speculate* that the members of the Petrine community would have understood themselves to be 'students' of Peter, but disciples of Jesus Christ" (3843; italics added). But did Peter represent a teacher with a special connection *to this* community of readers or was he *just one* of the authoritative apostles, or more generally, one of many pastors concerned for the flock? Soards does not prove that the name Peter had

influences on 2 Peter and if this is taken into account, the cumulative effect of similarities between these texts is not remarkable.

It may be that at a more fundamental level the idea of a school is inappropriate altogether. Bauckham points out that those who postulate Pauline or Johannine schools are attempting to explain theological and literary similarities between texts that are not believed to come from the same author. In the case of 1 and 2 Peter, "there are no such similarities to be explained" (1983, 146; cf. discussion under 4.2).

In his 1972 doctoral dissertation David Henry Schmidt examined 1 and 2 Peter, the *Apocalypse of Peter*, and the *Gospel of Peter* to explore whether they should be considered a Petrine corpus (neither Soards nor Ward interact with Schmidt's thesis). In his opinion, the evidence did not support this, and he notes, among other things, that (a) although they all draw from sources they do not appear to have made use of the same ones[47]; (b) each writing addresses a particular concern, but that these problems and their way of dealing with them are varied (199; cf., 190); and (c) the choice of the name Peter does not seem to have been made for any reason that would link these texts. Thus "there is no evidence of any common overriding factor which caused the Peter writings to be written under Peter's name. Instead we must find individual reasons behind each writer's attraction to identify with Peter" (200–01).

Beyond these general comments, it is reasonable to ask whether scholarly theories about the existence of schools behind the NT writings is at all influenced by presuppositions brought to the task of locating texts. The ancient world knew of schools associated with notable teachers (e.g., Socrates, Aristotle, Epicurus [see Alexander 1992 for an overview of Hellenistic schools]). But whether these precedents justify the conclusion that schools were widespread in first and second–century Christianity remains uncertain. The interest in postulating a Johannine or Isaianic or Petrine school is understandable; if correct it would explain the presence of similarities between texts. At the same time, apparent success in locating one group of NT texts within a school[48] may tempt some to look for similar phenomena elsewhere when there is even less evidence in support of it.

It seems that the value of scholarly consensus in this case (discussed in 3.2.9) is particularly relevant. Only a handful of scholars see evidence for a Petrine community/school. If one were to speculate further about why the school

---

special significance for this school or community. Schmidt did not find this to be the case in his study of Petrine writings (see below). The name may have been used only because Peter was a well known member of the apostolic circle.

[47]Matthew, he notes, appears to have been reflected in each of these texts "but the popularity of this gospel limits the significance that this usage might have" (199; cf. further 187–89).

[48]There is wide agreement that a Johannine school lies behind writings associated with that name (see esp. Culpepper [1975] and bibliography listed there; he also provides a survey of the history of this thesis, 1–34).

hypothesis has some appeal, it is tempting to suggest that early historical phenomena are being viewed through the lens of later events. Examples in later Christian history of rival orthodoxies, such as those found in the post–Reformation period (for which there are clear examples of party writings), or even the presence of clearly defined Christian denominations in modern Protestantism may suggest to historians that similar division into parties existed in the first and second centuries. This allows the historian to find some sense of order in the diverse writings of early Christianity.[49]

2.3.5 CONCLUDING REFLECTIONS ON DEVELOPMENTAL THEORIES

> Yes, I am a thief of thoughts / not, I pray, a stealer of souls / I have built an' rebuilt / upon what is waitin' / for the sand on the beaches carves many castles / on what has been opened / before my time / a word, a tune, a story, a line / keys in the wind t'unlock my mind / an't' grant my closet thoughts backyard air / it is not of me t'sit an' ponder / wonderin' an wastin' time / thinkin' of thoughts that haven't been thunk / thinkin' of dreams that haven't been dreamt / an' new ideas that haven't been wrote / an' new words t' fit into rhyme / (if it rhymes, it rhymes / if it don't, it don't / if it comes, it comes / if it won't, it won't)
>
> —Bob Dylan, "11 Outlined Epitaphs"

These words from a contemporary poet make the point that authors borrow and steal from what has been said and written before. These thefts, as a result, provide valuable keys to help unlock the mind of the later writer. However, they are of limited use, because writers build and rebuild, and their own creativity may obscure those earlier influences or make the significance of observed parallels difficult to determine. At times writers may seek to cover up their tracks, hiding any evidence of borrowed material.

As noted above, developmental models attempt to find a location for texts by seeking one or more of the following: a *terminus a quo*, a *terminus ad quem*, or a general milieu indicated by similarities with contemporaneous literature. There is certainly a place for all of these in establishing the location of texts, including 2 Peter. For various reasons however these models in themselves can distort the evidence, if certain factors are not taken into consideration.

---

[49]In 2.2.3 it was seen that Robinson was able to follow a line of progression in Paul's thought starting with the apostle himself and an early adaptation of his teachings (1 Corinthians), through a Pauline school in the years following his death (Colossians and Ephesians; cf. the Pastoral Epistles), and then to the later gnostic writings from Nag Hammadi. Following a similar trajectory of development in Peter's thought does not appear to be possible owing to the lack of unambiguous connection between the various Petrine writings. At the same time it is interesting to observe how Peter as a character in early Christian writings has been variously interpreted— there are times when he is a hero of orthodoxy on whom the church is built (e.g., the Acts of the Apostles; the *Acts of Peter*; cf. Matt 16:17–19) but others when he is presented in less than favourable light (e.g., the *Gospel of Mary*).

a) As said, there is no room given in each of these for the possibility that an individual author is a creative, original thinker. Moreover, an author may not be a mirror image of his or her environment. Naturally a writer speaks the language of the intended audience and, as much as possible, makes contact with experiences familiar to them in order to gain a hearing (cf. 2 Pet 1:1, 12–13; 3:1). But it does not necessarily follow that everything written automatically represents the views held by the intended community.

b) Often adequate consideration is not given to the possibility that a document may have contributed to the shape of the environment in which it is located. For example, while similarities between the thought of 2 Peter and second–century (early catholic) tendencies may suggest that 2 Peter belonged to that context, it is also possible that the context was shaped in part by 2 Peter.

c) At times these models limit the author too much. Not enough can be deduced about the author of 2 Peter from three short chapters to determine such things as theological perspective or affinities with/differences from other early Christian writings.

d) The difficulty of determining dates for other literature complicates the task. Second Peter was likely dependent on Jude, but this only helps to the extent that a date for that short letter is known. Here again scholars are dealing with tentative, approximate dates, not certain ones.

e) Authors may deliberately seek to blur a link to a given context for various reasons. They may attempt to create the impression that their work derives from a different setting (cf. any example of historical fiction); they may depict their environment as they wish it was (cf. perhaps apocalyptic literature with its depiction of justice for the oppressed); they may provide a description of their contemporary setting that is only partially correct and mixed with exaggerations in order to create satire (e.g., Aristophanes, *The Clouds*); or they may deliberately distort aspects of their context as a polemic.

Apart from the lack of information about the early centuries of the church, one of the greatest weaknesses in attempts to locate texts in broad movements or trends lies in the idiosyncrasies of authorship. Since the individuality of writers is always present in their work, they distinguish themselves from their contemporaries. Even scribes making copies of manuscripts—perhaps the form of writing with the most constraints requiring conformity—found many ways, deliberate and non–deliberate, of leaving their mark.[50] On the other hand, writers attempting to create a fiction in order to locate themselves in a tradition of writing or even a period of time may fail by including anachronisms.

To support this point about the idiosyncrasies of authorship, some insights are drawn from writers who have offered challenges to the findings of history of

---

[50] In some cases, this was obvious as when the scribe signed his name. There were also distinctive qualities in handwriting, spelling tendencies, and even patterns of scribal correction where mistakes were assumed to be present in the original manuscript.

religions research with respect to early Christian development. It is not a perfect analogy because, for them, the interest lies in the origin and development of concepts; this study is focused on texts (specifically the relationship of texts with one another). However, just as authorial individuality presents a challenge to conclusions about the location of texts, the creativity of Christians challenges conclusions about Christian origins reached by proponents of the history of religions school of thought. Three examples are given here.

a) Ben Meyer's search for a model other than evolution–by–borrowing and the "organic process"[51] led him to the conclusion that the model of transposition or translation is more appropriate for Christian origins.

> It supposes that every act of meaning is embedded in a context and that the maintenance of meaning is conditioned by the more or less creative act of transposing meaning from one context to another. In contradistinction to the model of evolutionary syncretism, it affirms, as the starting point of early Christian development, not a low christology, low ecclesiology, etc., but an experience of salvation—"the Easter experience of the disciples," the object of which was the risen Christ—with intrinsic implications of high christology, high ecclesiology, etc. What Dix called Christianity's "leap for life" from the Jewish to the Greek world imposed the task of signifying in new conceptual as well as new linguistic terms the realities first encountered and thematized by the first Christians of Jerusalem. In this as in all comparable cases something of the old was (both deliberately and indeliberately) lost in the translation and significant new elements were gained (1986, 190–91).

As said, in Meyer's study the focus is on the origin of concepts and ideas, whereas in the present study it is individual texts. However, this idea of *borrowing and creating/adapting* is helpful in clarifying the nature of literary relationships. Authors are more than imitators; they adapt, create, rewrite, and steal. This challenges the assumption that tracing influence from one text to the next is a simple process.

b) Another example of this approach to Christian origins is found in the work of Meyer's student Tom Robinson (1990, 225–50). He calls attention to historical realities that create difficulties in pinpointing contexts for early Christian writings. In his study of ecclesiastical structure in early Christianity, he illustrates three ways development is conceptualized. Some idolize the past. In this case, any departure from the beliefs and practices of the early church is viewed as apostasy (e.g., Pentecostals and Käsemann, though in different ways [228–29]). Others view development as somehow essential to the nature of Christianity (e.g., F. C. Baur).

---

[51]By this expression he points to Moule's study of Christology. Moule prefers the term development to evolution (the latter being implied by the history of religions approach): "if, in my analogy, 'evolution' means the genesis of successive new species by mutations and natural selection along the way, 'development', by contrast, will mean something more like the growth, from immaturity to maturity, of a single specimen from within itself" (1977, 2; cf. 140–41).

Finally, some see a substantial authoritative core in the primitive period while at the same time recognizing that this needs to be incorporated into new settings (e.g, Harnack [226–32]). All of these, Robinson finds, fail to address the issue of development in the early church appropriately. He argues that development occurred in the early church but goes on to illustrate how this development was neither a reduplication of what already existed (Judaism) nor an inevitable fulfilment of a pre–ordained future. Development is flexible, open to adjustment, and unpredictable in advance; it has novelty, tensions and quandaries, hesitations and illusions, trial runs and errors (249–50). This position offers an obstacle for those wishing to idealize the past or reduplicate it in the present.

    c) A final example of this emphasis on creativity among early Christians is found in the work of Larry Hurtado, who explored the issue of the early church's veneration of Christ in a predominantly Jewish, monotheistic context (1988, 11–15, 93–128). His procedure was to describe the resources available to help Christians "accommodate conceptually the exaltation of Jesus next to God" (93; this is done in the first four chapters of the book). He then observes what he calls "mutations" (2, 121–22, etc.) of Jewish concepts into distinctively Christian ones.[52] A strength of Hurtado's study is that he allows for original contributions of Christian thinking and not just a wholesale adoption of other's concepts. A weakness of the history of religions school, which has influenced subsequent NT scholarship, is the lack of recognition of Christian creativity. One comment on this point illustrates Hurtado's critique:

> There seems to have been the assumption that all characteristics of early Christianity (all beliefs, ethics, practices, and concepts) must have been borrowed from the surrounding religious environment. That is, the religious influences were seen as coming only from the surrounding world into early Christianity. There was insufficient readiness to entertain the question of whether influences might ever have run in the other direction. Nor was much consideration given to the possibility that the early Christians might have developed genuinely distinctive ideas and practices (9; see also ch. 5 "The Early Christian Mutation").

Texts do not necessarily correspond to overarching models of development. While heuristic schemes have a place, these are limited as tools for locating texts, because writers and their creations do not always follow predictable patterns. Each

---

[52]Cf. Meeks' comments on the Pauline communities: ". . . Paul and the other founders and leaders of those groups engaged aggressively in the business of creating a new social reality. . . . They developed norms and patterns of moral admonition and social control that, however many commonplaces from the moral discourse of the larger culture they might contain, still in ensemble constituted a distinctive ethos. They received, practiced, and explicated distinctive ritual actions. None of these was made *ex nihilo*. All drew upon the common language and culture of the Greek–speaking, Roman provincial cities as well as upon the special subculture of Judaism, which had already over generations adapted to those cities. The resultant, nevertheless, was an evolving definition of a new, visibly different subculture" (1983, 104–05).

text must therefore be treated individually, recognizing that similarities—parallels —between one writing and another do not in themselves necessarily provide sufficient evidence to show that they derived from a common theological environment, period of history, or geographical context.

CHAPTER 3
CRITERIA FOR DETERMINING
THE VALUE OF PARALLELS

No method in literary study is more objective or more fruitful than the comparison
of one work with another to determine the question of literary indebtedness—
which one shows acquaintance with the other, use of it, and dependence upon it.
—Edgar J. Goodspeed,
Foreword to Albert Barnett's *Paul Becomes a Literary Influence*

Virtually every study basing claims on literary parallels has elicited at least
one reviewer calling attention to the potential pitfalls in this approach. As theories
building on parallels in one way or another are legion, such review literature is
itself extensive.[1] For good reason, parallels figure prominently as an issue of
methodology in need of constant vigilance. The following discussion outlines a
variety of concerns related to methodology. Five lists are presented that suggest a

---

[1]To illustrate, and without going into the details of the two examples mentioned here, it
may be noted that the following studies have based their theories on parallels in ways that have
been subsequently challenged. Martin McNamara claims that the Aramaic Targums have
influenced the NT. Harrington expresses concern about the line of argument involved: "When
does the process of gathering parallels pass from circular reasoning to a true convergence of
evidence? How many parallels do we need?" (1973, 254); "The numerous similarities between
these Targums and the NT may simply point to a strong Palestinian tradition embedded in the
Targums rather than to an established text existing before NT times" (254). Appeal to parallels
is also found in the now popular comparison of Jesus with the Cynics. Wright makes the charge
against Burton Mack and other advocates of a Cynic–Jesus that their use of parallels is selective:
e.g., "Mack does not note the parallels between some of Jesus' aphoristic sayings and similar
sayings in Jewish texts" (1996, 37 n.33). Wright also calls attention to a review of Leif E.
Vaage's work that observes a tendency to concentrate almost exclusively "on certain external
similarities pertaining to the social image and [a neglect of] the more important dissimilarities
that determine the general framework and 'ideological' system of both ancient Cynicism and
early Christianity" (Denaux 1996, 138).

range of considerations necessary when parallels are cited as evidence for historical conclusions. To help with cross–referencing, see the brief outline given in appendices 3–7 (pp.154–58). These lists address the following: (1) What constitutes a parallel?; (2) Factors that lend weight to arguments claiming that parallels are due to literary dependence; (3) Complications with source theories: Factors that weaken claims of literary dependence, lead to mistaken claims of literary dependence, or obscure real dependence; (4) Conclusions possible on the basis of parallels; and (5) Parallels that are not reliable for reaching conclusions about dependency. It is proposed that due attention to the issues represented in these lists will provide some safeguard against the type of fallacies based on parallels noted by Sandmel, Donaldson, Stoutenburg, and others (see 1.3).[2]

3.1 WHAT CONSTITUTES A PARALLEL?

This question is often considered under the more specific matters of what constitutes a quotation or direct borrowing. In the case of the Book of Revelation for example, extensive use of the OT is usually recognized, though the extensive verbal parallels never constitute an actual quotation (MacKenzie 1997, 27).[3] Quotations are parallels, but this term has also been used to describe other perceived relationships between documents. What follows is an attempt to chart out a range of these similarities on a scale moving from the most definite form of parallel—quotation—toward less definite relationships.[4] At the opposite extreme from quotation is mere coincidence (cf. the list suggesting what parallels are evidence for [3.4]).

------

[2]Owing to the subject matter it could not be said that these lists are exhaustive. The aim here is to provide sufficient material to stimulate reflection on the issue of parallels and examples are drawn from various early Christian writings. The examples of parallels between 2 Peter and other literature are intended to be illustrative, not exhaustive. For further examples see ch. 4.

[3]Elsewhere MacKenzie responds to those assuming that John includes quotations of the OT: "it is clear that Revelation does not contain any direct quotations from the OT of the sort which are introduced by a formula such as 'it is written' or 'Isaiah says.' Furthermore, there are no portions of any length that are reproduced word–for–word from the OT. In view of this it would appear that John was for his own purposes deliberately avoiding clear citation of it" (1987, 56).

[4]Cf. Donaldson who speaks of stronger and weaker genealogical parallels, the difference being the extent of influence from one tradition to another (1983, 199–200). In recent studies of biblical intertextuality other terminology is used to describe text relationships. For example, "First and foremost, intertextual reading requires close, comparative reading of different literary texts. We speak in this text of specific quotations or near quotations of an earlier text in a later text (what we call 'micro–level intertextuality') or allusive echoes, be they faint or strong, which reverberate between a focal literary text and other texts (be they literary or social—what we call 'macro–level intertextuality')" (Chance and Horne 2000, xix).

3.1.1 QUOTATIONS OR SUMMARY OF OR REFERENCE TO A WRITING WHERE USE OF A SOURCE IS ACKNOWLEDGED BY THE AUTHOR (AND KNOWN TO THE MODERN READER)

On many occasions, NT writers signal their use of sources (e.g., Acts 2:16: "this is what was spoken through the prophet Joel"; Mark 12:35: "David himself, by the Holy Spirit, declared"). On others citation of a source is acknowledged but not clearly identified by the author. These sources are still recognizable to modern readers (e.g., Acts 17:28: "'In him we live and move and have our being'; as even some of your own poets have said, 'For we too are his offspring'" [Aratus]; Titus 1:12: "It was one of them, their very own prophet, who said, 'Cretans are always liars, vicious brutes, lazy gluttons'" [Epimenides]).[5]   Sometimes authors acknowledge their sources but instead of quoting choose to paraphrase them (e.g., *1 Clem.* 47:1–7; "Take up the epistle of the blessed Paul the Apostle. What did he first write to you at the beginning of his preaching?" [Lake, LCL]).

3.1.2 UNIDENTIFIED BUT PRECISE BORROWING: USE OF A SOURCE IS NOT ACKNOWLEDGED BY THE AUTHOR BUT RECOGNIZED BY MODERN READERS

Ancient writers often made use of sources without identifying them. In the NT this occurs frequently when writers make use of Scripture (e.g., the use of Deut 17:7 in 1 Cor 5:13b [cf. Deut 19:19; 22:21, 24; 24:7]). It could be argued that such references are properly called quotations, if in fact the author assumed that the readers would recognize the source. This procedure is referred to as borrowing here, because it is not necessarily true that all readers would have recognized it as a quotation. Quotations and borrowings are not identical. The former often function in the NT as proof–texts intended to strengthen an argument by appealing to an authoritative body of literature (i.e., Scripture). When authors borrow material from other texts without signaling this to their readers, appeal to authority is not intended.

3.1.3 IMPRECISE BORROWING WHERE THE IDENTIFICATION OF SOURCES IS RELATIVELY CERTAIN TO MODERN READERS BUT NOT ACKNOWLEDGED BY THE ANCIENT AUTHOR

Identification of the source is possible here, because similarities between texts are recognized, not just incidental points. This is illustrated by the use of biblical imagery in the Book of Revelation (see n. 3).[6] Another example is provided by the author of *1 Clement*, whose use of Hebrews is generally recognized by modern

---

[5]The reference to Menander in 1 Cor 15:33 ("Bad company ruins good morals") is different in that there is no hint in the context that this is a quotation. Its function in the text does not depend on it being recognized as a quotation.

[6]It may be stated here that the influence of one text on another is not always accurately measured by the extent to which the borrower takes over words, phrases, or sentences verbatim from the source. As said above, non–quotation of the supplying document may be deliberate.

scholars, though it was not named by the author.

3.1.4 INCIDENTAL SIMILARITIES BETWEEN TEXTS THAT ARE TOO IMPRECISE TO POSIT BORROWING

Of course, a number of elements in a text could be parallel, such as vocabulary, themes, and structure.[7] These types of parallels however are not remarkable and indeed should be expected among texts sharing a broad cultural context. Similarities in literary features may also be incidental. To illustrate, parallels exist between the ethical list found in 2 Pet 1:5–7 and similar lists in the writings of Hellenistic moral philosophers. This does not indicate direct dependence of one text on another but is rather evidence of the shared use of a common pedagogical device.[8]

Affinities between texts may be coincidental. Parallel ideas may indicate no more than that similar conclusions were reached independently by separate writers or groups. Ferguson recognizes this possibility:

---

[7] Formal literary conventions are a very general type of parallel. For example, 2 Peter uses an epistolary salutation and the genre of a farewell discourse. Normally no conclusions can be derived from such parallels. One interesting attempt to do so is found in an article by Amy Harvey. Noting that an important way Paul influenced the development of early Christianity was in the area of literary form, namely the use of letters, Harvey observes that not all writers were influenced by this model to the same degree. Some did not feel compelled to employ certain features characteristic of the epistolary form (e.g., they omit an opening greeting, as in Hebrews; or a closing valediction, as in James and Diognetus; or both as 1 John, Jude, *2 Clement*, and 2 Peter). Also unlike Paul (and other early letters, e.g., Hebrews, *1 Clement*, Barnabas), some documents did not employ biblical exposition and argumentation to the same extent. In 1 John, 2 Peter, Jude, and Diognetus the OT is rarely quoted. Rather, they tend to use examples from biblical stories or apocryphal tradition to illustrate their teachings. This suggests that various early Christian texts, including 2 Peter, found in Paul "only limited guidance and inspiration" (1990, 340; for the full discussion about Paul's limited influence on some of the literature, see 339–40). Given this, Harvey asks what other models were available for early Christian writers, a question raised with particular attention to 2 Peter. Turning to the Jewish literature written in Greek, she finds in the testament a model that was employed by the author of 2 Peter. In particular, the *Testament of the Twelve Patriarchs* is singled out as having several points of contact with 2 Peter suggesting an influence. Among points of contact, Harvey observes various shared themes, similar use of biblical examples, overlap in vocabulary, and use of the name Simeon, in addition to characteristic features of the testament genre. Similarities in terminology between Jude and the *Testament of the Twelve Patriarchs* (and the *Apocalypse of Baruch*) are pointed out by Dunnett (1988, 288).

[8] On the similarities between 2 Pet 1 and the moral grammar of the Stoa see especially Charles 1997 and 1998. In this case, the device is specifically associated with the moral philosophers but their contribution is limited to the method of presentation: "While the form and function of the ethical list is borrowed by NT writers, it should be emphasized that Hellenistic philosophical assumptions about moral progress are not carried over into the NT by its writers" (1998, 59). Such parallels may provide assistance in locating 2 Peter to a general milieu.

Perhaps the first thing to observe is that there are only a limited number of options in any given historical setting. Only a certain number of ideas are possible and only a certain number of ways of doing things are available. We need not wonder at similarities, which need not be necessarily a sign of borrowing, in one direction or the other. Many things in a given historical cultural setting will be arrived at independently by more than one group, simply because there is not an unlimited number of options available about how to do something (1993, 1).[9]

In such situations parallels do not indicate any necessary relationship.

This range of possible meanings and usages for the term parallel necessitates careful definition when it is used, though this does not always occur.[10]   When appeals to parallels are made without defining the term, confusion may result. If, for example, a writer suggests that a parallel exists only in the sense of similarity, without clarifying this, it can lead to the distorted impression that deliberate borrowing or imitation has occurred.

3.2 FACTORS THAT LEND WEIGHT TO ARGUMENTS CLAIMING THAT PARALLELS ARE DUE TO LITERARY DEPENDENCE

The previous list represents a range of parallels that may exist. Such terms as quotation and borrowing assume that conclusions about literary sources can be made, but this is true for only some parallels. Other parallels may be due to such factors as shared education, or shared intellectual, cultural, religious, or language milieu. What is needed is a basis to justify the conclusion that a literary relationship between two texts is the best explanation for similarities. The following list proposes some considerations in this regard.

---

[9]Stoutenburg applies similar reasoning when evaluating parallel concepts found in both the early church and Judaism, especially in the area of individual and community prayer. "Conceptual parallelism, no matter how verbally identical it is made to appear, does not necessarily indicate anything more than shared interest in a common problem in which the paths of resolution are humanly limited" (1996, 85). Similarly, Meeks writes with respect to the distinctive characteristics of early Christian groups: "To be sure, 'distinctive' never means 'absolutely unique.' A century of study by historians of religions has demonstrated that there is hardly a belief attested in the New Testament for which some parallel cannot be found somewhere in its environment or antecedents. But on balance these studies have also shown that these parallels, though often immensely illuminating, rarely explain the meaning and function of the given beliefs in their Christian contexts" (1983, 91).

[10]Of course many scholars are careful to state what they understand parallels/similarities to be evidence for. Bauckham for one writes of the significance of parallels between 2 Peter, *1 Clement, 2 Clement*, and Hermas that "[t]he relationships of 2 Peter with these three works are *not* of the kind which literary dependence could explain, nor is common authorship conceivable. The four writers, despite the links between them, remain highly individual writers, each with his distinctive traits of thought and language. The kind of similarities which this commentary demonstrates are those which derive from the use of shared Christian traditions and from belonging to a shared Christian language milieu" (1983, 150; his emphasis).

3.2.1 LENGTH OF THE PARALLEL SECTIONS

Obviously the greater the length, the more data there is to work with in order to evaluate the possible relationship (cf. Matthew and Luke's use of Mark). When only words and short phrases appear, it is hard to rule out coincidence as a legitimate explanation.

3.2.2 CLUSTERING OF PARALLELS

Clustering indicates a number of parallels in close proximity between texts where a genealogical relationship is suspected. An example of the use of this criterion is found in the discussion of 2 Peter's relationship to the *Apocalypse of Peter* (cf. 4.5; Bauckham 1998, 302–03; 1988, 4723; cf. Tuckett 1989, 200–01).

3.2.3 PARALLELS APPEARING IN THE SAME ORDER

It may be significant that texts not only share similar material but that these parallels appear in the same sequence. Hillyer lends weight to this when addressing the relationship of 2 Peter and Jude: "The frequency with which such parallels appear *in the same order* plainly points to some connection between the two documents that is probably not oral but literary" (1992, 13 [his emphasis]; cf. Davids 1993, 239–40 n.28). This line of argument is often used in studies of the Synoptic Problem. Proponents of the two–source hypothesis often observe that Matthew and Luke appear to follow Mark's sequence of events.

3.2.4 STRIKING PARALLELS

Possible use of one text by another may be indicated when parallels are not easily explained by other means. An example of this is found in the parallels between a first–century inscription and 2 Pet 1. The inscription preserves a decree of the inhabitants of Stratonicea in Caria honouring Zeus Panhemerios and Hekate that contains various parallels with 2 Peter. Adolf Deissmann appears to have been the first to comment on them ([1901] 1988, 360–68; the text of this inscription is found on 361–62). He suggests that the inscription may date prior to 22 C.E. (366) thus allowing that the author of 2 Peter may have been familiar with it. Deissmann ruled out coincidence as an explanation for the similarities between them and suggested that this evidence may be significant for determining the origin of the epistle (though he stops short of categorically asserting that 2 Peter was written from Asia Minor [366–67]). As well, J. Daryl Charles commented on the verbal and conceptual parallels between 2 Pet 1:3–7 and this decree (1997, 146–48; 1998, 71–72). He finds them to be remarkable and striking parallels that allow for the possibility of literary dependence. If in fact this "reflect[s] the local color of the readers' situation, interesting light is thereby shed on the destination of 2 Peter"

(1997, 148).[11]

Not all have been equally impressed by the parallels between 2 Peter and the Carian decree. Green for one, in agreement with Chase and Mayor, finds a satisfactory explanation for similarities in commonplaces of rhetorical study, set prefatory phrases and the like (1960, 9, 23; 1987, 25–26). Furthermore, it should be noted that they share no context and subject matter (3.3.8; Schmidt 1972, 104).

3.2.5 AN AUTHOR STRAYS FROM USUAL PATTERNS OF WRITING

Suspicion that a source is being used is raised when there is a shift in an author's customary writing habits (cf. e.g., Tuckett 1987, 84). Such departures from what is characteristic of an author sometimes leads to the observation that traditional Christian material (e.g., hymns) is imbedded in a text.[12] Care is necessary here, as there are potential complications, such as a deliberate shift by an author who is capable of writing different genres and willing to mix them together in a single document.[13]

3.2.6 AWKWARD EDITING MAY SIGNAL USE OF A SOURCE

Sometimes suggesting that text B is dependent on text A provides the best explanation for difficulties in text B, and so ambiguities in the later document are the result of poor editing of the source. Identification of borrowed material or interpolations is often based on the awkward incorporation of that material. In cases where there is suspicion of a genealogical relationship between texts, the

---

[11]Cf. comments on the geographical provenance of 2 Peter (2.1.2). For another example of parallels between 2 Peter and a Greek inscription from Asia Minor see Deissmann (1927) 1995, 317–18 and Charles 1997, 139–40. In this case there are similarities with the ethical list given by Peter in the opening chapter. However, since such lists of virtues were common (a variety of examples are listed by Charles in his ch. 5, "The Ethical Catalog as Pedagogical Device") there is no need to assume dependence. Charles finds that the similarities of individual virtues "give evidence that the letter originated in or was destined to a Gentile setting" (140; so too Fornberg 1977, 98).

[12]R. P. Martin (1993b, 420–21; drawing on E. Stauffer's *New Testament Theology*, 1956) outlines the following clues indicating the possible use of hymnic material in texts: (1) contextual dislocations where the "flow" of prose material is interrupted (e.g., Col 1:15–20); (2) terminology and style that is different from the wider context (1 Tim 3:16); (3) introductory phrases (e.g., "thus it says" as in Eph 5:14) and the initial relative pronoun "who" (as in Col 1:15; Phil 2:6); (4) the presence of an antithetic style that creates a contrast (Phil 2:6–11); and finally (5) vocabulary that is rare and perhaps ceremonial.

[13]With respect to the style of 2 Peter, especially as evident in the author's redaction of Jude, see Thurén 1996, 332 n.15, 337. He suggests that Peter's unusual Greek (illustrated for example in the high number of *hapax legomena*; 57 of them) may be part of the author's attempt at gaining *ethos* (345).

earlier passage may clarify an otherwise ambiguous passage in the later document.[14] If there is evidence that an author has misunderstood his source, or, put another way, if one text (the lender) explains the awkward language of another (the borrower), it may indicate that a later writer has used and adapted the source. Bigg notes the importance of this criterion for determining the direction of borrowing.

> When two writers, whose date cannot be precisely ascertained, are clearly in the position of borrower and lender, the question of priority must turn to a great degree on points of style, and these will always strike different minds in different ways. If the arrangement of the one writer is more logical, and his expression clearer, than those of the other, it may be thought either that the first has improved upon the second, or that the second has spoiled the first. This criterion is of necessity highly subjective, and no very positive result will be attained unless we can show that the one has misunderstood the other, that the one uses words which are not only not used by the other, but belong to a different school of thought, or that the one has definitely quoted the other (1901, 216).

His use of this criterion in defense of 2 Peter's priority over Jude (discussed in the next chapter and against the prevailing conclusion of current scholarship) illustrates the caution needed in its application.

3.2.7 EDITORIAL HABITS EVIDENT IN ONE TEXT APPEAR IN ANOTHER

Redaction criticism examines how writers (B) have edited their sources (A). In cases where an author's sources are known and the process of editing can be observed, it is possible to isolate certain tendencies of the editor (B). When characteristics of the editor's work (B) appear in yet another, later document (C), there may be some evidence that B was indeed the specific source behind C (as opposed to B's source[s], A). In such cases, a parallel indicates knowledge of the editorial activity of B. This may be illustrated as follows:

$$(A \leftarrow B) \leftarrow C$$

In this case, C (the latest text) used B which was itself using and editing A.

Christopher Tuckett's study of gospel traditions in the *Didache* makes this point. Building on a criterion stated by Helmut Koester (1957), Tuckett argues that if material owing its origin to the redaction activity of an evangelist appears in a later work, there is reliable evidence that his work provided source material (1989, 199). This is qualified: it is possible that two independent redactors added to the tradition and it should not be assumed that dependence demonstrated by this criterion necessitates a direct link between documents. Still, "this criterion is really

---

[14]The reverse may also be true if the borrower better understood the lending document than modern interpreters. Since arguments can go in both directions, this criterion is very subjective.

the only one which ultimately can determine whether a text like the Didache presupposes the finished gospels or whether it uses traditions which lie behind our gospels" (199–200).

Also valuable is Tuckett's reminder that, though authors use language in different ways, this does not rule out dependence. To deny dependence on this basis would involve the assumption that traditions are being quoted, when in fact there may only be an intended allusion or use of common language (207). Related to this, it is curious that the Didachist(s) was (were) familiar with and influenced by the canonical Gospels, yet chose not to quote them explicitly. Tuckett explains:

> It is . . . inappropriate to judge the Didache's use of synoptic tradition as if it were a case of explicit quotation and to expect exact agreement between the quoted version and the source used. The Didache's use of synoptic tradition is more one of free allusion (199).

A text may reflect similarities to an earlier source and actually be influenced by earlier texts, but the author may deliberately choose not to quote them. Rather, the author freely reworks the source material in his own writing, using his own language. By this Tuckett attempts to account for the fact that the later text does at times quote sources (e.g., *Did.* 1:6; 9:5; 14:2; 16:7) yet chooses not to quote the gospel material which (Tuckett believes) was available to the Didachist(s). This is similar to the non–quotation of the OT in Revelation (noted above), where likely the motive was to be on the same level as the source rather than secondary to it. In that case John claims to be a prophet rather than an OT exegete like Paul and the author of Hebrews (Rev 1:3; 19:10; 22:7). The *Didache* wants to be apostolic rather than patristic.

As will be seen in the later discussion of Peter's non–quotation of Paul (4.4), this consideration is relevant. The *Didache* incorporates a great deal of gospel tradition; the question therefore is whether there is direct dependence on the canonical Gospels. Similarly, the author of 2 Peter explicitly refers to Paul (3:15–16), though the apostle is nowhere quoted. This raises the question whether the author was in any way dependent on (or perhaps better, influenced by) him.[15] At the same time, Peter feels free to borrow other source material extensively (2 Peter's dependence on Jude; cf. the *Didache*'s incorporation of the Two Ways source[16]). Following through with Tuckett's line of argument, it would be

---

[15]Perhaps in a way analogous to John's use of the Scriptures, the author of 2 Peter did not want to be viewed as in any sense an interpreter of his sources. Rather, he wanted to be viewed as on the same level of his sources—including Paul, Jude, and the Scriptures. The latter also are not formally quoted in the text.

[16]This is an assumption as the Two Ways source is not extant. It should be noted that a source not signalled to the reader, as in the case of Peter's use of Jude, does not serve the same purpose as an acknowledged authority. Naming Paul in 2 Pet 3:15–16 introduces an authority figure that the readers must have known.

reasonable to expect that Paul was a source for 2 Peter in spite of the fact that he was not quoted (this is discussed further in 4.4).[17]

3.2.8 SIMILARITIES IN THE WIDER CONTEXT OF THE TWO TEXTS IN ADDITION TO THE PARALLEL(S) IN QUESTION

Do the two writings being compared resemble each other in content apart from the specific parallels under consideration? When similarities in the wider context of two writings exist, it suggests that shared language is being used to achieve similar ends and thus lessens the possibility that the parallels are the result of coincidence (cf. 3.3.8).

3.2.9 SCHOLARLY CONSENSUS

The suggestion that scholarly consensus is a valid criterion needs to be qualified, but there is some validity in noting the predominant conclusions reached by scholarship generally. This can be abused. Appeal to a prevailing view on a difficult issue can be a shortcut allowing one to avoid wrestling with a difficult and/or labour intensive matter. When such work is bypassed, weaknesses in a theory may be perpetuated.[18] Positively, if an opinion crosses the various boundaries that exist in biblical scholarship (e.g., confessional, geographical, institutional), the collective wisdom of scholarship should be recognized as a valid criterion.

---

[17]Ian Henderson provides a thorough discussion of Tuckett's methodology highlighting some of the limitations inherent in such redaction–critical analysis. He warns against an oversimplified assessment of an author's style that minimizes the role of the borrower. It is argued that writers (and orators) do not slavishly reflect only one style. As a result, "[t]he grammatical and redaction–critical traditions are limited as tools in the analysis of style by their resolute formalism, an approach which considers style as a congeries of 'features'" (1995, 192). What occurs in practice however is much more complex: "style is the whole relationship between the many speech choices of a text and the universal means of expression and persuasion" (194); "style is a series of choices which are integral to the production of meaningful texts" (195). If style is understood not as an author slavishly tied to constraints created by external factors, but rather, as Henderson suggests, reflecting a series of choices, it is therefore not a static, invariable phenomenon. It implies that identifying use and non–use of sources in writings is greatly complicated.

[18]In his discussion of intertextuality in Paul's writings Hays allows some weight to the history of interpretation as a control and offers an example to illustrate: "Have other readers, both critical and pre–critical, heard the same echoes? The readings of our predecessors can both check and stimulate our perception of scriptural echoes in Paul. While this test is a possible restraint against arbitrariness, it is also one of the least reliable guides for interpretation, because Gentile Christian readers at a very early date lost Paul's sense of urgency about relating the gospel of God's dealings with Israel and, slightly later, began reading Paul's letters within the interpretive matrix of the New Testament canon" (1989, 31). Cf. appendix 8 for a summary of Hays' criteria for discerning echoes of Scripture in the NT.

Some final reflections on identifying the use of source material are drawn from John Dominic Crossan's latest major publication on Christian origins. At one point he addresses the issue of how one can determine if similarities between texts provide evidence for the dependence of one document on another (1998, 104–08). In cases where too many similarities in order and content to suggest coincidence exist, four explanations are possible.

First, a common oral matrix may lie behind the documents. This is illustrated with the following example:

> Luke 12:35 (RSV): Let your loins be girded and your lamps burning.
>
> *Did.* 16:1: Let your lamps be not quenched and your loins be not girded.

Here there are shared symbols but in no particular order and a variation in the negation.

Second, a common literary source is likely indicated when there are verbatim agreements (e.g., Q material). In the example given by Crossan (Matt 3:7–10 and Luke 3:7–9), he notes that there are only four minor changes in over sixty words in Greek.

Third, it is pointed out that arguments for direct literary dependence are more complex.

> This explanation must be supported by two mutually supportive arguments: one is *genetic relationship* and the other is *redactional confirmation*. Genetic relationship means that certain elements of order and content that are characteristically Markan are found in Matthew and Luke. We are not talking of general tradition common to all three gospels but of specific editorial aspects of Markan sequence or style whose presence in those other two texts indicates copying. What we are seeking, as it were, are Markan literary fingerprints or Markan theological DNA present within the gospels of Matthew and Luke (105; his italics).

An example of this very thing is found in one of Mark's most distinctive compositional devices, his use of intercalation or sandwich (an $A^1 - B - A^2$ sequence that also implies the A and B events are interconnected in some way). Whereas Mark includes as many as nine examples of this pattern, Matthew has only five and Luke only four. One way of understanding this is to suggest that the later authors were not as interested in this construction and chose to omit some of the occurrences. Whether or not this particular example is accepted, this general criterion is helpful.

Such instances of genetic relationship can (at least in the Gospels) be supported by redaction criticism. Crossan is clear that this does not provide proof, but it does help test the theory to some extent (redactional confirmation). If it is accepted that Matthew and Luke used Mark, it should be possible to explain why

Mark's use of intercalation was omitted in certain instances or retained in others.[19]

Fourth, though more difficult, it is possible to determine if indirect literary dependence is the best explanation. By this Crossan refers to the occasional proposals that an author has read or heard a document in the past and later recalls it when writing. In such a case, the remembrance of a text heard or read in the past "would most likely lack any peculiar, individual, or personal identifying traits found in the original—such as Markan intercalations" (108).

3.3 COMPLICATIONS WITH SOURCE THEORIES: FACTORS THAT WEAKEN CLAIMS OF LITERARY DEPENDENCE, LEAD TO MISTAKEN CLAIMS OF LITERARY DEPENDENCE, OR OBSCURE REAL DEPENDENCE

The fact that two texts resemble each other does not always indicate an obvious, direct relationship between them.[20] For various reasons, assuming a direct connection between them may be misguided.

3.3.1 THE SUSPECTED SOURCE COULD NOT HAVE BEEN AVAILABLE TO THE PROPOSED BORROWER

When a source relationship is suspected, it needs to be asked whether the author could have possibly known this work (cf. Donaldson 1983, 201; Hays 1989, 29–30; and the illustration of source criticism p.150, point 'b'). Some source theories assume a late date for 2 Peter (e.g., those arguing it is dependent on Josephus [see 3.6] or the *Apocalypse of Peter* [see 4.5]). If in fact the epistle is earlier, then obviously such conclusions are incorrect.

3.3.2 AN AUTHOR MAY HAVE DELIBERATELY OBSCURED USE OF A SOURCE FOR A VARIETY OF REASONS

Allowing the presence of a source, an author's intention in using an earlier writing may be difficult to determine. For example, an author may disagree with

---

[19]This assumes of course that the redaction of Mark was always consistent but this was not necessarily so.

[20]At times an author may want his readers to recall an earlier text. If this is attempted with subtle allusions to that text, the connection could be missed. On occasion, an allusion may be intended to recall a wider context. Hays illustrates this by pointing to the allusion to Gen 1:3–5 in 2 Cor 4:6; Paul echoes only the words light and darkness. What is important to ask in such cases is "how distinctive or prominent is the precursor text within Scripture, and how much rhetorical stress does the echo receive in Paul's discourse?" In this example, "the source is the distinctive and memorable Genesis creation account, and Paul has placed the echo at the rhetorical climax of a unit in his letter" (Hays 1989, 30). For another example that is not as obvious on first reading, see Brawley's study of Acts 1:15–26 in 1995, ch. 5. Here the wider context of Pss 68 and 108 (LXX) are seen to be relevant when only brief quotations are made.

the source or feel a need to correct it (and so misrepresent it).[21] Or an author may want to capture a certain quality or tone by alluding to or imitating earlier material.[22]

3.3.3 THE PARALLEL MAY BE EXPLAINED BY AN INTERMEDIARY SOURCE

The assumption that text B used text A would be wrong if in fact author B used an intermediary source (X, which may not even be extant). The relationship here could be diagramed as follows:

$$A \;\leftarrow\; X \;\leftarrow\; B$$

Here A was used by X; B did not know A directly but only to the extent that A was an influence on the middle document.[23] Scholars assuming a genealogical

---

[21]Those involved in comparative religious studies need to be careful when postulating developmental theories. A tendency towards reductionism represents an inappropriate use of parallels, i.e., "the assumption that the function and meaning of a 'borrowed' element is essentially determined by its function and meaning in the original setting" (Donaldson 1983, 202).

For an example of correction possibly pointing to a source one may compare John 4:1 ("Jesus is making and baptizing more disciples than John") with 4:2 ("although it was not Jesus himself but his disciples who baptized"). It appears that the author inherited a tradition with which he was not too comfortable (so Tuckett 1987, 84–85).

[22]Some have found in Luke's infancy narratives an imitation of the prophets, thus creating an atmosphere to his work. Similarly, the language of Revelation which is often described as Semitic may in fact represent John's deliberate imitation of biblical (LXX) style (see MacKenzie 1997, 80, 113, 147, 168, and throughout).

It may be mentioned as well that, as a reader, a borrowing author may impose a particular perspective or meaning on an earlier text, even one that the author of that earlier text would not have accepted. Depending on the motive of the reader, this would differ from deliberately trying to obscure or correct the earlier source. An interesting example of this is provided by Birger A. Pearson in his study of the parallels between 2 Peter and the gnostic *Apocalypse of Peter* (a different text than the *Apocalypse of Peter* discussed in 4.5). He concludes that the different philosophical and theological perspectives represented in these two Petrine documents does not present an obstacle to the proposal that 2 Peter was an influence on the *Apocalypse* even if the former was a polemic against views similar to those represented in the latter: "2 Peter could have been, and was, freely used by the gnostic author of the Apocalypse of Peter. That is not, of course, to say that 2 Peter is really a gnostic text! In fact, it probably was an anti–gnostic text, so far as the original intention of its author is concerned. But it can be read 'gnostically,' and so it was in the case of its use by the author of the Apocalypse of Peter" (1990, 73).

[23]There need to be strong reasons for posing the existence of X. It should not become a double hypothesis (i.e., a hypothesis which needs another one to explain why it does not fit the evidence). For illustrations of how this fallacy appears in NT scholarship, see Wisse 1992: "Miraculously our hunches always fit, or rather, we make them fit by explaining away any objections. We are so attached to our historical speculations that we keep them alive, even when they do not fit the data, simply by creating other hypotheses which elegantly explain the

relationship between A and B are therefore incorrect, as X has been missed as the source for B.

Alternatively, the similarities between texts (B and C) may derive from their use of a common source (oral or written). In early Christian literature, the presence of the OT or early Jewish sources and imagery as a common resource deserves special consideration.

Here the similarities between B and C exist—they are legitimate parallels—but there is no basis to posit the dependence of one on the other (hence the small arrow); they have both made use of the common tradition A.[24] The parallels between B and C are not genealogical, so once again the conclusion of direct dependence would be wrong.[25]

Another example illustrates how difficult it is to pinpoint a specific source. Robinson and Koester put forward the thesis that traces of Q material may be found in 1 Corinthians (1971, 40–43, 186). Tuckett challenged this thesis because it is too difficult to distinguish Q material from other gospel traditions. One variable noted in this example is the matter of what stage in the tradition–history of Q provides the link with 1 Corinthians: is it Q as preserved in the canonical Gospels or Q in some earlier stage?

> . . . if one is seeking to establish a link between 1 Corinthians . . . and Q, this can only be substantiated if the sayings in question are shown to be part of Q. Links between 1 Corinthians and other parts of the synoptic tradition may be very interesting from the point of view of the use of gospel traditions in the early church, but they contribute nothing to an alleged link between 1 Corinthians and Q. This seems so obvious as to be almost trite. However, a careful study of the synoptic half in each alleged link between 1 Corinthians and Q appears never to have been undertaken to test whether one really is dealing with Q material. When this is done, many of the alleged links disappear (1983, 611).[26]

---

discrepancies" (36).

[24]As an example, Tuckett (1989, 201) refers to Helmut Koester's objection that parallels between *Did.* 16.4 and synoptic traditions may be explained as the common use of standard eschatological motifs and OT language (1957, 182).

[25]There is further ambiguity here. Direct text dependence is often the easiest explanation for similarities between texts. To deny such a genealogical relationship on the basis of common tradition potentially involves guilt of the fallacy mentioned above, namely, appeal to a further hypothesis to explain a problem in an argument. There needs to be strong reasons to resort to common tradition or oral tradition.

[26]One example he gives involves Paul's reference to divorce (1 Cor 7:10–11) which is found to be closer to Mark (10:11–12; Matt 19:9) than to Q (Matt 5:32; Luke 16:18). "The link between 1 Corinthians and Q is thus illusory: an examination of the gospel evidence shows that

CRITERIA FOR DETERMINING THE VALUE OF PARALLELS

Therefore, Robinson and Koester propose the following:

$$A \, (Q) \quad \leftarrow \quad B \, (1 \text{ Corinthians})$$

However, Tuckett suggests that an alternative source theory provides a better explanation:

$$A \, (Q) \quad \leftarrow \quad X \text{ (the Synoptic Gospels)} \quad \leftarrow B \, (1 \text{ Corinthians})$$

A final example is drawn from Birger Pearson's study of 2 Pet 2:4. Pearson argues that Greek mythology influenced *1 Enoch*, which in turn influenced Jude 6. Jude therefore was indirectly influenced by the Greek source material only as it was mediated by Enoch. However, though 2 Peter made use of Jude, 2 Pet 2:4 "has been formulated under direct influence from Greek mythology, with no independent use of *1 Enoch* at all in evidence" (1969, 75).

> Whereas the author of *Jude* derives all of his mythological traditions from Jewish sources—mainly from such apocrypha or pseudepigrapha as *1 Enoch*—the author of *II Peter* avoids any reference or allusion to these now unacceptable writings. Instead, whether consciously or unconsciously . . . he is influenced directly by pagan mythology (80).

And so, following Pearson's argument, Jude's sources can be diagrammed as follows:

$$(A \, [\text{mythology}] \quad \leftarrow B \, [1 \, Enoch]) \quad \leftarrow C \, (\text{Jude})$$

Second Peter's sources on the other hand appear as follows:

$$(A \, [\text{mythology}] \quad \leftarrow B \, [1 \, Enoch]) \quad \leftarrow \quad C \, (\text{Jude}) \quad \leftarrow$$
$$D \, (2 \text{ Peter})$$
$$X \, (\text{mythology}) \quad \leftarrow$$

According to Pearson's theory, the missing X was Peter's independent use of Greek mythology.

3.3.4 A PARALLEL MAY REPRESENT THE INFLUENCE OF AN EARLY TEXT ON THE WIDER GENRE IN WHICH A LATER AUTHOR IS WRITING

It is possible that the later document B is not directly dependent on the earlier document A, despite similarities (especially when there is a considerable amount of time between them). Scholars err if they assume that author B was directly

---

there is a link between 1 Corinthians and the Marcan tradition" (613).

indebted to author A, when in fact A was only indirectly influential. Authors may influence those who follow either by introducing innovations to their chosen form of literary expression[27] or by being so widely read that their ideas, vocabulary, and images find there way into other writings of the same genre. A writing produced later, in a genre influenced by such an earlier and widely influential author, may then resemble that writer in some respects. The influence however is indirect.[28]

3.3.5 AUTHORIAL CREATIVITY MAY MEAN THAT AN AUTHOR'S WORK IS UNLIKE OTHER LITERATURE IN HIS OR HER ENVIRONMENT

Parallels between texts do not necessarily indicate a shared context or period of history, though on occasion scholars may be inclined to group texts together, when they share general similarities (see examples given in ch. 2). The observation of parallels may lead to inappropriate conclusions because of unrealistic expectations.

Sufficient attention must be given to the role of the author in both creating material and in editing sources. This has various implications. For one thing, it must not be assumed that everything in a text is derived from earlier material. For another, it may be that source materials that have been used are sufficiently obscured so as to be unrecognizable (and this, it may be assumed, is often the case). Caution is thus necessary before making too quick an equation of author with environment.[29] There is no reason to assume that authors always reflect general characteristics of the period of time or the geographical or theological context in which they write. Also, when scholars appeal to general environment, a question must be asked: does this document reflect the proposed context or was it an influence that helped shape it? In a related issue, use or non–use of certain vocabulary is a weak indicator for identifying the presence of sources because what is distinctively Petrine or Pauline? (cf. p.75 n.50). Parallels involving only similar

---

[27]An example of this is found in the work of the English poet Edmund Spenser (1552–1599). He is known for having been an experimenter, introducing new rhyme schemes such as the Spenserian sonnet. At the same time, his influence was wide and later poets learned the art of versification from him. Among examples of later poems reflecting his innovations are Percy Bysshe Shelley's "Revolt of Islam", Lord Byron's "Childe Harold's Pilgrimage", John Keat's "Eve of St. Agnes", and Lord Tennyson's "The Lotus–Eaters" (Abrams 1987, 260–61).

[28]For an illustration of this possible complication, see appendix 1. There the suggestion is made that the similarities between Homer's *Odyssey* (book 11) and Luke 16:19–31 are best explained by Homer's influence on the wider afterlife genre used by Luke (i.e., the tradition of writing narratives depicting journeys to heaven and hell or other postmortem experiences).

[29]The assumption that the particular will normally reflect the general is fallacious. As an illustration, one need only compare student papers with one another. Assuming there is no plagiarism involved, an individual student's interests (reflected in choice of topic and resources), style of writing, and quality of work distinguishes his or her work from others in the class. Here there is a similar context shared by all students (a specific course in a particular school and one instructor) and yet the papers turned in have the potential for infinite variety.

language or terminology are an insufficient basis to postulate a source.

3.3.6 THE MODERN READER MAY BE GUIDED BY PRESUPPOSITIONS THAT MAKE THE DISCOVERY OF PARALLELS DESIRABLE OR UNDESIRABLE

It is of course critical that scholars be aware of all presuppositions brought to their work, and this is no less true for the study of parallels; at times the correspondence of one text or body of literature with another may be a desired conclusion. Stoutenburg offers useful comments about the relationship between modern translators and the identification of parallels between the Testaments that illustrates this point. With respect to christological proof–texts in the Christian Bible, translations of Hebrew and Greek Scripture can deliberately reinforce parallels. This is well illustrated, he suggests, by comparing translations of the OT, which clearly demonstrate a parallel with the NT, with translations of Tanak prepared by Jewish scholars (such as the JPS project, *The Tanakh*).

> Many of these apparent OT Christological proof–texts disappear; in such cases, no relation appears whatsoever when compared with the NT texts. The Christians [*sic*] charge that Jewish intention to avoid such Christological affirmations in their translation of the Hebrew Bible must be fairly countered by Jewish concern that Christian inclusion created the so–called parallels in the first place. This kind of debate proves circular and, therefore, unprofitable (1996, 83; cf. Sandmel 1962, 10 on the importance of scholarly impartiality).

See also comments under 3.5.4 regarding ambiguous translation.

3.3.7 APPEAL TO SIMILARITY IN ATMOSPHERE RUNS THE RISK OF OVERSIMPLIFICATION

The danger possible in appealing to vague terms like atmosphere is that too much weight is placed on subjective judgments, generalizations based on impressions rather than on clear criteria and sufficient evidence. Scholars at times find value in the less definite use of parallels that may be called something like atmosphere or spirit or quality. Here the affinities between texts may suggest more than the general milieu of Judeo–Christian religious life of the first or second century and point to a more specific pocket within that larger category. Though subjective, readers familiar with a wide body of ancient texts may appeal to this as a criterion. Some examples:

> . . . the superior spiritual quality of 2 Peter, when compared with second–century "Petrine" literature (*Gospel of Peter, Preaching of Peter, Acts of Peter, Apocalypse of Peter*) is only too obvious, even on a casual reading (Hillyer 1992, 11).

> . . . that the whole tone and conception of the *Apocalypse* [*of Peter*] is later than 2 Peter seems to me to be beyond doubt (Bigg 1901, 209).

When we discover an epistle which has the dignity and originality and high ethical
character of 2 Peter, in which are no anachronisms that the most searching
investigation can discover, and in which are found no absurd miracles or foolish
legends or heretical teaching contrary to the spirit and character of Peter, but in
which there are touches that remind one of the fiery apostle described in the Acts
and the Gospels . . . then it is a fair conclusion that we have here a genuine
message of the Apostle–Preacher Peter (Ebright 1917, 149).

This type of reasoning is too subjective to be of any real help, but is a common line
of argument. Reading 2 Peter under the rubric early catholicism (discussed in ch.
2) does this very thing. Under such a category, relative to Paul's authentic writings
or even 1 Peter, 2 Peter is thought "to breathe a different and inferior air" (Martin
and Elliott 1982, 119). This category was found to be problematic however,
because it involved too much value judgment based on the exegete's theological
presuppositions. Furthermore, since ancient writers were not constrained by their
context (cf. 3.3.5), such evaluations are not reliable guides in and of themselves.

Pursuing such lines of argument requires at least some supporting evidence.
To illustrate, several writers have suggested that the author of 2 Peter and the
readers for whom it was initially intended were largely Hellenistic in their world
view.[30] While there is evidence to support this, two points need to be kept in mind.

First, it is possible that a teacher can adapt a message to suit the context of the
audience (cf. Paul's Areopagus address, where he is seen to be conversant with
Greek philosophical thought [Acts 17:16–34]). As a result, it is not necessarily true
that texts provide unambiguous or direct evidence for the author's personal
perspective; the choice of vocabulary or method of presentation may indicate only
the strategic application of language as a vehicle to communicate a message.[31]

---

[30]Fornberg argued that the readers were most likely in a pagan context (1977, esp. ch. 6).
Neyrey observed parallels between the opponents addressed in 2 Peter and Plutarch's *De Sera
Numinis Vindicta* and concluded that the readers were facing opposition from sceptics whose
world view was influenced by Epicureanism (Neyrey 1993, 230–31). Charles has noted affinities
between the ethical list presented in 2 Pet 1 and those of the Stoics (1997, 156) and writes that
although exegetes disagree about whether 2 Pet 3 mirrors Epicurean or Stoic thought, "what is
clear is that the writer has incorporated aspects of contemporary Hellenistic cosmology in his
rhetorical response" (155). Riesner (1984) has compared 2 Pet 3 with the Stoic understanding
of ἐκπύρωσις. The vocabulary of 2 Peter, it has been observed, also resembles language
associated with Eleusinian mysteries. Klinger (1973, 153) goes so far as to say that the term
ἐπόπται *is taken from* the Eleusinian mysteries in which it designates the highest degree of
enlightenment, consisting of the fullness of knowledge, or 'all–embracing' knowledge"
(emphasis added). These few examples illustrate the parallels between 2 Peter and a Hellenistic
context. The fact that parallels exist is one thing, what they are evidence for is quite another.
[31]See also the example given in appendix 1. Charles (1998, 63–64) writes: "That the
writer is making use in 2 Peter 1 of pagan metaphysical language reveals an underlying
motivation: to demonstrate an awareness of and relevance to the social location of his audience."
In his defense of the traditional view of authorship for 2 Peter Moo writes: "Many scholars find
it difficult to believe that Peter, the Galilean fisherman, could have used some of the

Second, it is not necessarily true that the audience understood or accepted the author's message. This is often too quickly assumed. Comparisons of 2 Peter with Hellenistic philosophical schools of thought seem to imply that the readership was equally familiar with the Judeo–Christian belief system they have embraced (1:1) and the Epicurean or Stoic influenced world views being challenged by the author. Yet it is possible that the readership would more readily recognize Jewish apocalyptic imagery behind the language of 2 Pet 3:7–10 (e.g., Isa 24:19; 34:4; 66:15) than parallels with the Stoic doctrine of cosmic conflagration. Or again, the readership may have recognized the parallels between *1 En.* 6–11 and 2 Pet 2:4 more readily than those between 2 Peter and the stories of the *Titanomachia* (as found in Hesiod's *Theogony*).[32] The parallels between 2 Peter and Greek literature and ideas exist, but they do not necessarily provide reliable data for locating either author or audience because the author may be adapting his message as a rhetorical strategy and the readers may not have been familiar with the language used.[33]

It is reasonable to assume however that communication involves a certain amount of understanding between author and audience. The writer of 2 Peter claims to know his readers and has had some dialogue with them before (1:16; 3:1). At the same time, the writing is catholic in its scope (1:1), probably intended for a wide readership. If 2 Pet 3:1 points back to 1 Peter, it may be that the same readers are intended as the audience for 2 Peter (i.e., believers scattered throughout Pontus, Galatia, Cappadocia, Asia, and Bithynia [1 Pet 1:1]). If it is a circular letter, attempts to connect the text to the situation of the audience would be made difficult. The writer may have kept the message sufficiently general in its scope to make it meaningful for a wide range of readers and so it provides limited information about any specific community. Also, the language and concepts used in 2 Peter may have been understood by only a segment of the population addressed (i.e., the churches who received the letter may have been mixed, perhaps including both Jews and Gentiles, educated and non–educated).

3.3.8 CLAIMS OF TEXT DEPENDENCE ARE WEAKENED IF THERE IS LITTLE SIMILARITY IN THE CONTENT OF THE TWO WRITINGS BEING COMPARED

If passages resemble each other in details (vocabulary, phrases) but do not share similarities in the broader, literary context of the passage in question or in

---

philosophical and religious terminology that we find in 2 Peter. But we should see this as evidence that Peter adapted his message to his audience. By using 'religious' language that his readers would have been familiar with, he 'contextualizes' the gospel to meet their needs" (1996, 26).

[32] The latter suggested in Pearson's 1969 article discussed above.

[33] The move from choice of vocabulary and style to intended readers is always a great leap. In a text like 2 Peter, where the author identifies himself with the readers and points specifically to their faith stance (1:1), all that can be safely said about them is that they were Christians.

subject matter generally (cf. 3.2.8), suspicion about a genealogical relationship is justified. It may be asked why an author would consider borrowing material from a source that otherwise has little or nothing to do with the immediate project (cf. comments on the parallels between 2 Peter and Josephus [3.6] and an inscription found in Asia Minor [3.2.4]). This is equally relevant in the case of parallels where there is strong suspicion of dependence due to the extent of similar material. In some reflections on the significance of conceptual parallels between early Christianity and its environment (not referring specifically to extensive verbal parallels), Ferguson makes observations that are also helpful under this category:

> Where genuine dependence and significant parallels are determined, these must then be placed in the whole context of thought and practice in the systems where the contacts are discovered. Although Christianity had points of contact with Stoicism, the mysteries, the Qumran community, and so on, the total world view was often quite different, or the context in which the items were placed was different. Originality may be found in the way things are put together and not in the invention of a completely new idea or practice (1993, 3).

At the same time, it may be asked why Christian writers would borrow from such unlikely sources at all.

3.3.9 THE ABSENCE OF PARALLELS

Arguments from silence do not allow for definite conclusions and so dating or locating texts requires caution. For one thing, it cannot be assumed that the silence of history regarding a document (i.e., the lack of evidence for it in later writings) implies that a work was written late. Not all documents circulated widely, and it is possible that other writers found no need to use a particular writing in their own work—not all literature was influential.

Second, influence from one text to another may be obscured by the fact that there is continuous evolution in religious traditions over time. What is meant by this is that the earlier document (A) may have included an idea that a later writer (document B) chose to incorporate. However, the earlier idea from document A is transformed to make it more suitable for the new, later context (cf. 2.3.5). So even if the authors of documents A and B are writing for similar audiences (e.g., Christian communities), the borrowed concept originating in the earlier document was reworked. This can be illustrated from a study of Jewish literature in relation to the NT:

> Certain genuine parallels may exist between Judaic literature and the NT, especially the gospels. One would expect parallels to exist in literature exclusive to a single people group [i.e., Jews, whether Christian or non–Christian]. By the same token, differences will also exist because people groups differ from generation to generation—thoughts evolve and progress, habits mature and adjust to new environmental, social and political challenges, smaller communities within

the larger complex choose to be different (Stoutenburg 1996, 86).

This line of argument is further illustrated by Peter's redaction of Jude and other source material where adjustments to new environment challenges are evident. Unlike Jude, 2 Peter is addressed, some argue (see n.30), to a largely Hellenistic community (e.g., Fornberg 1977, 111; Charles 1997, 138–39), which may explain the disinterest in Jewish apocalyptic imagery (meaning here the omission of Jude's references and allusions to apocalyptic literature [*Assumption of Moses, 1 Enoch*]). This particular example (discussed further below) is open to debate.[34]

But when, if ever, are arguments from silence (including specifically the absence of parallels) significant?[35] This question needs to be asked as occasionally it is introduced in attempts to locate 2 Peter. A few examples (in no particular order) illustrate:

[in 2 Peter] traces of the second century are absent at those points where they might have been confidently expected to occur . . . (Bigg 1901, 242).

In spite of its heavy stress on Petrine authorship, II Peter is nowhere mentioned in the second century. The apologists, Irenaeus, Tertullian, Cyprian, Clement of Alexandria, and the Muratorian Canon are completely silent about it. . . . Even down to the fourth century II Pet was largely unknown or not recognized as canonical (Kümmel 1973, 433–34 [these comments are part of his argument against Petrine authorship]).

. . . I am impressed by the absence of any suggestion of chiliasm in 3:8 when quoting the very verse used by Barnabas, Justin, 2 Clement, Methodius and Irenaeus to support it. I find this almost incredible if 2 Peter did in fact come from a second–century hand. I am equally impressed at the contrast between the parousia teaching of 2 Peter and that of the early second–century *Apocalypse of Peter*. I am impressed by the absence of interest in church organization (one of the main preoccupations of second–century works like the *Didache* and the *Ascension of Isaiah*) . . . (Green 1987, 39).

To infer from the absence of any allusion to chiliasm that the epistle must be very old, is doubly erroneous; for (i.) chiliasm was not universal in the second century, (ii.) nor was the quotation from Ps 90[4] its starting–point, as Apoc 20[4f.] is enough

---

[34]This is a questionable conclusion because it is based on the erroneous assumption that a Hellenistic community would not be interested in Jewish imagery. This assumption illustrates the misuse of the category atmosphere/milieu discussed in 3.3.7. There is no evidence for this and there is in fact data suggesting the opposite (for various examples of Gentile interest in Judaism between the years 70 and 200 C.E., see Stephen Wilson's intriguing article "Gentile Judaizers" [1992, 605–16]; also, MacKenzie [1997] regarding the Book of Revelation). Readers did not think of apocalyptic writings as Jewish as much as they were divine revelations.

[35]This line of argument also appeared in my article "Reflections on the Authorship of 2 Peter" (2001, 304–05) where biblical scholarship was compared with Shakespearean studies in the area of authorship debates.

to show (Moffatt 1911, 362 n.).

> The letter gives no hint of a second–century environment or of problems such as
> the monarchical bishop, developed Gnosticism, or Montanism (Blum 1981, 261).

> Indeed if this is the sort of thing that was being produced in the first half of the
> second century [referring to the *Apocalypse of Peter*] it is the strongest possible
> argument for *not* placing II Peter there (Robinson 1976, 178 [his emphasis]).

> To commentators, the use of the double name Συμεὼν Πέτπος [*sic*] seems
> strange, as it occurs elsewhere only in Acts 15.14. It is noteworthy that 'Simon
> Peter' does not occur in any pseudo–Petrine writings of the second century
> (Charles 1997, 130).

> . . . it should be noted how the predictive character of the testament genre is used
> in 2 Peter. Nothing in the letter reflects the situation in which Peter is said to be
> writing; the work is addressed to a situation after Peter's death (Bauckham 1997,
> 924).

> . . . pseudepigraphic literature is normally connected to heretical groups. . . . [2
> Peter] has no evident heterodoxical agenda, bears no clear resemblance to any other
> pseudo–Petrine literature, and exhibits no references to any second–century
> doctrinal controversies (Kruger 1999, 670).

Arguments based on silence can be used in diverse ways, as these examples show.
They illustrate how the absence of parallels or reference to a writing is used to
support opposite conclusions—2 Peter *is* a second–century document and 2 Peter
is not a second–century document. This topic touches on several other issues
already addressed, but especially the observation that authorial creativity may mean
that the literature produced is unlike the work of contemporaries, and so parallels
should not be expected (3.3.5). The assumption that there is a direct and obvious
correspondence between author and context is potentially misleading.[36]
    A further example often cited in studies of 2 Peter involves the comparison
with Jude. Much is made of the fact that 2 Peter, as already said, does not include
pseudepigraphal material to the same extent that Jude does. In fact, the author of
2 Peter seems to excise traces of this material quite deliberately (Jude 6 cf. 2 Pet
2:4, 9; Jude 9 cf. 2 Pet 2:11; Jude 14–15 cf. 2 Pet 2:17). Does this say something
about 2 Peter's intended audience? Maybe they were not familiar with these Jewish
traditions, suggesting therefore a (primarily) Gentile readership (cf. nn.30 and 31).
Or, does it say something about the date of composition? Perhaps it signals a later
stage in the church when there was a reluctance to use pseudepigraphal writings.[37]

---

[36]A major factor here is that historians' knowledge of the church in the second century
is far less than comprehensive and so the presence or absence of certain elements in a document
is not a reliable basis for dating (i.e., it cannot be claimed that the absences are conspicuous).

[37]E.g., "Interestingly, Second Peter reflects the development of the canonical process. In
quoting Jude, it purges all references to works outside the Hebrew canon, expunging the

However, such reasoning reflects an oversimplified view of the early church. It is equally possible that *parts of the church* were uncomfortable with this literature (2 Peter), while other *parts of the church* felt free to make use of it (Jude).

3.4 CONCLUSIONS POSSIBLE ON THE BASIS OF PARALLELS

When a parallel is observed, one must recognize that a wide spectrum of conclusions is possible.[38]

3.4.1 DIRECT DEPENDENCE

Parallels may be due to direct dependence (B used A). In the NT, this is most clearly evident in the Synoptic Gospels. In this example, the case for literary dependence is strengthened by extensive word–for–word agreements (note 3.2.1, length of parallel material). The direction of that dependence is a separate issue.

3.4.2 COMMON AUTHORSHIP

Parallels may be due to common authorship (one author penned both A and B). For this to be true, one would expect some measure of consistency in style, vocabulary, and thought. J. A. T. Robinson has proposed this for 2 Peter and Jude, finding them to be the product of a single mind (1976, 193–95).

3.4.3 USE OF A COMMON SOURCE

Parallels may be explained by use of a common source (A and B both used X).[39] For this to be true, dependence of A on B or B on A does not adequately

---

allusions to the Assumption of Moses and Enoch" (Hauer and Young 2001, 352).

[38]This list is intended to illustrate that direct dependence of one text on another is not the only explanation for parallels (though it is one of them and therefore included here). The criteria given in 3.2 (factors that lend weight to arguments claiming that parallels are due to literary dependence) provide some clues indicating direct borrowing. The other possible explanations for the presence of parallels in literature given here would need to be ruled out before concluding that a genealogical relationship is the best explanation. Only rarely can certainty be achieved.

[39]A word of caution is necessary here. Parallels may indicate dependence of one text on another but they cannot provide certain evidence of a common source. The simplest and strongest explanation of the nature of dependence is text A used text B, or text B used text A. If neither is probable due to dissimilarities in the elements that are thought to be parallel, this means that the claim of the parallel being due to dependence is in question. The hypothesis of an unknown source X on which presumably both A and B depend is really a double hypothesis that intends to explain why the evidence does not fit direct dependence. Such a hypothesis runs the danger of trying to explain one ambiguity with the help of another. There are situations, however, such as manuscript traditions, where there is no question that parallels are due to dependence, when posing a manuscript X as a *Vorlage* for A and B is justified.

explain similarities and differences between them. For example, it is occasionally suggested that Matthew and Luke both made use of an earlier form of Mark's Gospel (*Urmarkus*). Here an attempt is made to account for various phenomena such as Luke's omission of Mark 6:45–8:26 and the minor agreements of Matthew and Luke against Mark. A common source for 2 Peter and Jude is occasionally postulated (e.g., Reicke 1964, 190) but this overlooks the simplest explanation— direct dependence of one on the other.

3.4.4 DELIBERATE IMITATION

Parallels may be due to deliberate imitation.[40] For this to be true, one would expect an otherwise inexplicable mix of affinities and contrasts with the suspected source(s).[41] A writer using the name of another may try to preserve the fiction by reproducing that author's style, vocabulary, and thought. At the same time, differences rule against common authorship. This may be true of the so–called deuteropauline letters (Ephesians, Colossians, 2 Thessalonians).[42] This type of reasoning can develop into very complex hypotheses, where perceived differences in content are thought to rule out the obvious explanation of common authorship. In this case, there is an external interference in the normal way of explaining striking parallels. Thus imitation is never a normal explanation for parallels but depends on there being sufficient reasons to rule out common authorship.

3.4.5 ORIGIN IN A SCHOOL

Parallels are sometimes thought to be the result of activity in a school. This possibility has been much discussed in relation to the Johannine writings. Here similarities in style and content are coupled with alleged differences in theological positions, ruling out common authorship.[43] As noted in chapter 2, the school

---

[40]It is difficult to distinguish imitation from literary dependence. Imitation differs in the author's purpose or motive, namely, to hide pseudonymous authorship.

[41]Distinguishing such imitation from non–deliberate imitation (influence) would also be very difficult. If texts written in the name of a prominent figure (pseudepigraphy) resemble the authentic writings of that same teacher, it is reasonable to postulate deliberate imitation. On the other hand, a writer's ideas, choice of language, and areas of interest may all be shaped by the writings/teachings of another to the point where that influence is not consciously repeated. Where similarities exist with that same teacher but where there is no claim to be the work of that individual, the imitation may be non–deliberate.

[42]To take another example from Spenser's poetry, it has been observed that in his "Shepheardes Calender" he deliberately used archaic language "partly out of homage to Chaucer . . . [and also] to achieve a rustic effect" (Abrams 1987, 260). In the NT some writers appear to have imitated characteristics of the Septuagint, presumably to lend a prophetic tone to their work.

[43]There is a need for caution here. Normally the case for a school is based on parallels in technical vocabulary (see Culpepper's outline of the characteristics of ancient schools, listed in 2.3.4). In cases where schools are postulated in biblical literature the simplest explanation—

hypothesis has also been postulated as an explanation for the similarities and differences found in the Petrine literature.

3.4.6 A SHARED MILIEU

Parallels are sometimes attributed to a shared milieu, if the similarities reflect features of a specific religious or geographical environment. For example, the book of Hebrews resembles aspects of Philo's Platonism, suggesting to some Alexandria as the place of origin (but cf. comments under 3.3.5).[44]

Though defining milieu is difficult, one way of understanding it can be suggested by an example. A number of near parallels between 1 Peter and OT pseudepigrapha has been observed by Davids. Given that there is one instance where there is almost certainly an allusion to *1 Enoch* (1 Pet 3:18–20), it is reasonable to ask if other traces of influence from this body of literature can be found. Davids lists well over thirty examples of similar material and describes these as:

> 1. places in which unusual words or expressions appear in both 1 Peter and the pseudepigrapha (although often in very different contexts), 2. places in which the same general idea appears in 1 Peter and the pseudepigrapha (although often expressed quite differently), and 3. some parallels in which there is both closeness of concept and some overlap of vocabulary (1993, 238; his list is presented on 237–38).

He does not find in these parallels sufficient evidence to prove that the author knew the pseudepigrapha in question, despite the cumulative nature of the evidence. What the evidence is sufficient to show however is that 1 Peter and at least some of the pseudepigrapha "move in the same thought–world," more specifically, "an apocalyptic world" (239, 243).[45] Perhaps milieu or tradition are also suitable terms

---

common authorship—is being dismissed on the basis of subtle differences in theology. Alternative explanations, such as shifts in the author's theology, should not be overlooked.

[44]Indeed it would be remarkable if there were not these general parallels between the literature of the NT and its environment (even when the originality of writers is taken into consideration). "The kind and significance of . . . parallels may be further clarified by commenting on the cultural parallels. That Christians observed the same customs and used words in the same way as their contemporaries is hardly noteworthy in itself. Those things belonged to the place and time when Christianity began. The situation could not have been otherwise for Christianity to have been a real historical phenomenon, open now to historical study. To expect the situation to have been otherwise would require Christianity to be something other than it is, a historical religion. Indeed, if Christianity did not have these linguistic and cultural contacts with the first–century Mediterranean world the presumption would be that it was a fiction originating in another time and place" (Ferguson 1993, 1–2).

[45]For very general reflections on the role of the OT pseudepigrapha in Jude and 2 Peter (with an emphasis on the former) see Dunnett 1988. He examines both *how* (quotations, allusions, reminiscences, catchwords) and *why* (e.g., the appeal of apocalyptic writing in

here. This observation is certainly valuable for exegesis; it assists the interpreter in understanding the vocabulary and imagery used in the text. This does not help isolate a location for texts however, as apocalyptic writing was not confined to any specific geographical setting or time period (apart from the very general time frame of, say, 200 B.C.E. to 200 C.E. that is often suggested). At this point, parallels are so general and vague that there is not much urgency to explain their presence. The appeal to a shared milieu may assist on occasions, for instance shedding light on the use of certain terms. For placing texts historically, however, such parallels offer little; the use of terms and concepts can rarely be located to a precise time or place.

At this point, a further illustration of the idea of milieu is introduced, though one that is again of limited value for locating texts to specific contexts. There are times when similarities with earlier material are insufficient for scholars to assume direct literary dependence, but they are still clear enough to posit knowledge of similar traditions. This phenomenon occurs when early stories undergo modification over time and writers reflect *a particular way of reading* shared with other texts (again drawing from Davids 1993).

This is illustrated in James' reference to biblical characters, where he demonstrates knowledge of the retelling of biblical narratives found in pseudepigraphal literature (esp. stories about Abraham, Job, and Elijah [possibly also Rahab]; 228–33). In Jas 5:11, for example, the author refers to the ὑπομονή of Job, a description that is not entirely consistent with the Book of Job itself, where he is seen protesting against God. An explanation of James' description may be found in the *Testament of Job* where, after suffering for seventeen years in a contest with Satan, Job says "Now my children you also must be patient in everything that happens to you. For patience is better than anything" (*T. Job* 27:6–7). This story seems to represent the basis for the idea found in Jas 5:11, but what is this parallel between James and the *Testament of Job* evidence for? Davids writes:

> . . . it is possible that James actually knew the work [the dating of the *Testament of Job* allows for this]. However, the data at hand are not extensive enough (mainly the use of the term ὑπομονή, 'patient endurance') to prove such a claim. The most we can argue is that James shows contact with the traditions incorporated in the *Testament* (232).

After discussing other examples that indicate familiarity with particular *ways of reading* the canonical stories, Davids suggests that the evidence is insufficient to indicate that James used any pseudepigraphal books, but it does provide evidence for traditions which shaped James' way of understanding canonical stories. These traditions represent "a contemporary grid" or "paradigm" that both supplemented and interpreted the biblical stories (233, 243). In the case of James, the source is not so much a specific text necessarily, but *a way of reading* earlier stories.

------

polemics) these materials were used in these canonical letters.

A similar phenomenon is found in 2 Peter. Peter's reference to Noah as a "preacher of righteousness" (2:5) introduces a description not found in Genesis but one well attested in other literature (e.g., *Sib. Or.* 1:148–98; *1 Clem.* 7:6). Similarly, the reference to the righteousness of Lot (2:7–8) goes beyond the picture of this character found in Genesis, but it is a familiar theme in extrabiblical texts (e.g., Wis 10:6; 19:17; *1 Clem.* 11:1).

As already noted parallels may involve nothing more than incidental similarities between otherwise unrelated texts. Texts written in the same language, at approximately the same time, addressing broadly the same topics (religion, Christ, ethics, and so on) are bound to resemble one another at times (in vocabulary [even phrases], or themes). No conclusions concerning the relative location of a text can be drawn from such parallels. As one moves down this list (3.4.1–6), it becomes more difficult to draw specific inferences about relationships between texts. Conclusions based on similarities are suspect unless there is an accumulation of parallels or some particularly striking feature.

It is obvious that dependency is not the only explanation for parallels. It is suggested that determining instances of direct, genealogical relationships between texts is possible, if high standards which rule out other possible explanations (see the criteria in 3.2 above and 3.5 below) are in place. The alternative explanations outlined here in 3.4 become increasingly vague as one moves down the list, and the conclusions they could allow, if proven, are less useful to the historian interested in locating texts to a specific time or place.

3.5 PARALLELS THAT ARE NOT RELIABLE FOR REACHING CONCLUSIONS ABOUT DEPENDENCY

At this point two issues introduced above are brought together. In chapters 1 and 2, some problems involved in locating 2 Peter to a precise historical location were presented. In chapter 3, to this point, issues related to the use of parallels were discussed. The question is now asked whether the observation of parallels between 2 Peter and other early Christian literature provides scholars with the type of data needed to fix this text to a more precise historical context.

The relative dating of a text of unknown origin through comparison with another text involves two questions (among other things): did the author use datable texts and betray knowledge of datable phenomena (i.e., a *terminus a quo*) and was this same text used by later, datable documents (i.e., a *terminus ad quem*). With respect to 2 Peter, the latter has been the greater concern (cf. p.4 above).[46] What

---

[46]Regarding a *terminus a quo*, Peter's use of Jude is likely but the date of Jude's composition cannot be determined with any precision and therefore it is of limited value for dating 2 Peter. A *terminus ad quem* of 200 C.E. is provided by both Origen, who was the first to refer to 2 Peter by name, and its presence in P[72]. There has been great interest, however, in seeking to lower that date by finding evidence of 2 Peter's influence on other, earlier literature (see ch. 4).

often occurs however is that *possible* instances of dependence on 2 Peter are not distinguished from *probable* ones. Too often lists of *possible* instances of dependence are presented (e.g., Bigg 1901, 199–210; Picirilli 1988; Kruger 1999, esp. 649 56[47]), leaving the somewhat distorted impression that 2 Peter was widely known to second–century authors. Of course all parallels between writings are of value—even if they are not instances of dependence they can still assist with interpretation. But for the task of locating texts (here specifically, determining a *terminus ad quem*), many of the parallels put forward by Bigg, Picirilli, Kruger and others should be excluded from consideration, because they do not unambiguously prove that the second–century author in question was familiar with 2 Peter.[48] The following list is therefore intended to eliminate questionable instances of dependence from consideration. It should be stressed that the goal here is not a distinction between impossible–possible but rather possible–probable (cf. Garnet's statement, quoted on p.81 n.1).

3.5.1 PARALLELS BETWEEN TEXTS POSSIBLY RESULTING FROM COMMON USE OF AN EARLIER SOURCE

In many cases, the parallels between 2 Peter and other texts could conceivably be the result of mutual use of an earlier third source. This can be illustrated as follows:

$$\begin{array}{ccl} & \leftarrow & \text{B (2 Peter)} \\ \text{A (e.g., Scripture)} & \updownarrow & \\ & \leftarrow & \text{B (a parallel in an early Christian text)} \end{array}$$

Parallels that can be explained in this way, it is suggested, are best eliminated from discussion. This is not fool–proof, as 2 Peter could be the medium through which an earlier tradition was passed on, in which case:

$$\text{A} \leftarrow \text{2 Peter} \leftarrow \text{B}$$

This criterion is frequently relevant with common use of OT passages.

---

[47]To illustrate, Bigg lists four *possible* instances of dependence in Ignatius, five words and phrases in Hermas which *may have* been suggested by 2 Peter, and six phrases in *1 Clement*.

[48]Instructive is a comparison with Sandmel who finds various sins in Strack and Billerbeck's *Kommentar zum Neuen Testament aus Talmud und Midrasch*, among them the excessive piling up of rabbinic references. "Nowhere else in scholarly literature is quantity so confused for quality as in Strack–Billerbeck. There mere abundance of so–called parallels is its own distortion, for the height of the pile misleads him who reads as he runs to suppose that he is dealing with sifted material. The distortion lies also in the circumstance that quantity lends a tone of authority all too often submitted to" (1962, 10). It is suggested that a similar problem occurs in studies of 2 Peter that create lists of *possible* instances of dependence on that text.

3.5.2 WIDELY ATTESTED PARALLELS

Similarly, widely attested parallels, meaning phrases or expressions found in a variety of places beyond 2 Peter and the text supposedly dependent on it, are best omitted.[49] Here it is difficult to determine precisely which text provided the source for the others. It is of course possible, as in the first point above, that 2 Peter could be the source for the various writings. However, 2 Peter's apparent limited circulation in the second century, suggested by the limited textual evidence, reduces the probability of this.

3.5.3 ARGUMENTS BASED ON STYLE OR TYPICAL WRITING/THOUGHT PATTERNS

Building on assumptions about what a writer would or would not do is a line of argumentation that is necessarily inconclusive. Few Christian writers in the ancient world have left sufficient samples of their work to justify arguments based on what is typical or usual in their writings.[50] Since 2 Peter is short and not unambiguously from the pen of an author known in any other source, this would be an unreliable basis on which to formulate conclusions about this document.

3.5.4 PARALLELS BASED ON SUSPECT TRANSLATION, OR INTERPRETATION OF DIFFICULT PASSAGES, OR ON WHAT APPEARS TO BE EXTENSIVE REDACTION

Parallels involving ambiguity in the meaning of difficult passages, or where extensive redaction is suspected, are best omitted. An example of this occurs in a parallel between 2 Peter and the *Apocalypse of Peter* (discussed in 4.5). When translated a certain way, the Ethiopic version of the *Apocalypse* does not parallel 2 Peter's meaning at all. See also the example discussed on p.37 n.37.

---

[49]This is distinguished from 3.5.1 in that there is not a clear, ultimate source for the parallel such as that provided by Scripture.

[50]As a point of interest, Lauri Thurén refers to Alvar Ellegård's *A Statistical Method for Determining Authorship: The Junius Letters, 1769–1772* (1962) in which it is argued that the text being analysed to determine authorship must have at least 19,000 words, the material of the author in question 100,000 words, and the contemporary comparative material 1,000,000 words (Thurén 1996, 332 n.15). Thurén himself suggests that such use of "style or word statistics is problematic, since we do not have enough material" (332). A further variable exists in that "the same author can produce very different types of language and style in different situations" (332 n.15). According to Green, there are 399 words in 2 Peter and 543 words in 1 Peter (1960, 12) so even if they are from the same writer, this is still a small portfolio.

3.5.5 PARALLELS BASED ON TEXTS WHERE THERE ARE UNRESOLVED TEXTUAL
DIFFICULTIES

As explained in 3.5.4, parallels in passages involving significant textual
problems are best omitted. By and large, the text of 2 Peter is not in dispute,
despite what appears to be limited early circulation, for most variants reasonable
explanations have been put forward to account for them. Some more significant
readings remaining somewhat uncertain are found in 2:4, 2:6, 2:18, and 3:10.[51] To

---

[51]In 2:4 there is an interesting textual question involving a choice between the terms
σειραῖς (cords, chains; P[72] K P Ψ et al.; this reading is given a 'C' rating by the UBS editors)
and σειροῖς (= σιροῖς; pits; ℵ A B C et al.). Assuming 2 Peter's dependence on Jude, it may
be that the author used the unusual σειραῖς for Jude's δεσμοῖς (v.6) "in accordance with his
habit of substituting more elegant and unusual vocabulary for Jude's" (Bauckham 1983, 244 n.a;
cf. Metzger 1971, 701–02). Others conclude that copyists were influenced by Jude 6 to use a
synonym for his δεσμοῖς (see Pearson 1969, 78; Kelly 1969, 331; Schelkle 1961, 207; and
Fornberg 1977, 52).

There is some uncertainty in 2:6 about the term ἀσεβέ[σ]ιν (given a 'C' rating by the
UBS editors). In P[72] B P and others the dative ἀσεβέσιν is found whereas the infinitive ἀσεβεῖν
appears in ℵ A C K Ψ and others. Since μελλόντων is frequently followed by the infinitive, a
change to this construction would be understandable. The dative, which the NIV here follows,
gives a better sense ("what is going to happen to the ungodly"; cf. the NASB, "to those who
would live ungodly").

The textual question in 2:18 has received a fair amount of attention by commentators.
Though given an 'A' grade by the UBS editors, there remains some uncertainty. Ὀλίγως (with
the sense of barely [NASB and NEB]?; or just [NIV and JB]?) is rare, not appearing elsewhere
in the NT or the LXX. Since copyists would be more inclined to replace an unfamiliar word with
a more common one, the appearance of ὄντως (ℵ* C K P et al.) is likely secondary. Mayor notes
that the latter "seems to involve a self–contradiction after δελεάζουσιν" and in the MSS the
two terms would have been nearly indistinguishable, making confusion quite understandable
(1907, cxcviii; see Metzger 1992, 187 for comments on the scribal error suggested by this
variant).

Finally, a variant in 3:10 raises the question whether the earth and the works in it will "be
found" (εὑρεθήσεται: ℵ B), "be found dissolved" (P[72]), "disappear" (C), or "be burned up" (A
048). The first reading listed above (given a 'D' rating by the UBS editors)—there are others as
well—may not be original but seems to explain the others best (Metzger 1971, 705–06; for a
defense of P[72] see Crehan 1982, 145–49, esp. 147–48). Variant readings, influenced by Matt
24:35 and Rev 20:11, emerged when sense could not be made of ℵ which derived its reading by
haplography. If εὑρεθήσεται is accepted as the best alternative, along with the UBS text, there
is still a need to explain its sense. Lenhard suggests the following on the basis of internal
evidence: "Die gesamte sichtbare Welt vergeht, nur der Mensch muß sein Handeln vor Gott
verantworten" (1961, 129). Others appeal to external parallels. Danker discusses this verse in
the light of Pss. Sol. 17:10 where εὑρεθῆναι is "understood in the sense of judicial inquiry
culminating in a penal pronouncement" (1962, 85). The concept of being found is present in
Jesus' eschatological parables and may provide the background for this perplexing language (so
Wenham 1987, 477–79). Neyrey finds 'being found' "a plausible and contextually appropriate
term" noting similarities with other NT passages (1993, 243–44). This reading is also supported
in an interesting article by Al Wolters in which he argues that the sense of the Day of the Lord

conclude that the text of 2 Peter has been reasonably well established is justified given this relatively small number of outstanding questions. If the changes from the UBS³ to UBS⁴ are any indication, there is increasing confidence in the text of 2 Peter. Thirteen times ratings in UBS³ improved by one letter grade and twice (1:3; 2:18) by two letters.[52]

Despite the general reliability of the text, variant readings still represent an area where caution is needed with respect to parallels. Since copyists themselves may have been influenced by other texts familiar to them, it is possible that parallels were created in transmission where none existed before. This phenomenon is evident in the Greek text of the *Apocalypse of Peter*, here many similarities with 2 Peter suggest the influence of the canonical text on later copyists; this means that the parallels do not suggest an influence on the original form of the work (see discussion 4.5). This is illustrated further in 2 Pet 1:20. Some minuscules of this verse have πᾶσα γραφὴ προφητείας (206 378 429 522 etc.) instead of πᾶσα προφητεία γραφῆς. This minor variant suggests the influence of 2 Tim 3:16 and its reference to Scripture (Metzger 1971, 701). There is a thematic parallel here, regardless of the wording but similarities in word order do not represent anything beyond this since the parallel was the result of later copyists (for comments on similarities between the Pastoral Epistles and 2 Peter, see 5.1).

3.6 SOME METHODOLOGICAL CONCLUSIONS

Parallels between texts written in the same language, addressing similar subject matter, and written at approximately the same time are not remarkable in themselves, and indeed they should be expected. Unless there are compelling reasons to think otherwise, it should not be assumed that text dependence is the best explanation. More general explanations like coincidence or the influence of a shared culture or educational background are to be preferred. Some compelling reasons to suspect the dependence of one text on another were given in 3.2. Even when such clues exist, source theories can still be in error (3.3). Furthermore, in addition to direct dependence other possible explanations for parallels must be considered (3.4). In what follows, an example of a hypothesis based on parallels is summarized for two reasons. First, it serves to make the point that when there is insufficient attention given to alternative explanations, the discussion of parallels between texts often results in the development of source theories. Second, the

---

is not a conflagration that will annihilate everything but rather it is like a smelting process from which the world will emerge purified (1987, esp. 408). He notes that this is the sense of the flood judgment which Peter refers to as a parallel to the future day of judgment (3:6–7; i.e., the world of that day did not vanish, it was purified).

[52]Only four remained unchanged (2:6; 2:20; 3:10; 3:11b). One reading was omitted (2:21; given a 'C' in the earlier edition), and five new variants were added (1:2; 1:4; 1:5; 2:13b; 2:14). It should be remembered that the criteria for the newer grading scheme was somewhat revised from the earlier one (see UBS⁴, xii).

example given discusses 2 Peter's relation to another body of literature not often appearing in current research on this text (further illustrating the importance of scholarly consensus, cf. 3.2.9).

In the nineteenth century, Edwin Abbott suggested that 2 Peter was dependent on Josephus (1882, 49–63) and, in a related effort, Farrar (1888, 58–69) argued the reverse relationship. Discussion about the relationship between 2 Peter and Josephus was continued by James Moffatt in his survey of NT literature (1911, 28–29, 366). Various verbal and thematic correspondences between the preface to the *Jewish Antiquities* and 2 Peter can be observed.[53]

Josephus	2 Peter
θεοῦ πρῶτον φύσιν κατανοῆσαι (*Ant.* 1.4.19)	θείας κοινωνοὶ φύσεως (1:4)
τοῖς μύθοις ἐξακολουθήσαντες (*Ant.* 1.4.22)	Οὐ ... μύθοις ἐξακολουθήσαντες (1:16)
τὴν ἀρετὴν ἔχοντα τὸν θεόν (*Ant.* 1.4.23)	[God, by his own] δόξῃ καὶ ἀρετῇ (1:3)
τὴν μεγαλειότητα τοῦ θεοῦ (*Ant.* 1.4.24)	τῆς ἐκείνου μεγαλειότητος (1:16)

Similar terms are also used in the account of Moses' last address (*Ant.* 4.8.177–319) and 2 Peter: τοιάδε (cf. τοιᾶσδε, 2 Pet 1:17), μνήμην (2 Pet 1:15), εὐσεβεία (2 Pet 1:6; 3:11), and καταφρονεῖν (2 Pet 2:10). One longer passage from the historian includes several similarities:

Josephus	2 Peter
δεῖ με τοῦ ζῆν ἀπελθεῖν . . .οὐ μέλλω βοηθὸς ὑμῖν ἔσεσθαι . . . δίκαιον ἡγησάμην (*Ant.* 4.8.177–78) (i.e., knowledge of impending death)	ταχινή ἐστιν ἡ ἀπόθεσις τοῦ σκηνώματός μου (1:14); δίκαιον δὲ ἡγοῦμαι (1:13)
τήν τ᾽ ἐλευθερίαν ἡγεῖσθε μὴ τὸ προσαγανακτεῖν οἷς ἂν ὑμᾶς οἱ ἡγεμόνες πράττειν ἀξιῶσι (*Ant.* 4.8.187; i.e., a warning against an abuse of freedom)	ἐλευθερίαν αὐτοῖς ἐπαγγελλόμενοι (2:19)
use of ἔξοδος, ἀνάμνησις, and βέβαιος in close proximity (*Ant.* 4.8.189, 192)	ἔξοδος (1:15); ὑπομιμνήσκω (1:12); βέβαιος (1:10, 19)

Taken together these are remarkable parallels and they correspond to some of the criteria suggested as positive indicators of literary relationships (clustering of

---

[53]References to Josephus are taken from the LCL.

parallels, 3.2.2; parallels in the same order, 3.2.3). Moffatt's conclusion is of interest, especially for the reasons he gives for direct borrowing. These illustrate various issues involved in determining genealogical relationships:

> The occurrence in Josephus of several unusual words and phrases which are characteristic of 2 Peter would not of itself be decisive, as some also occur in Philo and elsewhere. Even the common use of midrashic traditions[54] does not involve literary filiation. But a number of the coincidences of language and style occur not only in the compass of two short paragraphs of Josephus, but in a sequence and connection which is not dissimilar; and, even after allowance is made for the widespread use of rhetorical commonplaces, these coincidences can hardly be dismissed as fortuitous. Their weight tells in favour of the hypothesis that the author of 2 Peter was familiar with Josephus,—an inference which is the more plausible as in any case the epistle belongs to the second century (28–29).

Here again evidence cited in favour of dependence is convincing to some but not others. As is so often the case, parallels are not the sort of evidence sufficient to prove conclusively a location for texts. In this particular example, no modern scholars affirm a connection between Josephus and 2 Peter, let alone dependence in a specific direction (cf. 3.2.9). Granted, the similarities observed are impressive (and only a few examples are given here). However, they can be explained by recognizing literary conventions (such as the farewell discourse), shared use of literary language, common ideas derived from the influence of Jewish traditions, and coincidence. There is no need to appeal to literary dependence as an explanation.[55]

Despite such dangers, it is suggested that parallels can still serve an important role in determining at least an approximate location of texts in history (in the case of 2 Peter, first or second–century Greek speaking Christianity). Parallels can also shed light on such things as the language and religious milieu of early Christianity.[56] However, in the same way that Sandmel and others have warned about the exaggerated claims in history of religions research, the present project is exploring the limitations of parallels for locating NT writings with no fixed historical markers. By doing so there is an attempt to provide criteria that distinguish between parallels that allow historical inferences—those that are

---

[54]By this Moffatt means the allusion to the Jewish legend that Adam predicted the twofold destruction of the world by deluge and by fire (*Ant.* 1.2.2 cf. 2 Pet 3:5–6; 28).

[55]This example provides a reminder that even when there are reasons to suspect a relationship between texts (here especially overlapping vocabulary), the evidence may still be deceptive.

[56]Cf. two important articles discussing the role of parallels in biblical studies: "the subsidiary explanatory potential of parallels–study is not to be minimized. Parallels, both stronger and weaker, are important for the illumination and insight that they can provide in the study of specific aspects of the NT" (Donaldson 1983, 203–04); "I am not seeking to discourage the study of parallels, but, especially in the case of the Qumran documents, to encourage them" (Sandmel 1962, 1).

dependable and reliable for locating texts—from those that are not.[57] It is suggested that the most productive model for locating texts is one that moves beyond an emphasis on verbal or thematic correspondence alone—in themselves, these are not sufficient to locate a text.

The influence from one writing to another can take many shapes: texts can *suggest subject matter* for the later writer to explore; texts can *raise questions* for a later writer to answer; texts can *answer questions* sufficiently well that a later writer sees no need to explore a topic further (possibly explaining a text's silence on a topic); texts can *suggest a genre* by which a later writer can communicate; and so on. Such general influences are too broad to measure, and therefore scholarship is not always in a position to say absolutely that this text was known or not known. This limits the ability of the historian to determine a *terminus a quo* or *terminus ad quem*. Furthermore, themes and ideas from earlier texts may be incorporated in such a way that the source cannot be recognized. The borrower's skill as an author may mean that the source is hidden, leaving only inconclusive traces of the earlier document if anything at all.

As noted in chapter 1, the information needed to determine an absolute historical location is lacking for many early Christian texts, leaving historians with frustrating gaps in their understanding. Selected attempts to reconstruct the context of 2 Peter specifically were introduced in chapter 2. There it was seen that assumptions involved in the various theories were problematic. In the present chapter, the evaluation of parallels has highlighted further weaknesses involved in those developmental models, at least to the extent that they depend on parallels for support. It is concluded that other types of evidence are needed, if any gains are to be made in determining historical contexts, though parallels may of course support conclusions reached on other grounds (cf. the evaluation of Reicke). Some specific examples of claimed genealogical relationships between texts will be examined in chapter 4, which illustrate the criteria and concerns presented in chapter 3 and will simultaneously introduce and evaluate theories of text relationships between 2 Peter and other early Christian literature.

---

[57]The criteria for determining what is significant for *the historian seeking to locate a text* is more stringent than the criteria for *the interpreter seeking to explain the meaning of a text*. If parallels do not meet the criteria suggested here for use in historical work, they remain valuable for interpretation.

CHAPTER 4
ANALYSIS OF 2 PETER

Having presented some guidelines in the last chapter to assist with the evaluation of parallels, the focus in the present chapter will be on some of the proposed literary relationships between 2 Peter and other early Christian texts. Specific parallels will be examined and observations will be made on their possible value for locating 2 Peter. Frequently a phrase found in one document may resemble language found in another but be too brief to assume dependence or influence, and it is therefore not admitted as evidence.[1] It is better to err on the side of caution. Or, when there are instances of legitimate genealogical parallels, it may be that there are no further insights gained to assist in locating 2 Peter to a specific time or place (as, for example, when the supplying text itself cannot be dated precisely).[2] In cases where specific location of texts proves to be impossible, texts can still be grouped more generally—a relative location is still useful.

This chapter considers proposed examples of genealogical relationship—both

---

[1] Similar caution in methodology is illustrated by Paul Garnet in the context of manuscript identification. He offered a review of Jose O'Callaghan's claim that fragments of NT writings were found among the Dead Sea Scrolls. Even 2 Peter was represented (7Q10=2 Pet 1:15). In response, Garnet writes: "In these fragments very few letters are clear, so that many identifications would be possible in principle. It should be emphasised that 'possible', 'feasible' or 'plausible' identifications are of no help to the historical researcher. They have to be at least 'probable', viz. more likely than not" (1973, 11).

[2] Though the emphasis in this chapter is on genealogical relationships between texts it was seen in the previous chapter that parallels can also be evidence for less specific relationships, especially a broader milieu. Possible indicators of such wider environments (similar vocabulary, themes, and the like) do appear in the following pages, though given the possible complications involved (see 3.3) and the ambiguity of conclusions about shared environments, greater attention is given to genealogical text relationships.

possible sources behind 2 Peter[3] and texts thought to demonstrate knowledge of 2 Peter. One helpful way to do this would be to consider first those writings thought to provide source material for it (or influence on it) and then those writings demonstrating use of 2 Peter (or showing traces of being influenced by it). This is made difficult, however, since in two cases (Jude and the *Apocalypse of Peter*), the documents would have to be considered under both categories, as the direction of dependence is disputed. Rather than treating Jude and the *Apocalypse* under both headings, each writing will be considered only once. The order of presentation that follows is not intended to be significant (though there is a general arrangement of those texts *more likely* to be sources towards those texts *more likely* to be influenced by 2 Peter). The parallels noted in this chapter do not represent exhaustive lists.[4] Rather, they are intended to serve as examples of methodological considerations.

---

[3]That the Scriptures were an influence on 2 Peter is self–evident and so they will not be treated separately. The following allusions to OT passages are found in 2 Peter (in canonical order): Gen 1:1, 6–9 (3:5); 6:17 (2:5); 7:11–21 (3:6); 8:18 (2:5); 19:1–16 (2:7); 19:24, 29 (2:6); Numb 22:7 (2:15); 22:21–35 [esp. v.28] (2:15–16); 24:17 (1:19); Pss 2:6–7 (1:17–18); 8:5 [LXX 6] (1:17); 90 [LXX 89]:4 (3:8); Cant 2:17 (1:19); Isa 34:4 (3:10, 12); 52:5 (2:2); 60:22 (3:12); 65:17 (3:13); 66:22 (3:13); Dan 7:14 (1:17); 7:27 θ, LXX (1:11); Hab 2:3 (3:9, 12–14). The only quotation is Prov 26:11 (2:22 [though this is possibly a familiar saying as opposed to a deliberate use of Scripture]). See lists of allusions in UBS[4], 891–901 and more thoroughly, though cautiously, Bauckham 1983, 138. Some of these may have been drawn from the author's sources (e.g., Jude's use of Gen 19 [cf. Jude 7]; Gen 22:7 [cf. Jude 11]) and at this point criterion 3.3.3 would be relevant (intermediary source). Generally the author uses the LXX but this is not always the case. (Any discussion of the author's use of Scripture is greatly complicated by the fact that different versions of the Scriptures in Greek were available around the time 2 Peter was written). When the author is not relying on the LXX rendering of a passage, he is in most cases likely using a source other than the Scriptures. Bauckham lists the following passages not derived from the LXX: Cant 2:17 (1:19); Prov 26:11 (2:22); Hab 2:3 (3:9, 12–14); Isa 60:22 (3:12). He notes that "in all except the first of these cases the author has probably taken the allusion from an intermediate source" (138). This would tell against the position exemplified by Falconer (1902): "One cannot avoid the impression that the author of 2 Peter was better acquainted with the Hebrew Bible than with the LXX" (461; full survey of OT influence, 460–63).

[4]In 3.1 (What constitutes a parallel?) it was seen that the term parallel means many things. Since not everything that is rightly called a parallel is relevant for the purposes of locating texts it was decided to focus here on possible genealogical relationships between 2 Peter and those writings where there are other grounds to suspect connections (e.g., Peter's reference to Paul in 3:15).

4.1 JUDE

Much has been said about the relationship of Jude to 2 Peter.[5] While discerning the direction of dependence has been a major concern, more recent work has focused on the distinctive contributions made by each author.

As said in the last note, three options are possible regarding the relationship between 2 Peter and Jude (if John A. T. Robinson's interesting, though unusual proposal that a single writer is behind both is omitted [1976, 193–95][6]): 2 Peter is dependent on Jude, Jude is dependent on 2 Peter, or 2 Peter and Jude are both dependent on a common source, whether oral or written.

4.1.1 SECOND PETER IS DEPENDENT ON JUDE

Some of the main arguments for 2 Peter's dependence on Jude can be outlined briefly.

a) Length may be considered relevant for two reasons. First, similarities between these texts are frequent enough to question coincidence as an explanation. And second, source–critical studies assume that writers tend to expand their sources (cf. Matthew and Luke's use of Mark), though this is not conclusive in itself (cf. 3.2.1; regarding the example of the Synoptic Gospels, this rule does not always hold true).

b) The sequence of examples from the OT in Jude 5–7 (Israel's deliverance

---

[5]The following treatments illustrate different positions on the matter. Among those concluding that 2 Peter is prior to Jude, see e.g., Spitta (1885, 381–470), Zahn (1953, 2:194–38), Bigg (1901, esp. 242–47), and Wolff (1960, 26–27). Douglas Moo is also favourably inclined toward this position (1996, 17–18, 28). Confident statements by those concluding that Jude is prior are not hard to find. Kümmel for one (1975, 430–31) argues that the evidence shows that "it is II Pet which is the dependent factor." Lindemann writes "2 Petr ist mit Sicherheit literarisch abhängig von Jud" (1979, 91). Arguing for a common source behind 2 Peter and Jude, Hillyer writes: "that both writers have employed a common written source, seems more probable, for while the same topics are touched upon in the same sequence, the differences in treatment are palpable" (1992, 13–14). The complexity of the latter line of argument is its greatest weakness. By introducing a hypothetical document to the discussion the simplest explanation is overlooked —direct dependence. Only if there are compelling reasons to overlook direct dependence should this step be taken.

[6]Briefly, Robinson argues that Jude's desire to write to the readers about their common salvation was interrupted by a crisis requiring a more hurried written response (vv.3–4). "I suggest that what he was composing in the name of the apostle was II Peter" (193). Jude represents the shorter, hurried work prepared to meet the immediate crisis. Smith comments: "This hypothesis [i.e., common authorship] would account very well for both the limited amount of close verbal agreement and the close similarity of theme and content: the writer used different words to talk about the same thing. In addition, 2 Peter's puzzling omissions would be explained, for there would be little need to repeat everything already contained in the first letter [i.e., Jude, which is referred to in 2 Pet 3:1]. Why, however, on this hypothesis, did the author need to write both Jude and then 2 Peter?" (1985, 77).

from Egypt and time in the desert [v.5], fallen angels and their judgment [v.6], Sodom and Gomorrah and their judgment [v.7]) is arranged in chronological order in 2 Pet 2 and modified (fallen angels [2:4], *Flood* [2:5], Sodom and Gomorrah [2:6], *Lot* [2:7–8]). It is easier to imagine Peter correcting and supplementing than the reverse scenario, namely Jude breaking up the existing sequence.[7]

c) The statement in 2 Pet 2:10b–11 makes sense only if Jude 8–9 is understood to lie behind it. One interpreter has found that "[i]t is clear that 2 Pet presupposes Jude's statement, for without it the former's vague indication would remain mysterious" (Kahmann 1989, 108; similar statements are made by Kümmel 1975, 431).

> Bold and willful, they are not afraid to slander the glorious ones (δόξας), whereas angels, though greater in might and power, do not bring against them (κατ᾽ αὐτῶν) a slanderous judgment from the Lord (2 Pet 2:10b–11).

> Yet in the same way these dreamers also defile the flesh, reject authority, and slander the glorious ones (δόξας). But when the archangel Michael contended with the devil and disputed about the body of Moses, he did not dare to bring a condemnation of slander against him [i.e., the devil], but said, "The Lord rebuke you!" (Jude 8–9).

It is widely held that Peter has here attempted to delete references to apocryphal writings and in the process has obscured the meaning of the text.[8] What is meant by δόξας in 2 Peter? Who is meant by κατ᾽ αὐτῶν? In Jude, δόξας clearly refers to good angels. It has been pointed out however that this does not necessarily hold true for 2 Peter. For Peter, the glorious ones appear to deserve condemnation before the Lord (2:11), and therefore they are evil angels. The following appears to be the situation presented by the two passages.

2 Peter	Jude
2:10 the glorious ones (δόξας) are evil angels	8 glorious ones (δόξας) are good angels
2:11 these angels are good angels (and therefore not the same as the glorious ones of 2:10b)	

---

[7]Helpful here is a comparison with the methods used by textual critics. In general, the more difficult reading is preferred in cases where manuscripts disagree. Scribes, it is argued, would be tempted to make emendations to the text in an effort to clear up any apparent difficulties (see e.g., Metzger 1992, 209). This is generally considered a strong argument.

[8]Some see in this an indication of chronological distance between Jude and 2 Peter, the latter having a clearer understanding of the limits of the canon (e.g., Brown 1997, 764; see too the citation on p.68 n.37). It could also reflect the different purposes of the authors.

against them (κατ᾽ αὐτῶν) refers back
to the glorious ones of 2:10b, not the
angels of 2:11

Second Peter, some argue, involves a development of the Jude material in a very different direction.   Whether this is the result of misunderstanding or reinterpretation cannot be determined though it seems evident that omission of the apocryphal material was a concern. Bauckham summarizes:

> The true significance of Jude 9 depends on a knowledge of the apocryphal story to which it alludes . . . . Probably the author of 2 Peter did not know the story, and therefore he misunderstood the point of Jude 9 . . . . He thought the story of Michael and the devil must be intended as an example of an angel's respect for the devil, contrasting with the false teachers' disrespect for the δόξας (Jude 8). This implied that the δόξας were, or at least included, evil angels, of whom the devil is one. Not wishing to baffle his readers with Jude's obscure allusion to the story of Michael and the devil but wishing to retain what he took to be its significance, the author of 2 Peter substituted a general reference to the behaviour of angels. For Jude's ὁ Μιχαηλ ὁ ἀρχάγγελος . . . he wrote ἄγγελοι . . . . and for Jude's τῷ διαβόλῳ . . . he wrote αὐτῶν . . . , referring back to δόξας . . . . (1983, 261).

Whether or not this particular reading of the passage is accepted,[9] the general point can still be made that recognition of Jude as the source behind 2 Peter allows for clarification of Peter's thought. This corresponds to criterion 3.2.6 (awkward editing) and supports the view that 2 Peter is dependent on Jude.

This conclusion needs to be qualified. Usually the earlier reading is the more difficult one (see n.7). If the earlier Jude clarifies the later 2 Peter, and the latter is the more difficult reading, it must be assumed that this is not a normal case but rather an instance of clumsy editing.[10]

d) Since the quotation from a noncanonical writing in Jude 14–15 (*1 En.* 1:9; 60:8) is lacking from 2 Peter, and because other allusions to (an) apocryphal source(s) in Jude (6, 9) are also omitted by the author of 2 Peter, some have argued that a later stage in the development of the church is implied (Kümmel 1975, 431; Kahmann 1989, 110–11).[11]

---

[9]Alternative readings of this passage exist. Cf. e.g., Reicke's reading discussed in ch. 2 above.

[10]A similar phenomenon occurs in studies of the Synoptic Gospels where Mark is usually thought to be the earliest text. There are occasions when Matthew and Luke (believed to be dependent on Mark) preserve what appear to be earlier readings. Sanders and Davies write: "Which one 'looks' earliest, of course, is a matter of subjective judgment, but there are enough cases in favour of each of the gospels to make us doubt that one has a monopoly on priority" (1989, 97). They refer to Matt 5:23–24 and Mark 11:25 as an example, citing Bultmann who found in the Matthew passage a more original form of the expression (98).

[11]This makes sweeping assumptions about the development of the church and does not allow for the possibility that *during the same time period* some parts of the church may have

e) In 3:3–6 there is a description of those who deny the Parousia. This points to a later period than Jude, who makes no mention of the problem of the delayed return of Christ (cf. discussion of 2 Peter as an example of early catholicism).[12] This is of course an argument from silence.

f) Some have found an important clue in the structure of the two writings. Whereas Jude 4–18 is a piece of writing "whose detailed structure and wording has been composed with exquisite care," 2 Peter is structured somewhat more loosely (Bauckham 1983, 142).[13]

In summary, if 2 Peter already existed, it is hard to imagine why Jude was needed. This same line of reasoning lends weight to the argument of Mark's priority over Matthew and Luke. It is hard to see what purpose Jude would have served, given that most of its thought is represented in 2 Peter (albeit in a different way).

4.1.2 JUDE IS DEPENDENT ON 2 PETER

Arguments in favour of 2 Peter's priority are not common in contemporary scholarship. Douglas Moo is an exception when he expresses sympathy toward this view: "if I were forced to the wall, I would probably opt for the theory that has Jude borrowing from Peter" (1996, 18). Defence of 2 Peter's priority over Jude often occurs in conjunction with a defence of Petrine authorship (though not all who defend traditional authorship necessarily assume Jude was the borrower).[14] An

---

rejected this literature while others embraced it.

Farkasfalvy (1985, 15 n.24) raises the interesting possibility that the quotation attributed to the apostles of Jesus Christ generally about scoffers in the last times (Jude 17–18) might fall in the category of apocryphal references in Jude. Such predictions are attributed only to Paul (2 Tim 3:1; Acts 20:29) in the NT. In 2 Peter this theme is connected to Peter himself: "First of all you must understand this, that in the last days scoffers will come" (3:3; cf. 2:1–3).

[12]Some have argued that the delay of the Parousia is not the issue being addressed by 2 Peter. "The primary issue, from the standpoint of the writer, is not the *timing* but the *fact* of a day of reckoning" (Charles 1997, 26 [his emphasis]). On the possibility that concern for the delayed Parousia provides a clue to a more specific period of dating see Bouchat's theory summarized in the opening pages of this dissertation.

[13]This is not to say that 2 Peter was poorly put together. On the rhetorical structure of this document, see Watson 1988.

[14]On the traditional view of authorship, see p.15 n.1. It is often argued that pseudepigraphy was not tolerated in the early church. A main objection was that it violated the ethical standards that the NT itself encourages. Since the practice of pseudepigraphy was not accepted, and because concurrently 2 Peter was accepted into the canon by the early church, it must be apostolic (see discussion in Carson, Moo, and Morris 1992, 368–70; Guthrie 1990, esp. 1011–28). To some, this line of reasoning is somewhat circular—it is apostolic because it is in the canon, it is in the canon because it is apostolic. It could also be argued that since pseudepigraphy involves a deception the church may have included it in the canon under the false assumption that Peter wrote it. In fairness to conservative scholarship, however, their presuppositions allow for divine supervision in the establishment of the canon. This means that

early dating of 2 Peter (usually the mid 60s) allows Jude to be the borrower (though note that some who believe 2 Peter is pseudepigraphal still hold to a first–century date, e.g., Reicke, Bouchat). It is also suggested that Jude (who was relatively unknown in the early church) would more likely borrow from an apostle than the other way around.

Some of the main reasons for arguing 2 Peter's priority over Jude can be briefly noted.

a) Jude 4 ("certain intruders have stolen in among you, people who long ago were designated [οἱ πάλαι προγεγραμμένοι] for this condemnation as ungodly") has been understood to refer to 2 Peter.[15] At the same time, Jude 17 ("remember the predictions of the apostles of our Lord Jesus Christ") has been taken as a reference back to 2 Peter as well (see previous note).

b) In 2 Peter, the future tense is used to speak of the coming false teachers (e.g., 2:1: ἐν ὑμῖν ἔσονται ψευδοδιδάσκαλοι), whereas Jude uses the present (e.g., v. 12: οὗτοί εἰσιν . . . σπιλάδες). Thus it is argued that (the earlier) 2 Peter foretold events that were being realized at the time Jude was writing his letter. This prophecy–to–fulfillment argument is weakened by the fact that Peter does use the present tense at times (2:10, 12–14, 17–18, 20; cf. use of past tense in 2:15, 22).[16]

c) Bigg explores the possibility that Jude betrays a misunderstanding or reinterpretation of 2 Peter. This is seen in a comparison of 2 Pet 2:4 (σειροῖς

---

arguing backwards from the established canon to conclusions about authorship is not circular reasoning, it just begins from a different premise (see also p.33 n.30).

[15]E.g., Zahn: "Assuming, then, that 2 Pet. ii. 1–iii. 4 is not copied from an older document which Jude also had before him, it is clear that Jude is referring to 2 Peter. . . . This conclusion is confirmed by 17f. The readers are told to keep in remembrance the words of the apostles of Christ formerly spoken. . . . The reference is to words which the apostles addressed to the readers of Jude, and so also to the readers of 2 Peter. Accordingly, in ver. 4 it is assumed that the readers are familiar with a written prophecy of the entrance among the readers of the libertines which has now taken place" (1953, 2:250).

[16]Bauckham argues that the alternation between future and present is a deliberate attempt to demonstrate how the apostolic predictions are being fulfilled with the coming of false teachers. This indicates that Petrine authorship is a fiction that the real author does not consistently carry through. Bauckham is not convinced that the author would inadvertently slip from future to present tense because this document shows signs of being carefully written. Allowing all of this, he concludes that Petrine authorship represents a transparent fiction that readers would readily recognize (the most complete argument is in 1983, 131–63 but see also the brief summary in 1997, 924). Marshall's review of his theory of authorship is quite interesting. It illustrates a cautious but open–minded reaction by one conservative: "Various pieces of evidence indicate that the letter is not in fact by Peter but emanates from the church at Rome and was motivated by pastoral concern for other churches. Understood in this way pseudonymity is compatible with canonicity since in this case the device is 'not a fraudulent means of claiming apostolic authority, but embodies a claim to be a faithful mediator of the apostolic message' ([Bauckham]161f.). If this concept of a non–fraudulent use of the literary genre is defensible, then it is clear that evangelical Christians need not react against the possibility that 2 Peter was not written by Peter" (1985, 78).

ζόφου ταρταρώσας) and Jude 6 (δεσμοῖς αἰδίοις).[17] Bigg suggested that, in this case, Jude may have had a copy of 2 Peter containing σειραῖς, which he paraphrased, or that he read σειροῖς and misunderstood it. If σειροῖς was the correct reading—which appears to have been the consensus when Bigg wrote— "we have a strong argument for the priority of 2 Peter" (1901, 274–75 cf. 216–17). Bigg's reasoning is sound, but the textual variant weakens the argument (see 3.5.5 regarding unresolved textual difficulties).

Another example is found in a comparison of 2 Pet 2:11 (οὐ φέρουσι κατ' αὐτῶν παρὰ κυρίῳ βλάσφημον κρίσιν) and Jude 9 (οὐκ ἐτόλμησε κρίσιν ἐπενεγκεῖν βλασφημίας). Here again is a textual variant.[18] Bigg argues that Jude's insertion of the story from the *Assumption of Moses* (the dispute between Michael and Satan) has "altered and spoiled St. Peter's point" and necessitated the omission of παρὰ κυρίῳ, because the dispute over Moses' body did not occur in the presence of the Lord (217 cf. 280).

According to Bigg, Jude uses certain terms that may be called Pauline and are certainly not Petrine. Among these he notes κλητός, ἅγιος (in the sense of Christians), πνεῦμα (in the sense of indwelling Spirit), and ψυχικός.

> Perhaps we cannot lay great stress on the first of these words, but the second most probably, and the third and fourth certainly, are alien from the Petrine vocabulary. To St. Peter ψυχή means the soul, the seat of the religious life, and he could not possibly use ψυχικός in the sense of carnal. Now it is surely far more natural to suppose that Jude was in the habit of using Pauline language, and slipped these words in without any sense of incongruity, than that 2 Peter, while following Jude slavishly elsewhere, cut out these words on doctrinal grounds (217).

This line of reasoning is problematic. Even if it is allowed that 1 Peter and 2 Peter are from the pen of the same author, it is too small a sampling to determine characteristic vocabulary (this same could be said of the Pauline corpus; see criterion 3.5.3, arguments based on typical patterns of writing). Furthermore, it must be remembered that authors were (and are) not tied to particular writing habits. If certain vocabulary was not used in earlier writings, it does not mean it

---

[17]This particular example is complicated by the fact that Bigg (whose ICC commentary was published in 1901) did not have access to P[72] as it was only acquired by M. Martin Bodmer in 1959. Still, it is worth considering as an illustration of a criterion noted in the previous chapter and its limitations (3.2.6 [awkward editing]). P[72] supports an alternative reading for 2 Pet 2:4 (namely, σειραῖς [cords, chains] as found in the UBS edition; cf. p.76 n.51). On P[72] see Metzger 1992, 40–41 and in relation to 2 Peter and Jude directly, King 1964. The UBS[4] gives 2:4 a C rating (in the third edition, it is D).

[18]Of the readings παρὰ κυρίου (P[72] 056 0142 et al.) and παρὰ κυρίῳ (א B C K P et al.), the UBS committee points out that the genitive is the more difficult. A change to the dative avoided attributing βλάσφημον κρίσιν to God as did the omission of the prepositional phrase altogether (A Ψ 33 et al.). The omission "may also reflect scribal recollection of the parallel account in Jude 9" (Metzger 1971, 703).

could not have been used in later ones (see 3.3.5 and 2.2).
A final argument put forward by Bigg may be noted.

> First of all you must understand this, that in the last days scoffers will come, scoffing and indulging their own lusts and saying "Where is the promise of his coming?" (2 Pet 3:3–4).

Cf. Jude 17–18:

> But you, beloved, must remember the predictions of the apostles of our Lord Jesus Christ; for they said to you, "In the last time there will be scoffers, indulging their own ungodly lusts."

In this parallel Bigg points out that Peter gives the warning as his own, whereas Jude gives the words as a quotation, an apostolic commonplace which could have been derived from any one of the apostles (e.g., Paul, Acts 20:29; 1 Tim 4:1). What is relevant for Bigg at this point is that "this particular form of the prophecy is found only in 2 Peter" and therefore "[t]here is strong reason for thinking that Jude is here quoting 2 Peter" (218). An alternative explanation is that a pseudepigrapher would not need to refer to a generic apostolic warning, because he was assuming the mantle of Peter.

In the end, Bigg's arguments are not convincing. The textual variants weaken the first two examples considerably as do the assumptions made in the last two.

4.1.3 SECOND PETER AND JUDE ARE BOTH DEPENDENT ON A COMMON SOURCE

At this point, a word should be said about the possibility of a common source behind 2 Peter and Jude. M. E. Boismard is one who maintains the influence of a third source: "J'étais arrivé à la conclusion que les deux épîtres utilisaient un document commun, de ton eschatologique."[19] Somewhat similar is Harvey's explanation. She finds in 2 Peter and Jude two writings dealing with similar subjects, addressing similar situations, using standard illustrations and comparable vocabulary and phraseology. But verbatim repetitions of material, "such as would be required to prove 'literary dependence'" (Harvey 1990, 342), are not found. Between these writings variations in vocabulary, grammatical structures, and phrases could, she admits, be explained by literary dependence but other alternative explanations can be suggested:

> The two authors may have been in close association, using . . . the same models and expressing themselves in similar ways; or the two 'letters' could be the work of a single author who was moved to compose two essays on much the same theme

---

[19]Personal correspondence to Michael Green (acknowledged in 1987, 61 n.4). This same view is held by Robson 1915, 52 and Reicke 1964, 190.

using similar literary resources. There is no need to decide between these possibilities. The important point gained is that we are not compelled to assume that one is a reworking of the other (343).

Harvey finds in the similarities that exist between 2 Peter, Jude, and the *Testaments of the Twelve Patriarchs* an explanation. Here the parallels do not warrant an assumption of literary dependence on this Jewish testament, rather, they point to a literary milieu that suggested style, examples, and vocabulary to both writers (344; cf. 3.4.6, a shared milieu). Finally, dependence by both texts on a common early Christian oral tradition is theoretically possible (so Osburn 1992, 311) but unlikely given the overlap in vocabulary.

While these explanations (common source; common milieu) are not impossible, they are certainly hard to prove. The simplest solution is direct borrowing one way or the other. Various reasons outlined in the previous chapter support this conclusion. First, the sustained parallels between 2 Peter and Jude (3.2.1–2, length and clustering of parallel material). Parallels are found in all three chapters, though those found in chapters 1 and 3 are not as striking as those in chapter 2. Some examples of the parallels outside chapter 2 include the following.[20]

2 Peter	Jude
1:5 σπουδὴν πᾶσαν παρεισενέγκαντες	3 πᾶσαν σπουδὴν ποιούμενος
1:12 Διὸ μελλήσω ἀεὶ ὑμᾶς ὑπομιμνήσκειν περὶ τούτων καίπερ εἰδότας	5 Ὑπομνῆσαι δὲ ὑμᾶς βούλομαι, εἰδότας [ὑμᾶς] πάντα
3:18 αὐτῷ ἡ δόξα καὶ νῦν καὶ εἰς ἡμέραν αἰῶνος. [ἀμήν.]	25 μόνῳ θεῷ ... δόξα ... καὶ νῦν καὶ εἰς πάντας τοὺς αἰῶνας, ἀμήν.

Even apart from these[21] and other similarities, the relationship of Jude and 2 Pet 2 is impressive on the basis of the quantity of contact between them.[22]

These arguments are not all of equal weight, but the case for 2 Peter's dependence on Jude remains more convincing than the reverse (cf. summary of the evidence for 2 Peter's priority above). Scholarly consensus (3.2.9) should be

---

[20]For a similar list, see Fornberg 1977, 33–34. There are disagreements about whether dependence is implied by all of these parallels. Bauckham for one (1983, 141) finds that most of those points of contact observed between Jude and 2 Pet 1 and 3 are likely no more "than accidental, except perhaps Jude 5 and 2 Pet 1:12."

[21]Fornberg also lists Jude 3, 20 cf. 2 Pet 1:1; Jude 21 cf. 2 Pet 3:13; Jude 24 cf. 2 Pet 1:10; and Jude 24 cf. 2 Pet 3:14.

[22]In 3.2.4 the term striking was used and it would apply in this case. "The similarities between the two texts . . . not only cover the reasoning but also details and vocabulary. Consequently a literary connection must exist; either one text provided the original for the other, or they have a common prototype" (Fornberg 1977, 34).

considered. Apart from some notable exceptions, there is overwhelming agreement that Jude was the source for 2 Peter.

4.2 FIRST PETER

Canonical arrangement makes a comparison of 1 and 2 Peter an obvious place to look for a literary (genealogical) relationship. Both texts claim to come from the pen of the Apostle Peter, and one seems to recall the other (2 Pet 3:1).[23] As the similarities and differences between these writings have been observed at least since the time of Jerome (*Epist.* 120.9), there is no need to rehearse all of the data here.[24] Again, the primary interest of this section is method, particularly regarding the value of such parallels as those found between 1 and 2 Peter in locating texts in a historical context.

The question of whether and to what extent 1 Peter influenced 2 Peter is debated. The case for influence from one to the other was presented most thoroughly by G. H. Boobyer (1959), though his argument is at times strained. Many writers have agreed with his main conclusion, but others have challenged the validity of some of the parallels observed (e.g., Dalton 1979, 547; Schelkle 1961, 222; Kelly 1969, 352–53; Fornberg 1977, 12–15). Still others have found no traces of influence from 1 Peter at all.[25]

---

[23]As a point of interest, Lenski's arguments about the priority of 2 Peter over 1 Peter may be mentioned. Assuming Petrine authorship for both writings, he goes on to argue first of all that the audience of the two letters must be different. Whereas 1 Peter is addressed to churches in Asia Minor (1 Pet 1:1) who were suffering (or expecting to suffer) for their faith, 2 Peter is not concerned with this at all but is, by contrast, concerned to warn readers about libertinists who scoff at hope in the coming of Christ. The earlier letter implied in 2 Pet 3:1 cannot therefore refer back to 1 Peter since it says nothing about such scoffers and 2 Peter is the second letter to do just that. Lenski concludes that "[b]oth of Peter's warnings antedate First Peter" and this means that the letter containing the first warning has therefore been lost (1945, 238). Others postulate a lost epistle referred to in 3:1. Green for one points out that the author of 1 Peter does not appear to have a close relationship with the readers of 1 Peter, but this does not hold true for 2 Peter thus arguing against identifying 1 Peter as the first letter (1987, 134–35).

[24]See especially Mayor's extensive discussion at this point (1907, lxviii–cxiv). Among the more helpful and thorough presentations of similarities and differences between these writings is that offered by Chase (1898–1904, 3:812–14).

[25]Illustrating the distance between these writings, Selwyn states in his study of 1 Peter: "I have deliberately excluded from my purview consideration of the rest of the 'Petrine' literature, and on this point will only say that I cannot believe the Second Epistle to reflect the same mind or spring from the same circles as the First" (1952, 1). Pheme Perkins writes: "Unlike the Johannine epistles or 1 and 2 Timothy, 2 Peter is not related to 1 Peter in either language and style or in its setting and theological development, a fact recognized by Jerome. . . . Second Peter 3:1 refers to itself as the 'second letter I have written to you.' That suggests knowledge of the existence of 1 Peter. However, there are no explicit verbal links between the two. If 2 Peter had been following 1 Peter as a model, one would have expected a reference to the readers as 'exiles of the Diaspora' in the greeting and perhaps elsewhere in the text" (1995, 159; similarly

The examination of similarities and differences between 1 and 2 Peter is often part of arguments attempting either to prove or disprove Petrine authorship. If the first letter is accepted as authentic, observed similarities are sometimes cited as evidence that the second letter also comes from Peter (e.g., Kruger 1999, 659–61). At the same time, others may argue that similarities are evidence that the author of the second letter was imitating the first (cf. 3.4.4; it appears that the reverse has never been suggested). In this line of argument, 1 Peter provides a standard by which 2 Peter is measured. The value of such discussion may be compromised depending on whether and to what extent amanuenses were involved (cf. 1 Pet 5:12) and if secretaries had freedom when writing letters.[26]

A few instances of shared vocabulary can be mentioned. Among various terms that are either rare or used in similar ways are the following: ἀρετή used in reference to God (1 Pet 2:9; 2 Pet 1:3); the similarity between χορηγεῖ (1 Pet 4:11) and ἐπιχορηγήσατε (2 Pet 1:5). The rare verb ἐποπτεύω (1 Pet 2:12; 3:2) may have suggested use of the noun ἐπόπτης (2 Pet 1:16; these verses represent the only use of these terms in the NT [both are also found in the LXX]).

At other points, similar phrases or themes have been taken to indicate the influence of one on the other. A few examples support this conclusion.

a) 1 Pet 1:1–2: χάρις ὑμῖν καὶ εἰρήνη πληθυνθείη; 2 Pet 1:2: χάρις ὑμῖν καὶ εἰρήνη πληθυνθείη. This expression has impressed some scholars.[27]

b) 1 Pet 1:19: ἀμώμου καὶ ἀσπίλου; 2 Pet 2:13: σπίλοι καὶ μῶμοι; 3:14 ἄσπιλοι καὶ ἀμώμητοι. This parallel in vocabulary is striking, though the differences in usage should be recognized as well. In 1 Peter these terms (with the alpha–privative) are used in references to the unblemished and spotless Christ, whereas in 2 Pet 2:13 the terms (without the alpha–privative) are used to describe the enemies of God; in 3:14, it is a goal Christians are to strive for (though with the alpha–privative). The order is also reversed in 2 Peter.

c) Both texts refer to Noah and those with him who were saved (1 Pet 3:20; 2 Pet 2:5), and both connect the fallen angels to the flood judgment (1 Pet 3:18–20; 2 Pet 2:4–5). The introduction of this example to Jude's material (vv.6–7) anticipates his further use of flood imagery in 3:6.

d) There is a connection between the patience (μακροθυμία) of God and repentance (1 Pet 3:20; 2 Pet 3:15; cf. the similar idea in 3:9).

Bauckham 1983, 143–46). In response, why should such an expectation be placed on the author? The greeting in 2 Peter is no less appropriate for Christian readers than is the greeting in 1 Peter. Cf. the two addresses to Timothy which are not identical.

[26]Longenecker (1974, 288) argues that the extent to which secretaries had freedom in drafting personal letters is "beyond determination from the evidence presently at hand, and may well have varied from case to case." See also Charles 1997, 60–63. Cf. n.28.

[27]Chase mentions Warfield (cited only by last name; articles on the canonicity and genuineness of 2 Peter in the *Southern Presbyterian Review*, Jan. 1882 and Apr. 1883) as finding this parallel significant because it is found only in 1 and 2 Peter (1898–1904, 3:812). See also Fornberg 1977, 12–13 and Kruger 1999, 659.

e) Boobyer observed the parallels between the opening chapters of both letters, specifically 1 Pet 1:3–9 and 2 Pet 1:3–11. He sets out the sequence of thought as follows.

1 Pet 1:3–9	2 Pet 1:3–11
Through the resurrection of Jesus Christ, we have hope of an incorruptible and undefiled inheritance, reserved for us in heaven.	Christ's divine power and glory are sources of all things pertaining to life and godliness, as well as of precious promises, enabling us to become partakers of the divine nature and avoid terrestrial corruption.
This inheritance is for those guarded by faith until salvation in the last time, and is a cause of rejoicing in the grief of present trials and temptations.	To faith other virtues must be added. This will promote the necessary knowledge of Jesus Christ and be in keeping with cleansing from former sins.
But faith, tested, and proved, will issue in glory, honour and the salvation of your souls 'at the revelation of Jesus Christ' (i.e., the second advent).	In this manner, make your calling and election sure, as well as your entry into Christ's eternal kingdom (i.e., at the Parousia).

The differences between these openings (among them the addition to faith of other moral virtues in 2 Pet 1:5–7, whereas 1 Peter stresses the importance of faith [1:5 and 7]) are similar to the differences seen between Paul and James. Boobyer suggests that, in the same way James may have been correcting a misunderstanding of Paul, so too the author of 2 Peter was responding to the false teachings of libertines who were twisting that apostle's words (3:15–16; 1959, 40–41).

One reason Boobyer suggests influence from 1 Peter in this section is based on 2 Pet 1:12–13: "Therefore I intend to keep on reminding you of these things, though you know them already and are established in the truth that has come to you. I think it right, as long as I am in this body, to refresh your memory." It is argued that περὶ τούτων points back to the exhortation found in 2 Pet 1:3–11, which may mean that what he was writing (2 Pet 1:3–11) was a "review and amplification" of 1 Pet 1:3–9. This would explain the inclusion of the words "though you know them already" (2 Pet 1:12): "They knew 'them', partly because they had been reminded of them in First Peter" (41; cf. also 37 on 2 Pet 1:12–13).

These similarities do not lend support to the view that the author of 2 Peter was familiar with 1 Peter. The parallels in and of themselves are not so striking as to demand this assumption. Except for the fact that there are other reasons to suspect a relationship with 1 Peter (namely 3:1 which most naturally points back to 1 Peter), little connects these two documents other than the name Peter.

That the writing styles of 1 and 2 Peter are quite dissimilar is widely recognized, but the significance of this fact is open to debate.[28] More valuable for comparison are those similarities and differences in doctrine that may be observed. With respect to Christology, 1 Peter presents Christ as an example for believers (e.g., 2:21; 3:17–18; 4:1), and references to him are concrete. Second Peter, however, presents Christ as the object of knowledge, suggesting a more abstract and distant concept (e.g., 1:8; 2:20; 3:18; Fuchs and Reymond 1980, 31). Also, some have noted how 1 and 2 Peter compare in their respective use of the OT. First Peter contains extensive use of the OT with both formal quotations and wide influence on the imagery and vocabulary of the letter. In 2 Peter, on the other hand, are no formal quotations of the OT (the reference to Prov 26:11 in 2:22a is likely part of a longer proverb of which this biblical passage was a part). This is not necessarily significant; the author's purpose and audience may have influenced the decision either to make extensive use of the OT (1 Peter) or to include only allusions to it (2 Peter). It has been observed that 2 Peter alludes to Psalms, Proverbs, and Isaiah, all of which are quoted in 1 Peter (Guthrie 1990, 832; he acknowledges Falconer at this point), though this does not indicate much, as many writers did the same.

Also pertinent is the early attestation of these writings. Comparatively speaking, 1 Peter was much more readily received in the early church than 2 Peter. Though Origen, the first to refer to 2 Peter by name, spoke about two Petrine letters (e.g., *Hom. in Josh.* 7.1), other early writers recognized that authorship was disputed. Eusebius for one provides evidence for this question facing the church:

> And Peter, on whom the Church of Christ is built, against which the gates of Hades shall not prevail, has left one acknowledged epistle, and, it may be, a second also; or it is doubted (*Hist. eccl.* 6.25.8).

Elsewhere he describes 2 Peter as disputed (ἀντιλεγομένων [*Hist. eccl.* 3.25.3]).

The influence of the Apostle Paul is another point for comparison. Whereas

---

[28]On the one hand some are struck by the extent of the differences between the two documents. For example: "Le *style* simple et spontané de 1 P n'est en rien comparable à celui, baroque, de 2 P, recherchant les effets" (Fuchs and Reymond 1980, 30); "The style of 1 P is simple and natural, without a trace of self–conscious effort. The style of 2 P is rhetorical and laboured, marked by a love for striking and startling expressions" (Chase 1898–1904, 3:813). Others arguing for traditional authorship of both texts downplay this distance by postulating the influence of a secretary or secretaries in the writing process which would explain how such different writings could come from the same author. For discussion on amanuenses see Guthrie 1990, 768–70; "If the linguistic characteristics are considered too divergent to postulate common authorship [of 1 and 2 Peter], the difficulties would, of course, be considerably lessened, if not obviated, by the amanuensis hypothesis for one epistle. If Peter, for instance, were author of I Peter, with the assistance of Silas (Silvanus) as amanuensis, and author of 2 Peter, it would be possible to account for these stylistic differences and similarities" (833). The line of argument on both sides of the debate is compromised by the fact that there is so little material for comparison (3.2.1). Cf. n.26.

1 Peter has many points in contact with Paul, 2 Peter, as noted below (4.4), exhibits little if any Pauline influence though it does hold this apostle in high regard.

> On peut encore faire des constatations du même ordre à propos de la pensée de *Paul*: 2 P cite nominalement l'apôtre (3,15), mais la pensée de Paul ne joue pratiquement aucun rôle dans l'épître; au contraire en 1 P, où le nom de Paul n'est pas prononcé, l'influence de la théologie pauliniene est constante et importante (Fuchs and Reymond 1980, 31).

To be sure, the extent of Paul's influence on these letters is different, but what does this prove? It may be that the subject matter addressed in one occasioned the use of Paul, whereas in the other, there was no particular need to appeal to Pauline authority (Peter was an apostle himself after all).

What is found in the relationship of 2 Peter to 1 Peter is analogous with the relationship between 2 Peter and Paul (cf. 4.4). First Peter is most likely referred to, which suggests the author recognized it as an authority (i.e., he assumed it to be authentic and was attempting to gain authority for his own work). For whatever reasons, the author chose not to reflect its style or content. Why this decision was made is open to debate, but if in fact 2 Pet 3:1 does point back to 1 Peter, it is reasonable to assume that the author of the second letter would not want to repeat material already found in the first. If 2 Peter is pseudonymous, establishing authenticity was of greatest concern: 'I am Peter, author also of that other letter recognized as authoritative in your community [or communities].' In such a scenario, signaling knowledge of a writing does not necessarily mean that influence or dependence should be expected. It is interesting to note a similar phenomenon with respect to Paul.[29]

4.3 THE CANONICAL GOSPELS

Second Peter makes several allusions to gospel traditions.[30] It is not so clear if the author's knowledge of this material is dependent on the canonical Gospels or familiarity with oral tradition. The later one dates 2 Peter, the less likely it is that it is oral tradition. In any case, the written Gospels have the first claim and one should only resort to oral tradition for compelling reasons.

a) The most obvious example of gospel tradition in 2 Peter is the reference to the transfiguration in 2 Pet 1:16–18. Some maintain that 2 Peter's version of the

---

[29]Cf. Tuckett's reflections on the non–quotation of the Gospels in the *Didache* (3.2.7).

[30]In terms of texts, similarities are found primarily between 2 Peter and the Synoptic Gospels. There are not many parallels with John's Gospel but Peter's awareness of his imminent death (2 Pet 1:14) brings Jesus' words in John 21:18–19 to mind—whether the author was deliberately echoing that Gospel or not.

transfiguration represents a tradition independent of the Gospels.[31] Significant differences exist, to be sure. To begin with, substantial omissions in Peter's version are obvious (though these prove nothing): Peter's companions James and John, details of Jesus' appearance, the presence of Moses and Elijah, and Peter's suggestion regarding the tents are not recorded. This does not prove independence from the synoptic accounts since omissions could simply reflect the author's purpose. Also, 2 Peter's brief account employs distinctive terminology: τῆς ἐκείνου μεγαλειότητος (2 Pet 1:16); τιμὴν καὶ δόξαν (2 Pet 1:17); and φωνῆς ἐνεχθείσης αὐτῷ τοιᾶσδε ὑπὸ τῆς μεγαλοπρεποῦς δόξης (2 Pet 1:17). This terminology is consistent with the author's style and may only show that he has put the tradition into his own words (Bauckham 1983, 205). Finally, in 2 Pet 1:18 the voice came ἐξ οὐρανοῦ whereas it came ἐκ τῆς νεφέλης in the Gospels (Matt 17:5; Mark 9:7; Luke 9:35). The sense is obviously the same (see further below).

There is a basis for suggesting that the author of 2 Peter was familiar specifically with Matthew's version of the transfiguration story. In the accounts of the divine affirmation, only Peter and Matthew include a word of divine approval:

Matt 17:5b: "with him I am well pleased" (ἐν ᾧ εὐδόκησα; cf. also 12:18)

2 Pet 1:17: "with whom I am well pleased" (εἰς ὃν ἐγὼ εὐδόκησα)[32]

According to Miller (1996, 623–24), the phrase in Matthew appears in this context as a result of Matthean redaction; it is taken from the divine voice mentioned in the baptism narrative (Matt 3:17 cf. Mark 1:11) and added to his source for the transfiguration narrative (Mark 9:7). Miller argues that proposals of an independent source behind 2 Peter's version of the transfiguration introduce unnecessary complications.[33] This methodological concern is expressed when discussing the provenance of the divine voice. Miller writes:

---

[31]E.g., "The story of the Transfiguration is recounted in a notably abbreviated form and clearly according to a tradition which is secondary to that of the Synoptists" (Käsemann 1982a, 186). Bauckham (1983, 205–10) also finds the evidence to suggest an independent tradition.

[32]Again, where did the voice come from? The idea of a voice from heaven is common apocalyptic imagery (e.g., Dan 4:31; *1 En.*13:8; Rev 10:4; 11:12; 14:13). The affirming voice in John 12:28 is "from heaven" though in a different context. The version of the transfiguration in *Ps.–Clem.* 3:53 reads εἰς ὃν εὐδόκησα which Bauckham suggests "may depend on a tradition related to 2 Peter's" (1983, 206). The simplest explanation is direct influence from 2 Peter and/or Matthew.

[33]Miller is dialoguing in this article with Richard Bauckham (1983, 205–12) who observes various differences between Peter and the synoptic accounts that lead him to suggest the following: "We may conclude that the evidence is strongly in favor of the view that in his account of the Transfiguration the author of 2 Peter was not dependent on the synoptic Gospels but on independent tradition, which could perhaps be his own knowledge of Peter's preaching, or else the oral traditions current in the Roman church" (210).

My judgment [namely, the variant is too minor to warrant an appeal to an otherwise unknown source] is based on the methodological axiom that, all other things being equal, the simplest explanation is the most preferable. In a case like this one the operative principle can be formulated as follows: if two expressions are interchangeable [namely cloud and heaven in apocalyptic writing] in their meaning and literary function and if no obvious tradition–historical significance can be discerned in an author's choice of one over the other, then there is no need to posit a hypothetical source to account for the presence of an alternative way of saying the same thing. To reject or ignore this principle is to open the door to a proliferation of unverifiable source theories (621–22).

The inclusion of the phrase "with whom I am well pleased" in 2 Peter appears to be based on Matthew specifically, as there is evidence at this point of Matthew's redactional activity (see 3.2.7; evidence of editorial habits from the proposed source found in a later text). Farkasfalvy also argues that Peter was dependent on Matthew (1985, esp.5–8).[34]

b) One proposed connection between 2 Peter and Luke is again associated with the transfiguration. Both make a double reference to the vision of glory (Luke 9:31 and 9:32; 2 Pet 1:17; see Farkasfalvy [1985, 6–7], who finds the author of 2 Peter combining elements from Matthew and Luke).

Luke   2 Peter

ὀφθέντες ἐν δόξῃ . . . εἶδον τὴν δόξαν   λαβὼν . . . τιμὴν καὶ δόξαν . . . ὑπὸ τῆς . . .
                                        δόξης

This particular example is not too convincing on its own. For one thing, there is not an exact correspondence in the meaning of δόξα between the two writings. For Luke it refers in the first instance to Moses and Elijah and in the second to Jesus, whereas in 2 Peter it is used to speak of Jesus and then God (the Majestic Glory speaking from heaven). It is also possible to find similar parallels with Paul and John (cf. 2 Cor 4:4–6; John 1:14). Recognizing these factors, Farkasfalvy goes on to note the similar use of ἔξοδος by both writers (Luke 9:31 and 2 Pet 1:15 [7]). But here, different subject matter is involved; Moses and Elijah are speaking of Jesus' death in the former, Peter of his own death in the latter. Finally, it is observed that Peter (2 Pet 1:14–15) speaks of "the tent" (his body), which again links 2 Peter to the transfiguration accounts in the Gospels (cf. 2 Cor 5:1). While the term ἔξοδος may be a little unusual, the term δόξα is not, making the arguments here less convincing. There is also some affinity with Luke in the use of the rare term μεγαλειότης (splendor, magnificence; Luke 9:43; Acts 19:27; 2 Pet 1:16 [only here in the NT]; cf. Dan 7:27 LXX). Finally, one further similarity between 2 Peter and Luke is their reference to Lot (only twice in the NT: Luke 17:28–32; 2 Pet 2:7). Luke and Peter use the

---

[34]Note also 2 Pet 2:9 (ἐκ πειρασμοῦ ῥύεσθαι) cf. Matt 6:13 (πειρασμόν . . . ῥῦσαι).

illustrations of Noah and Lot in the same order (though this may only be chronological). It does not seem obvious that the author of 2 Peter made any use of Luke's Gospel. Those arguments that have been put forward are not so remarkable that they cannot be explained by coincidence (3.1.4) or common use of the LXX (3.5.1).

c) In 2 Pet 2:20 there is a near exact quotation of Q material (Matt 12:45/Lk 11:26):

2 Peter	Q
γέγονεν αὐτοῖς τὰ ἔσχατα χείρονα τῶν πρώτων	καὶ γίνεται τὰ ἔσχατα τοῦ ἀνθρώπου ἐκείνου χείρονα τῶν πρώτων

(See further comments on this passage in n.35 below). A further connection with Q is noticed in the use of Noah as an illustration (Matt 24:37–39/Luke 17:26–27; cf. 2 Pet 2:5; elsewhere Noah appears only in Luke 3:36 [a genealogy]; Heb 11:7; and 1 Pet 3:20). Peter inserts this reference (along with the example of Lot [2 Pet 2:7; only here and Luke 17:28–32]) in a passage otherwise dependent on Jude.

The Day of the Lord is said to come like a κλέπτης in 2 Peter (3:10) and in Q (Matt 24:43/Luke 12:39; cf. also Paul [1 Thess 5:2] and John [Rev 16:15]). On the basis of criterion 3.5.2 (widely attested parallels) this is an unreliable basis to argue literary dependence.

d) Thematic parallels can be noted, such as the similarities that exist between 2 Pet 2:21 and Matt 18:6 (cf. Mark 9:42; 14:21; Luke 17:2; cf. 1 Clem. 46:8) and Matt 26:42 (cf. Mark 14:21; Luke 22:22). Peter's phrase ("it would have been better for them never to have known the way of righteousness than, after knowing it, to turn back from the holy commandment that was passed on to them") resembles sayings attributed to Jesus:

> If any of you put a stumbling block before one of these little ones who believe in me, it would be better for you if a great millstone were fastened around your neck and you were drowned in the depth of the sea (Matt 18:6).

> The Son of Man goes as it is written of him, but woe to that one by whom the Son of Man is betrayed! It would have been better for that one not to have been born (Matt 26:24).

These parallels are too general to prove literary dependence though there is definitely common ground here (and use of one of the Gospels remains the simplest explanation): those who try to thwart the plan of God and those who hinder others in their relationship with God deserve severe judgment. In this context, Peter is describing his opponents who lead others astray after they have (ὀλίγως meaning recently or barely?) escaped the error of their ways (2:18). The idea of turning back to inappropriate behaviour after conversion is found in both earlier writings (e.g., Ezek 18:24) and other Christian texts (Heb 6:4–6; Jas 4:17).

The similarity of 2 Pet 3:4 to Mark 9:1 (cf. Matt 16:28; Luke 9:27) and Mark 13:30 (Matt 24:34; Luke 21:32) is also worthy of note. Like Käsemann, many commentators suggest that the occasion for 2 Peter is stated in 3:3–4, namely, that some were scoffing at the delay of the Parousia. "To the anger of the writer, the rejection of the primitive Christian hope has sunk to the level of derision" (1982a, 170). Part of the accusation—"ever since the fathers fell asleep"—seems reminiscent of Jesus' words: "Truly I say to you, there are some of those who are standing here who shall not taste death until they see the kingdom of God after it has come with power" (Mark 9:1; Matt 16:28; Luke 9:27; note, this statement precedes the transfiguration which is also found in 2 Peter; cf. Mark 13:30; Matt 24:34; Luke 21:32). Among differences, it is significant that while the Gospels place these words in Jesus' mouth, in 2 Peter it is the false teachers who are speaking. The contexts are different (3.3.8; cf. 3.2.8). While there are similarities in language, nothing suggests dependence.

Several of these vague parallels to the gospel traditions are employed in 2 Peter specifically in its challenge to opponents. The transfiguration functions as an apologetic argument in defense of the expected Parousia (Neyrey 1980a), and at least part of the description of the false teachers is derived from Jesus' teaching (assuming 2 Pet 2:20 refers to the false teachers).[35]

By way of conclusion, though there are no citations, clear allusions to Gospel

---

[35]The language of 2:17–22 is ambiguous. In 2:20 it is not clear who is addressed: "For if after they have escaped the defilements of the world by the knowledge of the Lord and Savior Jesus Christ, *they* are again entangled in them and are overcome, the last state has become worse for them than the first" (NASB). Who are "they"? False teachers? Their followers? Both? Among those arguing that the false teachers are intended are Mayor, Bauckham, Green, and Käsemann. For the conclusion that the victims or followers of these opponents are intended, see Spitta, Bigg, and Kelly. A more general position is offered by Horst Balz and Wolfgang Schrage (1973, 140) who see both groups in these verses. Arguments in favour of seeing the false teachers in this passage include (a) the proximity of the reference to these characters in v.19, making them the normal antecedent; (b) εἰ γάρ is a natural connection between vv.19 and 20; (c) the verb ἡττάομαι (to be overcome) is found in both vv. 19 and 20 (only here in the NT); (d) the false teachers are the subject of the whole chapter. Furthermore, (e) the language of vv.20–22 seems too strong for the recently converted who have not yet relapsed into sin. At the same time, support for understanding the victims of false teachers exists: (a) "for", it is argued, looks back to v.18, not v.19, therefore enlarging on the consequences of being caught in the false teachers' snare; (b) "after escaping" (ἀποφυγόντες) must be intended to pick up "just escaping" (ὀλίγως ἀποφεύγοντας) in v.18 and furthermore the mention of being plunged again in the "pollution of the world" seems an echo of the fleshly passions of v.18; (c) the repetition of "overcome" is not conclusive; its use in v.19 illustrates the servitude of the false teachers but it contains a caution for all; (d) the language of vv.20–21 is hypothetical, and therefore reads like a deterrent to readers facing temptation but who have not yet given in to it. Clearly the heretics have been given up as lost and so (e) even though the language is strong, it is an anticlimax after the prophecies of destruction made about these in the previous section, and yet is not inordinately harsh if interpreted as a severe warning to recent converts (so Kelly 1969, 347–48). Both positions are based on reasonable arguments and a conclusive verdict seems out of reach.

narratives presuppose no other source than the written Gospels themselves. The influence of Matthew specifically on the author of 2 Peter seems plausible.[36] Appeal to oral tradition as an explanation introduces a variable that cannot be tested but its greatest weakness is that it introduces a hypothesis that is not necessary to explain the parallels. Peter's knowledge of texts is the simplest and therefore strongest explanation.

4.4 PAUL

What is the relationship between 2 Peter and Paul's writings? This important question presents itself, because the author explicitly refers to Paul's letters, claims that there are shared concerns between his letter and Paul, and even knows something about the content of Paul's writings ("some things in them"; 2 Pet 3:15–16). Does the writer's high praise of Paul ("wisdom given him") and the friendly "our beloved brother" point to a later period of the church when there was a concern to heal the old wounds created by the schism between these two apostles? (cf. discussion of Baur's developmental model in ch. 2). Is this an attempt to lend authority to a pseudepigraphal writing? (so Farkasfalvy 1985, 8–9).

Mixed opinions have been expressed about the extent of the influence of Paul's letters on 2 Peter. At one end of the spectrum is Lindemann, who finds no allusions to Pauline material (1979, 263). At the other are those who confidently assume the apostle's influence on 2 Peter and speak of a variety parallels between it and his letters. Farkasfalvy illustrates the latter. He finds numerous points of contact with Paul and gives very little indication that this is a disputed point (1985, 8–14 [including the Pastoral Epistles]; Fornberg is also somewhat positive, 1977, 24–27). Again, it is not the goal to present here an exhaustive list of proposed instances of literary dependency. Some of the stronger arguments for connecting Paul and 2 Peter will be noted.

An attempt to complile and evaluate the case for dependency on Paul is found in Paul Barnett's *Paul Becomes a Literary Influence* (1941). He lists nine parallels

---

[36]As a point of interest, Klinger has pointed out that the author of 2 Peter differs from the Gospels in the reasons given for asserting Peter's authority. Whereas in the Gospels this authority is given by Jesus in such words as "you are Peter, and on this rock I will build my church" (Matt 16:18), "feed my sheep" (John 21:15–17), or "I have prayed for you that your own faith may not fail" (Luke 22:32), 2 Peter claims authority on the basis of the transfiguration. Peter is an ἐπόπται, eyewitness, of that event (1973, 153). Klinger's concern in this paper is not source criticism, but he seems to assume the author's knowledge of the written Gospels. The significance of this observation for Klinger's argument is that it establishes a basis of authority not shared by the Apostle Paul (hence the lack of reference to Peter being an eyewitness of the resurrection because Paul too could claim this [1 Cor 15:5 cf. 9:1]). As the mystery of the resurrection did not give Peter any advantage over Paul, access to another mystery, namely the transfiguration, was necessary (160). Klinger's view of the false teachers is the basis for this line of argument; he understands the liberalism of false disciples of Paul to be the problem addressed by 2 Pet 2 (155–57, 165).

between Paul and 2 Peter, as well as sixteen possible instances of literary reminiscence. Along with each parallel, he provides an evaluation not unlike the grading systems used by the United Bible Society for textual variants or the Jesus Seminar for sayings and activities attributed to Jesus. 'A' represents practical certainty, 'B' a high degree of probability, and 'C' a reasonable degree of probability "of literary indebtedness on the part of the passages quoted." Further evaluation is implied by the fact that the possible reminiscences are distinguished from the parallels in that they are not printed out in the text and they receive no letter grade (in his tabulation of the results, they are listed as unclassed). His study of Paul's influence on 2 Peter finds two 'B' parallels (one from Romans, one from Ephesians); seven 'C' parallels (three from Romans; one each from 2 Corinthians, Galatians, Ephesians, and 1 Thessalonians).[37]

Barnett clearly places greater weight on verbal correspondences as the most meaningful parallels. Others, in their consideration of the parallels between Paul and 2 Peter, have paid greater attention to thematic parallels with different results (again, for the range of possible meanings for the term parallel, see 3.1). Neyrey for one finds closer ties with 1 Thessalonians (tentatively allowing that the author may have known it, see further below) than Barnett's tabulation seems to imply (one 'C' rating; one unclassed).[38] The following discussion gives attention to both thematic and verbal parallels.

a) Second Peter 1:10 recalls themes and vocabulary found in Romans (see particularly 8:28–30): σπουδάσατε βεβαίαν ὑμῶν τὴν κλῆσιν καὶ ἐκλογὴν ποιεῖσθαι (2 Pet 1:10). Two terms should be noted: ἐκλογή is found only in Acts 9:15; Rom 9:11; 11:5, 7, 28; and 2 Pet 1:10 in the NT; πταίω only in Rom 11:11; Jas 2:10; 3:2; and 2 Pet 1:10b. In both Romans and 2 Peter, the latter is used in discussion of ἐκλογή (Barnett 1941, 224). This may indicate no more than coincidental use of common language (3.1.4 [incidental similarities]) or perhaps technical language, if by the term technical, language used among Christians is meant.

b) Second Peter 2:19 resembles the thought of Rom 6:16:

... people are slaves to whatever masters them (2 Pet 2:19).

Do you not know that if you present yourselves to anyone as obedient slaves, you are slaves of the one whom you obey, either of sin, which leads to death, or of obedience, which leads to righteousness? (Rom 6:16).

Barnett finds that "the general point of the two contexts is so nearly the same as to

---

[37]For an explanation of his methodology, see ix–x; for his analysis of 2 Peter see 222–28.

[38]It should also be pointed out that the Pastoral Epistles are not included in Barnett's study. These three letters are treated instead as writings influenced by Paul (i.e., they are pseudonymous) and so are not considered as possible influences on 2 Peter. Some parallels between the Pastorals and 2 Peter are discussed in 5.1 below.

create the strong presumption in favor of literary dependence" (224 [though he gives it only a 'B' rating]). Similarities in context were listed among criteria possibly indicating a textual relationship (3.2.8; cf. 3.3.8). This parallel is strong.

c) Second Peter 3:9 is an important passage for comparison with Paul's thought.

οὐ βραδύνει κύριος τῆς ἐπαγγελίας, ὥς τινες βραδύτητα ἡγοῦνται, ἀλλὰ μακροθυμεῖ εἰς ὑμᾶς, μὴ βουλόμενός τινας ἀπολέσθαι ἀλλὰ πάντας εἰς μετάνοιαν χωρῆσαι (2 Pet 3:9).

ἢ τοῦ πλούτου τῆς χρηστότητος αὐτοῦ καὶ τῆς ἀνοχῆς καὶ τῆς μακροθυμίας καταφρονεῖς, ἀγνοῶν ὅτι τὸ χρηστὸν τοῦ θεοῦ εἰς μετάνοιάν σε ἄγει; (Rom 2:4).

Paul also explains the delay of the Parousia in terms of God's patience in Rom 9:22 (cf. 1 Pet 3:20; 2 Pet 3:15). Mayor argues that καθὼς . . . ἔγραψεν (3:15) "can only refer to the preceding injunction, the importance of which injunction is shown by the reiteration in *vv.* 9 and 15, to the effect that the long–suffering of God was to be regarded as an evidence of His goodwill to men" (1907, 164). This would suggest Paul's teachings in Rom 2:4; 3:25–26; 9:22–23; and 11:22–23.[39] (Use of the term μακροθυμία with reference to God's actions can be found in 2 Pet 3:9, 15 and Rom 2:4; 9:22).[40]

First Timothy 1:16 parallels both Peter and Paul, and 2 Peter more closely resembles the 1 Timothy reference (see discussion in 5.1 below). A conceptual link is found between 2 Peter and Romans. This is further supported by the connection to 2 Pet 3:15, where again the ideas of patience and salvation are mentioned (καὶ τὴν τοῦ κυρίου ἡμῶν μακροθυμίαν σωτηρίαν ἡγεῖσθε) and explicitly connected to Paul.

d) It has been observed that the twisting of Paul's teachings (3:16) might be compared to the situation addressed by Paul in 1 Cor 10:23 and elsewhere, namely the misuse of his teachings on liberty to justify license in behaviour.[41] This is far

---

[39]Some, including Mayor, have seen in this connection reason to support the view that 2 Peter was addressed to the Roman church (164).

[40]Among those supporting the influence of Romans on 2 Peter are Farkasfalvy (1985, 9–10) who also notes Fuchs and Reymond (1980, 123 n.1).

[41]Peter apparently charges his opponents with twisting Paul's teachings in the interest of ethical libertinism (cf. 2 Pet 2:19). "While he furnishes no details, we know from Irenaeus and Tertullian that similar–minded, though more advanced and sophisticated, Gnostics of the second half of the 2nd cent. constantly appealed to such passages as Rom. viii. 21; 2 Cor. iii. 17; Gal. v. 13 as supporting antinomianism. We can only speculate what texts the trouble–makers interpreted as favouring their scepticism about the Parousia (the Apostle himself complains in 2 Thess. ii. 2 that he has been misrepresented as teaching that it has already taken place), but later Gnostics made considerable capital out of passages like I Cor. xv. 50; 53, or again Rom. vi. 3ff., arguing that they contained a more 'spiritual' doctrine of resurrection than the 'materialist' one of the orthodox" (Kelly 1969, 373–74). On the trajectory between Paul's

too general to be of help in determining a shared context or a textual relationship.

e) Farkasfalvy is impressed with shared theological ideas between Paul (2 Cor 4–5) and 2 Pet 1:12–19. These include:

(1) death as the unfolding of this tent and thus bringing the apostle to heaven;
(2) God's glory shining and seen on the (face of the) glorified Christ;
(3) revelation as light shining in darkness;
(4) God's light shining in the human heart (1985, 11).[42]

General similarities are present to be sure, but specific dependence on Paul at this point is not easy to defend given that the parallel is not at all close or distinct. Farkasfalvy's "probability" of a conscious use of 2 Corinthians is again overstating the case. Barnett is impressed particularly by the connections between 2 Pet 1:13–14 and 2 Cor 5:1 and finds here a possible case of literary dependence (1941, 224; he gives this a 'C' rating).

f) Second Peter's address (1:1–2) recalls 1 Peter but also, according to Barnett, Ephesians with its catholic character. He goes so far as to write that this "writing was probably its model" (223; he gives this a 'B' rating). The main evidence for this is the prominence of the theme of knowledge as the basis for personal religion (ἐν ἐπιγνώσει τοῦ θεοῦ, 2 Pet 1:2) which, he suggests, betrays the influence of Ephesians (esp. 1:17). This is not particularly compelling; it is at best a case of possible dependence, but there is nothing that makes it probable.

g) Second Peter 3 is concerned that Christians be patient and firm in their faith and above all live holy lives (3:11–12, 14, 17–18). This emphasis is found in Paul's writings, particularly in 1 and 2 Thessalonians (1 Thess 4:13–5:11; 2 Thess 1:7–10; 2:1–12; Reicke for one notes similarity in emphasis, 1964, 82–83). Furthermore, it has been observed that 1 Thess 5:2 is particularly close to the language of 2 Pet 3:10:

For you yourselves know very well that the day of the Lord will come like a thief in the night (Paul).

But the day of the Lord will come like a thief (Peter).

Though Farkasfalvy goes so far as to call this a quotation of Paul (1985, 9), this is in fact a widely used phrase (Matt 24:43–44; Luke 12:39–40; Rev 3:3; 16:15) that cannot be traced back to a specific source with any confidence (3.5.2, widely

---

opponents and Gnosticism, see Robinson and Koester 1971, 34–39.

[42]He also notes the more general similarity that "2 Corinthians 4–5 contains an understanding of eschatology according to which the apostle's death might precede the parousia" (12). He concludes: "This text has a large number of data capable of making the author of Second Peter think that his interpretation of Pauline eschatology is authentic and correct. This, of course, strengthens the probability that Second Peter was written with a conscious use of 2 Corinthians 4–5" (12).

attested parallels).

Neyrey tentatively concludes that the author of 2 Peter "knows at least Romans and 1 Thessalonians, and possibly 1 Corinthians" (1993, 134). His reasoning is based both on use of vocabulary and shared themes. Allowing that many overlaps likely derive from shared traditions (and even Paul depends on earlier traditions at times), Neyrey is still impressed with the mutual interest in the delay of the Parousia as a gift (Rom 2:4–6 ; 2 Pet 3:15), the thief in the night expression (1 Thess 5:4; 2 Pet 3:10), and the similarities between the reference to Paul's wisdom and the apostle's own list of credentials (2 Pet 3:15 cf. 1 Cor 3:10; 15:10; also Rom 12:3; 15:15 [1993, 134]).

Clearly the author was familiar with Paul's writings—he states this. Unconscious dependence is a possibility when one author is very familiar with another (cf. Crossan 1998, 107–08). The author of 2 Peter was certainly capable of borrowing from other sources, as seen in his use of Jude (cf. discussion of the *Didache* in 3.2.7). In any case, not too much should be made of this. Like Paul, the author of 2 Peter was an original thinker and writer, and the non–use of other texts is not necessarily evidence for disagreement with earlier writers or a lack of knowledge of their work. Without the reference to Paul made in 2 Peter, it seems unlikely that the parallels noted above would suggest dependence on his letters; there is no attempt to cite explicitly or make obvious connections to his letters. The criterion of quantity does not help build the case for dependence on Paul (3.2.1); various parallel phrases have been noted, but nothing of any significant length. It seems reasonable to suggest that the author was aware of Pauline teaching, but this need not have derived from first–hand knowledge of the writings. It may simply be that the reference to Paul points to the apostle's teachings generally:

> . . . Peter may be alluding simply to Paul's constant teaching in all his letters about the need for holy, patient, steadfast, peaceable living (especially in the light of the parousia). These are, of course, the very subjects Peter himself has just been discussing. This seems the simplest solution (Green 1987, 158–59).

How can the author's knowledge but non–use of Paul's writings be explained? Various comments have been made about this. Perhaps he did not find Paul's letters pertinent to his particular argument (Lindemann 1979, 262–63). Or, was the author's theology formed before he had much contact with Paul's thought (Bauckham 1983, 148)?[43] There is an implied assumption involved when this line of questioning is pursued (i.e., exploring the influence of Paul on Peter), namely,

---

[43]Bauckham points out that a collection of Paul's writings was taking shape around the time that 2 Peter was written (late first century). "It is quite possible that Pauline letters were already an established authority in the churches of Asia Minor, to which he wrote (hence 3:15–16), but, apart from Romans, had only recently become known in the church of Rome, from which he wrote" (148). For further discussion of Bauckham's view of provenance and audience, see 149–51, 157–62.

that an author is always going to reflect other texts he knows. As said above, an author's originality must be respected (3.3.5). Since there is a significant adjustment of a known source (Jude), it must be allowed that possible Pauline influences on the author may have been so significantly reworded as to be unrecognizable.

Parallels between 2 Peter and Paul exist, though they do not meet the criteria that indicate (unambiguous) literary dependence. There are no striking parallels (3.2.4), and those points of contact that do exist can be explained in ways other than direct use of the letters in question.

4.5 THE *APOCALYPSE OF PETER*

According to a recent essay, "The relationship between 2 Peter and the Apocalypse of Peter, though much discussed in the older literature, has never been satisfactorily clarified" (Bauckham 1998, 290). Not only do both of these documents lack certain historical location, but there is also a complicated textual tradition for the *Apocalypse*. According to a minority of scholars in the late nineteenth and early twentieth centuries, 2 Peter made use of this early apocryphal writing.[44] But this is not the consensus view today. John A. T. Robinson, quite certain that, if there is any dependence between them, the *Apocalypse* is later, writes "[h]ow Harnack can have thought otherwise must be counted as one of those aberrations of scholarship which fresh discoveries induce, and it has long since been abandoned even by those who view II Peter as a second–century document" (1976, 178). Before commenting on this theory specifically, some preliminary words of introduction are in order, especially given the *Apocalypse*'s complex textual history.[45]

Eusebius knew about the *Apocalypse of Peter* and referred to it negatively:

---

[44]". . . also hat der Verfasser des Briefes die Apokalypse benutzt" (Harnack 1897, 1:471–72). The most recent advocate of Petrine dependence on the *Apocalypse* seems to be Moffatt. He bases this on the popularity of the *Apocalypse* in the second century, the fact that it is attested earlier than 2 Peter, and the opinion that the occurrence and sequence of the various shared phrases are more natural in the *Apocalypse* than in the epistle. Moffatt admits that a firm conclusion is elusive for three reasons: (a) scholarship remains ignorant of the conditions in which the Petrine literature of the second century was composed; (b) it is possible that both the *Apocalypse* and 2 Peter drew on common sources; and (c) the extant *Apocalypse* is in a fragmentary state. Still, he is persuaded that it "is more likely . . . that the existence of the apocalypse was one of the motives which inspired the composition of 2 P. (in its apocalyptic outlook) than that 2 P [*sic*] 2–3 led to the fabrication of the apocalypse" (1911, 367). Further proponents of this view are listed in Bauckham 1988b, 4721 sec.2a (though notice the misprint; it reads "the Apocalypse was dependent on 2 Peter" when clearly the reverse relationship is meant).

[45]A thorough summary of research is found in Bauckham 1988b, 4712–50 and 1998, ch. 11. On the relationship of the *Apocalypse* to 2 Peter see also Smith 1985, 43–59; Schmidt 1972, 106–35; James 1924, 505–24; and Maurer 1965, 2:663–68.

> Among the books which are not genuine must be reckoned the Acts of Paul, the work entitled the Shepherd, the Apocalypse of Peter, and in addition to them the letter called of Barnabas and the so–called Teachings of the Apostles (*Hist. eccl.* 3.25.4; cf. 3.3.2).

Clement of Alexandria (d. ca. 215) also knew of it (*Ecl.* 41; 48; 49; Eusebius, *Hist. eccl.* 6.14.1) and the work appears to have made use of *4 Esdras*, which thus provides a *terminus a quo* of ca. 100 B.C.E. (Maurer 1965, 2:664). It was also used in the *Sibylline Oracles* (2) and is mentioned in the Muratorian canon (ca. late second century at the earliest): "We receive also the Apocalypse of John and that of Peter, which some of us refuse to have read in the Church" (taken from Bettenson 1943, 41).

These various lines of evidence place the text firmly in the second century. It has been suggested that a more specific time of composition can be determined on the basis of the *Apoc. Pet.* E2:

> Hast thou not grasped that the fig–tree is the house of Israel? Verily, I say to you, when its boughs have sprouted at the end, then shall deceiving Christs come, and awaken hope (with the words): 'I am the Christ, who am (now) come into the world.' And when they shall see the wickedness of their deeds (even of the false Christs), they shall turn away after them and deny him to whom our fathers gave praise (?), the first Christ whom they crucified and thereby sinned exceedingly. But this deceiver is not the Christ. And when they reject him, he will kill with the sword (dagger) and there shall be many martyrs.[46]

This false Christ may be a reference to Bar Kokhba. If so, it has been argued, this necessitates a *terminus a quo* of 135 B.C.E. (the end of the revolt). Vielhauer, for one, writes:

> Das älteste Zeugnis für die PetrApk stammt von Clemens Alexandrinus. Man nimmt daher an, daß sie in der ersten Hälfte des 2. Jh.s entstanden ist; wenn die Deutung des Feigenbaumgleichnisses (Äth 2) auf die Christenverfolgung durch Bar Kochba zutreffen sollte (was allerdings nicht zu kontrollieren ist), so wäre der Terminus a quo 135 nChr (1975, 508).

Bauckham reasons that "the absence of reference to Bar Kokhba's defeat necessitates a date during the revolt, 132–35" (1988b, 4733).[47] It must be allowed however that the passage in question does not unambiguously suggest the Bar Kokhba revolt so an absolute date remains impossible.

---

[46]All citations from the *Apocalypse of Peter* are taken from the translation by Maurer (Greek [Akhmim]) and Duensing (Ethiopic) in Hennecke's *New Testament Apocrypha* (1965, 2:663–83).

[47]See also his argument in 1985, 269–87 and esp. 1994, 7–111. The last study has been republished in 1998, 160–258 (see esp. 176–94 regarding date). Cf. discussion in Smith 1985, 47–48.

The *Apocalypse of Peter* is preserved in the following sources. (a) Quotations from early church fathers. Prior to the discovery of the first fragment, only a few quotations of the *Apocalypse* were known.[48] (b) The Akhmim (Greek) fragment (AAP) was discovered in 1887 and published in 1892. (c) The Ethiopian version (EAP) was first published 1907–1910 by Abbé Sylvain Grébaut.[49] Determining the relationship between AAP and EAP remains a significant challenge in reconstructing the original text. When they parallel one another, EAP tends to offer a fuller reading than AAP. In addition to this, they differ in order—in AAP Jesus reveals paradise and then hell, whereas in EAP, the order is reversed. (d) The Bodleian (Greek) text was published in 1911, and (e) the Rainer (Greek) text was first published in 1924 (though not correctly identified as part of the *Apocalypse of Peter* until 1929). These last two are both fragmentary.

According to scholarly consensus, EAP comes closest to the original form of the *Apocalypse of Peter* and AAP should be considered an altered and abbreviated version of the EAP (see e.g., Bauckham 1988b, 4718; Schmidt 1972, 107, 110–11; both note the contributions of James 1911, esp. 362–83, 573–83; and Prümm 1929, 79). The reasons for this include: (a) EAP more closely resembles the quotations found in the church fathers;[50] (b) EAP more closely resembles the Rainer and Bodleian Greek fragments (see James 1911, 367; idem 1931, 271; and Schmidt 1972, 108–10);[51] and (c) the order of EAP agrees with the second of the *Sibylline Oracles*. The latter is thought to be dependent on the *Apocalypse of Peter*, and it progresses from hell to paradise (so EAP; Schmidt 1972, 109–10). On the basis of these arguments, Schmidt concludes:

> . . . it is evident that the Ethiopic is based on an older text than the Akhmim, and the Bodleian and Rainer fragments may represent the Greek original on which the Ethiopic was based. This would be the Greek version which those who have argued for the priority of the Akhmim text desire. Then the Akhmim fragment can be judged for what it is, a later inferior text (1972, 111).

This seems to represent a consensus on the matter.

The similarities between 2 Peter and the *Apocalypse of Peter* have been summarized and explained in various ways: either 2 Peter was dependent on the *Apocalypse*, the *Apocalypse* was dependent on 2 Peter, or, both derive from the

---

[48]Clement of Alexandria (*Ecl.* 41.1; 48.1); Methodius of Olympus (*Symp.* 2.6); Macarius Magnes (*Apocritica* 4.6–7); an old Latin homily on the Ten Virgins (the texts of each of these is found in James 1924, 506–07). Maurer adds that Theophilus of Antioch (*Autol.* 2.19) alludes to the *Apocalypse of Peter* (Akhmim fragment, 15) around 180 C.E. (1965, 664).

[49]The EAP provides a more complete text though it has been recognized to be a careless translation (Bauckham 1988b, 4717; Smith 1985, 44).

[50]These are placed in parallel columns in James 1911, 367 and Schmidt 1972, 108.

[51]With respect to (a) and (b), EAP uses the future tense in describing hell like the church fathers and the Bodleian fragment whereas AAP uses the past tense (James 1911, 367–69; Schmidt 1972, 110).

same circle or made use of (a) common source(s).

4.5.1 THE *APOCALYPSE OF PETER* IN GREEK AND 2 PETER

The conclusions of the earliest studies on the background of the *Apocalypse of Peter* needed to be reconsidered following the publication (and identification) of the Ethiopic translation in 1910–1911, because, as noted above, the EAP is closer to the original form of the writing. Still, there are several points of contact between the later, Greek edition (AAP) and 2 Peter that raise the question of a possible relationship. The thesis that 2 Peter was dependent on the *Apocalypse*, based on affinities between AAP and 2 Peter, can be illustrated with examples.

a) AAP 1

Many of them shall be false prophets and shall teach ways and diverse doctrines of perdition

πολλοὶ ἐξ αὐτῶν ἔσονται ψευδοπροφῆται καὶ ὁδοὺς καὶ δόγματα ποικίλα τῆς ἀπωλείας διδάξουσιν

2 Pet 2:1

. . . false prophets also arose among the people, just as there will be false teachers among you who will secretly bring in destructive opinions

Ἐγένοντο δὲ καὶ ψευδοπροφῆται ἐν τῷ λαῷ, ὡς καὶ ἐν ὑμῖν ἔσονται ψευδοδιδάσκαλοι, οἵτινες παρεισάξουσιν αἱρέσεις ἀπωλείας

b) AAP 21

But I saw also another place, opposite that one, very gloomy; and this was the place of punishment, and those who were punished there and the angels who punished had dark raiment, clothed according to the air of the place

τόπον αὐχμηρόν

2 Pet 1:19

You will do well to be attentive to this as to a lamp shining in a dark place

αὐχμηρῷ τόπῳ

c) AAP 22, 28

And some there were there hanging by their tongues: these were those who had blasphemed the way of righteousness (cf. EAP 7).

These were those who blasphemed the way of righteousness and slandered it

βλασφημοῦντες τὴν ὁδὸν τῆς δικαιοσύνης

2 Pet 2:2, 21

because of these teachers the way of truth will be maligned

it would have been better for them never to have known the way of righteousness

ἡ ὁδὸς τῆς ἀληθείας βλασφημηθήσεται / τὴν ὁδὸν τῆς δικαιοσύνης

These examples, along with others (see lists in Bigg 1901, 207–09; Chase 1898–1904, 3:814–15; Mayor 1907, cxxi–cxxii) have not proved convincing to all. According to Schmidt, "[m]ost of the similarities are single words or very short phrases which indicate nothing more than the fact that the Akhmim writer was familiar with some of the same vocabulary as the writer of II Peter" (1972, 116; cf. 3.1.4 [incidental similarities]; 3.4.6 [shared milieu]). Furthermore, as AAP represents an edition further removed from the original (see above), a direct relationship at the stage of composition—either way—seems unlikely (see 3.5.4, parallels based on translation or extensive redaction).

Others however are sufficiently impressed by similarities to argue for some influence one way or the other. In addition to verbal parallels between AAP and 2 Pet 2:1–3, Smith calls attention to the distinctive characteristics found in both writings which are not found in Matthew, a source for AAP (so Smith argues [1985, 46–47]) and perhaps also 2 Peter.[52] For one thing, the description of the false prophets in AAP 1–3 more closely resembles 2 Pet 2:1–3 than Matt 24:11–13, which also offers points of contact with AAP. This is evident in the following: (a) both 2 Peter and AAP describe these villains in terms of teaching activity, whereas Matthew speaks of signs and wonders (Matt 24:24); (b) Matthew does not mention explicitly the fate of the false prophets, whereas AAP and 2 Peter both do; (c) the false teaching is referred to as a "way" in AAP 1 and this parallels the language of 2 Pet 2:15; (d) the phrase "way of righteousness" (AAP 28) occurs also in 2 Pet 2:21. Smith suggests that these similarities rule out chance as an explanation and therefore some kind of relationship seems likely. But he is cautious in stating this conclusion.

> Apart from the small cluster of similarities in these sections, the resemblances extend only to single words and short phrases, some of which, nevertheless, are not commonly found elsewhere. It is apparent that the 2 Pet/Apoc Pet relationship is not of the same nature as that between 2 Peter and Jude . . . . As far as common vocabulary is concerned . . . [some] cannot be regarded as providing evidence of a literary relationship, and [others] . . . though found in 2 Peter and rarely elsewhere in the New Testament, are common enough in other literature of the period to rule out the possibility that one writer *must* have copied them from the other (50, his emphasis; full argument, 49–50).

Smith finds it more plausible that the author of AAP adapted the language of 2 Peter than some alternative explanations (i.e., 2 Peter was influenced by AAP or a single author was responsible for both). He prefers those theories that posit a common source or those attributing the writing of both texts to the same school of thought (51; see bibliography given for each of these positions). At the same time,

---

[52]There is some debate here as shown in 4.3. In a recent article Miller questions whether oral tradition best explains the gospel material in 2 Peter. He concludes: "while it is possible that 2 Peter preserves an independent attestation of the transfiguration, it is far more likely that 2 Pet 1.16–18 is dependent on Matthew" (Miller 1996, 625).

AAP should be read as a document with its own transmission and redaction history. The parallels found between it and 2 Peter are strong enough that a relationship exists, though not at the stage of composition. Perhaps a later copyist responsible for AAP was familiar with 2 Peter and influenced by it.

4.5.2 THE *APOCALYPSE OF PETER* IN ETHIOPIC AND 2 PETER

Reflection on the possible relationship between 2 Peter and the *Apocalypse of Peter* cannot be limited to the Greek Akhmim text. The Ethiopic version must also be considered, as it too presents many intriguing parallels. A few examples are given.

a) EAP 1 is dependent primarily on Matt 24 for its description of the mockers but the influence of 2 Pet 3:3–4 has also been suggested.

> Take heed that men deceive you not and that ye do not become doubters and serve other gods. Many will come in my name saying 'I am Christ' (EAP).

> First of all you must understand this, that in the last days scoffers will come, scoffing and indulging their own lusts and saying, "Where is the promise of his coming? For ever since our ancestors died, all things continue as they were from the beginning of creation!" (2 Peter).

This example is not at all striking.[53]

b) Some have connected EAP 2, which describes those who turn after the false Christ, with 2 Pet 2:1.

> And when they shall see the wickedness of their deeds (even of the false Christs), they shall turn away after them and deny him to whom our fathers gave praise (?), the first Christ whom they crucified and thereby sinned exceedingly (EAP).

> But false prophets also arose among the people, just as there will be false teachers among you, who will secretly bring in destructive opinions. They will even deny the Master who bought them—bringing swift destruction on themselves (2 Peter).

If, as some understand, EAP here refers to the denial of the crucified Christ, this parallel can be considered close.[54] However, this is disputed, and it may be that the

---

[53]Dependence is possible according to Smith (1985, 53). These passages also resemble other texts (*1 Clem.* 23:3; *2 Clem.* 11:2 [cited below]; cf. Herm. *Vis.* 3.4.3). Criterion 3.5.2 would be operative here, namely, that parallels with multiple attestation are not sufficient to support theories of dependence.

[54]The nature of the denial in 2 Pet 2:1 has been discussed among interpreters with some favouring one sense over others. It has been understood, for example, as a denial of the Parousia, given the interest in the letter as a whole (so Chaine). It has also been viewed as a denial of Christ stemming from the teaching and practicing of immorality (so Bigg 1901, 272: "by impurity men practically reject their Lord's authority and deny his δύναμις"; and Bauckham

one denied is the false messiah described in the same context, both before and after this passage.

> Verily, I say to you, when its boughs have sprouted at the end, then shall deceiving Christs come, and awaken hope (with the words): 'I am the Christ, who am (now) come into the world.' . . . . But this deceiver is not the Christ. And when they reject him, he will kill with the sword (dagger) and there shall be many martyrs.

If, in fact, the proposed parallel refers to a false Christ,[55] 2 Pet 2:1 and EAP are not parallel. Criterion 3.5.4 (parallels which are ambiguous with respect to meaning) would be relevant here.

c) The similarities between EAP 4 and 2 Pet 3:12 deserve attention, as they are quite close to one another.

> Behold now what they shall experience in the last days, when the day of God comes (EAP)

> waiting for and hastening the coming of the day of God, because of which the heavens will be set ablaze and dissolved (2 Peter)

Bauckham finds this parallel striking "because the designation 'day of God' for the day of judgment is found only in these two passages in early Christian literature before 150, though Rev 16:14 has 'the great day of God the Almighty'" (1998, 295; cf. also *2 Bar.* 55:6). This is indeed a striking parallel (3.2.4; a possible clue indicating a literary relationship), but it is very brief and coincidence cannot be ruled out as an explanation.

d) Similar themes are found in EAP 5 and 2 Pet 3:7, 10–12 but again there is insufficient evidence to confirm a direct relationship between them.

> . . . and obscurity and darkness shall come up and cover and veil the entire world, and the waters shall be changed and transformed into coals of fire, and all that is in it (the earth?) shall burn and the sea shall become fire; under the heaven there shall be a fierce fire that shall not be put out and it flows for the judgment of wrath. And the stars shall be melted by flames of fire, as if they had not been created, and the fastness of heaven shall pass away for want of water and become as though they had not been created (EAP)

> But by the same word the present heavens and earth have been reserved for fire,

---

1983, 241).

[55]This is argued by Hills (1991, 560–73, esp. 565–66). In his interpretive paraphrase, he translates the Ethiopic as follows: "This end–time coincides with and is signaled by the coming of false messiahs (2.7). But the new sprouts are not deceived—they shall 'turn away from' the pretender, disbelieving him because they have been warned by Enoch and Elijah (2.8, 12). This false messiah is hailed by his followers as 'the glory of our fathers'; but an earlier generation of 'our fathers' erred in killing the true Christ, he who was Christ from the beginning (2.9)" (572).

being kept until the day of judgment and destruction of the godless. . . . the heavens will pass away with a loud noise, and the elements will be dissolved with fire (2 Pet 3:7, 10).

Both EAP and 2 Peter speak about the destruction of the world. Schmidt finds two reasons to question a relationship here: the account in EAP is much longer than 2 Peter and the theme of the earth being formed of water and destroyed by water (2 Pet 3:5–6) is absent from the *Apocalypse*, suggesting "that the two traditions of II Peter and the apocalypse are not close to one another" (1972, 115; in the final analysis, Schmidt finds "no significant relationship . . . between II Peter and the Ethiopic apocalypse" [116]). Another argument against direct borrowing is the theory that a Jewish apocalyptic source is behind 2 Peter at this point (see 4.6). If so, the points of contact between 2 Peter and the *Apocalypse* may be explained by their use of a common source (3.4.3).

e) Much more general are the similarities between EAP 7 (= AAP 22) and 2 Pet 2:2, 21.

> Then will men and women come to the place prepared for them. By their tongues with which they have blasphemed the way of righteousness will they be hung up (EAP).

> . . . many will follow their licentious ways, and because of these teachers the way of truth will be maligned. . . . it would have been better for them never to have known the way of righteousness (2 Peter).

Because the similarity at this point relies on two different verses in 2 Peter and use of common language (cf. e.g., *Barn.* 1.4; 5.4), it does not indicate any specific relationship between the texts (3.5.2, widely attested parallels).

f) A final example involves a longer section of the *Apocalypse*. Various phrases in EAP 15–17 (= AAP 4–20) recall passages in 2 Peter.

> And my Lord Jesus Christ, our King, said to me, "*Let us go into the holy mountain*" [cf. 2 Pet 1:18]. And his disciples went with him, praying. And behold, there were two men, and we could not look on their faces, for a light came from them which shone more than the sun, and their raiment also was glistening and cannot be described, and there is nothing sufficient to be compared to them in this world. And its gentleness . . . that no mouth is able to express the beauty of their form. For their aspect was astonishing and wonderful. And the other, great, I say, shines in his appearance more than hail (crystal). Flowers of roses is the likeness of the colour of his appearance and his body . . . his head. And upon his shoulders and on their foreheads was a crown of nard, a work woven from beautiful flowers; like the rainbow in water was his hair. This was the comeliness of his countenance, and he was adorned with all kinds of ornament. And when we suddenly saw them, we marvelled. And I approached *God Jesus Christ* [cf. 2 Pet 1:1] and said to him, "My Lord who is this?" And he said to me, "These are Moses and Elias." And I said to him, "(Where then are) Abraham, Isaac, Jacob and the other righteous fathers?" And he showed us a great open garden. (It was) full of fair trees and

blessed fruits, full of the fragrance of perfume. Its fragrance was beautiful and that fragrance reached to us. And of it . . . I saw many fruits. And *my Lord and God Jesus Christ* [cf. 2 Pet 1:1] said unto me, "Hast though seen the companies of the fathers? As is their rest, so also is the *honour and glory* [2 Pet 1:17] of those who will be persecuted for my righteousness' sake." And I was joyful and believed and understood that which is written in the book of my Lord Jesus Christ. And I said to him, "My Lord, wilt thou that I make here three tabernacles, one for thee, one for Moses and one for Elias?" And he said to me in wrath, "Satan maketh war against thee, and has veiled thine understanding, and the good things of this world conquer thee. Thine eyes must be opened and thine ears unstopped that . . . a tabernacle, which the hand of man has not made, but which my heavenly Father has made for me and for the elect." And we saw (it) full of joy. And behold *there came suddenly a voice from heaven* [2 Pet 1:18] saying, "*This is my Son, whom I love and in whom I have pleasure* [cf. 2 Pet 1:17], and my commandments. . . . And there come a great and exceeding white cloud over our heads and bore away our Lord and Moses and Elias. And I trembled and was afraid, and we looked up and the heavens opened and we saw men in the flesh, and they came and greeted our Lord and Moses and Elias, and went into the second heaven. And the word of Scripture was fulfilled: This generation seeketh him and seeketh the face of the God of Jacob. And great fear and great amazement took place in heaven; the angels flocked together that the word of Scripture might be fulfilled which saith: Open the gates, ye princes! After that the heaven was shut, that had been opened. And we prayed and went down from the mountain, and we praised God who hath written the names of the righteous in heaven in the book of life.[56]

As both the EAP and 2 Peter present transfiguration accounts, they provide natural points for comparison. Among the parallels, the use of "the holy mountain" is worth noting. It does not appear in Matthew, which is usually recognized as a source for the *Apocalypse* at this point. Bauckham admits that the use of the phrase in these writings could be coincidental, "but it is a striking coincidence, especially in combination with other points of contact in the same context" (1998, 301). At the same time, this expression does appear elsewhere (e.g., LXX Ps 47:2 [= MT Ps 48:1]), and so it could be no more than the coincidental use of an earlier source (3.5.1). Also, it is hard to imagine the author of the *Apocalypse* picking out a few words from Peter's version of the story while paraphrasing Matthew.

It may be relevant that both the *Apocalypse of Peter* and 2 Peter understand the transfiguration as connected in some way to the second coming of Christ. This is evident in the *Apocalypse* when the closing verses of the transfiguration story (EAP 17) are compared with the opening verse of this writing and its description of the second coming:

For the coming of the Son of God will not be manifest, but like the lightning which shineth from the east to the west, so shall I come on the clouds of heaven with a great host in my glory, with all my saints, my angels, when my Father will place a crown upon my head, that I may judge the living and the dead and recompense

---

[56]Editorial notes in the Hennecke–Schneemelcher–Wilson edition have been omitted.

every man according to his work (EAP 1).

For the author of the *Apocalypse*, the transfiguration is closely related to the second coming.[57] This is also true for 2 Peter, where the glory of Jesus provides a link between the transfiguration and the Parousia (Neyrey 1980a, 513), and Neyrey suggests that Peter understands the one to serve as a genuine prophecy of the other.

> The author defends the δύναμις of the Lord and the fact that God was the source of this glory [1:16]. But this usage of the transfiguration is understood by the author as a genuine prophecy of the parousia. The defense of the δύναμις καὶ παρουσία will work only if the author is convinced that he is defending the parousia–glory while discoursing about the transfiguration's "honor and glory" (514).

In this case, the transfiguration is a prophecy of that still unfulfilled event, namely the return of Christ.[58]

Finally, it may be significant that many similarities between the *Apocalypse* and 2 Peter appear in close proximity. This can be observed in the transfiguration accounts (EAP 15–17 = AAP 4–20 [cited above]; cf. 2 Pet 1:16–18).

> The fact that these correspondences occur in close proximity in both works suggests a literary relationship between the two works. Since the Apocalypse of Peter's transfiguration narrative is almost certainly dependent on Matthew and in any case unquestionably dependent on Synoptic tradition, while 2 Peter's account of the transfiguration is probably independent of the Synoptic tradition; and since the Apocalypse of Peter has put the transfiguration tradition to a secondary use, as a revelation of the glory of the redeemed rather than of Jesus Christ, it is clear that the dependence must be of the Apocalypse of Peter on 2 Peter, not *vice versa* (Bauckham 1998, 302–03).

He argues that these combined parallels strongly suggest a literary connection. But this conclusion is weakened by the two issues raised earlier: (1) it is hard to see why the author of the *Apocalypse* would borrow a few words and phrases from Peter when using Matthew, and (2) one of the key striking parallels in the argument can be explained in another way ("holy mountain" may be taken from the LXX).

---

[57]Various reasons are put forward by Neyrey (1980a, 512–13). For one thing, the context of the transfiguration is an eschatological discourse about the second coming of the Lord. Also, "Moses and Elijah's glory [EAP 15–17] is a proof and sample of heavenly glory awaiting those saved at the second coming, and Jesus' transfigured glory clearly resembles the glory he will have when he returns as the Son of Man" (513; see also James 1924, 520). Smith (1985, 51–52) suggests that this point of similarity between the *Apocalypse* and 2 Peter "might argue for their having come from the same segment of early Christianity."

[58]It could be argued however that linking the transfiguration to the Parousia is such an obvious step for the Christian reader that there is no need of an antecedent to think of it. This would suggest that the similarity noted here is not significant.

If Bauckham is correct that 2 Peter was used by the author of the *Apocalypse*, and if his date for the *Apocalypse* during the Bar Kokhba revolt is also correct, then 2 Peter must be dated before 135.[59] It is concluded here however that Bauckham has failed to prove dependence of the *Apocalypse* on 2 Peter, and so a *terminus ad quem* for the epistle is equally lacking.[60]

4.6 THE APOSTOLIC FATHERS

Sidebottom states "that evidence [of 2 Peter] is wanting in the Apostolic Fathers" (1967, 99).[61] He follows this statement with an example of parallel language,[62] and it is in such instances of *possible* knowledge of the epistle that the majority of evidence for 2 Peter in the post–apostolic period prior to Origen is to be found. Many proposed instances of dependence on 2 Peter have been put forward, though none has met with general agreement. There are scholars who are confident, however, that evidence of the use of 2 Peter in the second century can be found. One study claims that "[o]ne thing has been proved . . . one *cannot* dogmatically affirm that there *certainly* are no allusions to 2 Peter in the Apostolic Fathers" (Picirilli 1988, 74; his emphasis).[63] Such a claim is not helpful; the issue is the presence or absence of probable allusions. The burden of proof is on those who want to claim dependence on 2 Peter by second–century literature; parallels must meet high standards before they can be considered sufficient proof of this. A selection of parallels with the Apostolic Fathers are treated below.

a) The phrase ταῦτα, ἀγαπητοί, οὐ μόνον ὑμᾶς νουθετοῦντες ἐπιστέλλομεν, ἀλλὰ καὶ ἑαυτοὺς ὑπομνήσκοντες (*1 Clem.* 7.1) is similar to 2 Pet 1:12; 3:1. Here is common use of the term "remind" in an epistolary writing but no other striking parallel (3.1.4, incidental similarities).

b) *First Clement* 7:5; 11:1 and 2 Pet 2:5–9 all refer to Noah and Lot. The significant amount of space between the two Clementine references in that document suggests this seems to be no more than coincidental reference to OT heroes (3.1.4). In *1 Clem.* 7:6 the phrase Νῶε ἐκήρυξεν μετάνοιαν can be compared to 2 Pet 2:5. In this case, it is possible that Clement derived this

---

[59]A date during the conflict is assumed because there is no reference to Bar Kokhba's defeat.

[60]The *Apocalypse*'s dependence on 2 Peter is often confidently asserted. For example: "There is . . . ample evidence that the *Apocalypse of Peter* (c. 110) was dependent upon 2 Peter in its construction" (Kruger 1999, 654).

[61]Cf. Kümmel: "II Pet is nowhere mentioned in the second century" (1975, 433); Elliott: "It left no certain early traces among the churches of Antioch, Asia Minor, Africa, or Rome" (1992, 5:283).

[62]In this case from the epistle of the churches of Lyons and Vienne, preserved in Eusebius, *Hist. eccl.* 5.1.45 cf. 2 Pet 1:8.

[63]Such a statement does not really say anything, rather it attempts to put a positive spin on the situation. More helpful would be an open admission that there is no unambiguous evidence. Appeal to possibilities only clouds the issue.

description of Noah from the *Sibylline Oracles* (e.g., Chase 1898–1904, 799).
c) The similarities between *1 Clem.* 8:2, 5 and 2 Pet 3:9 are clear.

1 Clement	2 Peter
"For as I live, said the Lord, I do not desire the death of the sinner so much as his repentance" (8:2 [= Ezek 33:11]; [Lake, LCL])	not wishing for any to perish
Thus desiring to give to all his beloved a share in repentance (8:5a; [Lake, LCL]).	wishing . . . all to come to repentance

Both writers may have been independently familiar with the Ezekiel reference (cf. 3.5.1; common use of an earlier source). The suggestion of literary dependence between the Clementine passage and 2 Peter cannot be supported.

d) In *1 Clem.* 9:2 τοὺς τελείως λειτουργήσαντας τῇ μεγαλοπρεπεῖ δόξῃ αὐτοῦ resembles 2 Pet 1:17. Given the widespread use of the term μεγαλοπρέπεια in the LXX, the parallel of vocabulary is not striking. At this point, *1 Clement* and 2 Peter use language that resembles Pss 20 (21):6 (δόξαν καὶ μεγαλοπρέπειαν), 144 (145):5 (τὴν μεγαλοπρέπειαν τῆς δόξης τῆς ἁγιωσύνης σου), and 144 (145):12: τὴν δόξαν τῆς μεγαλοπρεπείας τῆς βασιλείας σου. Here the parallels indicate only the influence of the Scriptures (3.5.1, parallels derived from earlier sources) or mutual use of common religious terminology (3.4.6, shared milieu; cf. also 3.5.2, widely attested parallels).

e) The phrase ἀκολουθήσωμεν τῇ ὁδῷ τῆς ἀληθείας (*1 Clem.* 35:5) is quite close to 2 Pet 2:2. Here both authors make use of very common language, which prevents specific conclusions (3.4.6 [shared milieu]; 3.5.2 [widely attested parallels]).

f) Second Peter 3:10 is quite close to *2 Clem.* 16:3. Given the close similarity in subject matter between 3:10 and the preceding verses, it has been suggested that the author of 2 Peter is continuing use of the Jewish apocalyptic source mentioned in *1 Clem.* 23:3–4 and *2 Clem.* 11:2–4.[64]

> But you know that "the day" of judgment is already "approaching as a burning oven (ὡς κλίβανος καιόμενος), and some of the heavens shall melt," and the whole earth shall be as lead melting (τακήσονται) in the fire, and then shall be made manifest (φανήσεται) the secret and open deeds of men (*2 Clem.* 16:3; [Lake, LCL]).

> But the day of the Lord will come like a thief, and then the heavens will pass away with a loud noise (ῥοιζηδὸν), and the elements will be dissolved with fire

---

[64]"Let this Scripture be far from us in which he says 'Wretched are the double–minded who doubt in their soul . . .'" (*1 Clem.* 23.2 [Lake, LCL]); "For the prophetic word also says: 'Miserable are the double–minded that doubt in their heart . . .'" (*2 Clem.* 11.2 [Lake, LCL]).

(καυσούμενα λυθήσεται) and the earth and everything that is done on it will be disclosed (εὑρεθήσεται; 2 Pet 3:10 [on the variant reading found here, see p.76 n.51]; cf. 3:11–13).

Is *2 Clement* here dependent on 2 Peter?[65] More likely the texts resemble one another, because of their common use of the LXX (Malachi and Isaiah).

Mal 4:1: διότι ἰδοὺ ἡμέρα κυρίου ἔρχεται καιομένη ὡς κλίβανος καὶ φλέξει αὐτούς, καὶ ἔσονται πάντες οἱ ἀλλογενεῖς καὶ πάντες οἱ ποιοῦντες ἄνομα καλάμη, καὶ   ἀνάψει αὐτούς ἡ ἡμέρα ἡ ἐρχομένη, λέγει   κύριος παντοκράτωρ, καὶ οὐ μὴ ὑπολειφθῇ ἐξ αὐτῶν ῥίζα οὐδὲ κλῆμα

Isa 34:4: καὶ ἑλιγήσεται ὁ οὐρανὸς ὡς βιβλίον, καὶ πάντα τὰ ἄστρα πεσεῖται ὡς φύλλα ἐξ ἀμπέλου καὶ ὡς πίπτει φύλλα ἀπὸ συκῆς

(Isa 34:4 [B, L]: και τακησονται πασαι αι δυναμεις των ουρανων[66])

At times the Clement passage incorporate elements present in the prophets but not in 2 Peter (such as the reference to a burning oven [cf. Mal 4:1]). Clement's "some of the heavens shall melt" is similar to Peter but closer still to the Isaiah passage (cf. B and L). The probability therefore exists that Peter and Clement independently made use of Scripture or perhaps common tradition, and so this parallel does not meet the criterion for dependence (see 3.5.1, use of material earlier than the proposed source). At the same time, Clement's reference to the deeds of men being made manifest is unlike both Malachi and Isaiah but quite similar to 2 Peter (though different terms are used).[67]

Since there is closer similarity to the biblical passages in some details, a straightforward borrowing from 2 Peter seems unlikely. If the proposal that a Jewish apocalyptic source underlies this part of 2 Peter is correct, the epistle could not have been the vehicle through which *2 Clement* received this material, for the latter makes use of it to a greater extent. It does not seem that 2 Peter was dependent on *2 Clement*, though this cannot be ruled out.

---

[65]Bigg writes: "The author [of *2 Clement*] here quotes Mal.iv.1; Isa.xxxiv.4, but his view of the world–fire is that of St. Peter" (1901, 209).

[66]Cf. the MT: ונמקו כל־צבא השמים ("All the host of heaven shall rot away"); cf. Matt 24:29 and Rev 6:13–14).

[67]For discussion see Picirilli 1988, 62–65. Donfried (1974, 91) concludes that both *2 Clement* and 2 Peter are indebted to a common tradition. The view that a common Jewish apocalyptic source lies behind both has been argued by von Allmen (1966, 260–61). Bauckham (1983, 304–05, cf. 283–84) agrees, suggesting that the Jewish apocalyptic writing that lies behind *1 Clem.* 23:3–4 and *2 Clem.* 11:2–4 is also used in *2 Clem.* 16:3. This source was used (and adapted freely [284]) by Peter in 2 Pet 3:4–13. There have been attempts to identify this source. J. B. Lightfoot speculated that it was the lost book of Eldad and Modat mentioned in Herm. *Vis.* 2.3.4 (1989, 73 n.22). Not all are convinced that there is a common Jewish apocalyptic source behind *2 Clement* and 2 Peter here (e.g., Wolters 1987, 411 n.29).

Corresponding to criterion 3.2.6 (awkward editing of source), recognition of an underlying source preserved in *2 Clem.* 16.3 could help to explain the otherwise unusual language of 2 Pet 3:10. Bauckham finds that the puzzling words at the end of 2 Pet 3:10 are illuminated if *2 Clem.* 16:3 represents their source (i.e., γῆ καὶ τὰ ἐν αὐτῇ ἔργα εὑρεθήσεται). He argues as follows:

> Since φανησεται [*sic*] ("will appear") and φανερά ("open, apparent") are here used [i.e., in *2 Clem.* 16:3, see above] rather awkwardly together, it is not impossible that the original text of the source quoted in *2 Clem.* had εὑρεθήσεται, which 2 Peter 3:10 reproduces, rather than φανήσεται, and that the author of *2 Clem.*, though correctly understanding εὑρεθήσεται, found it slightly odd usage and substituted the more natural φανήσεται. If *2 Clem.* 16:3 really does represent 2 Peter's source, then it will be seen that the author of 2 Peter, by omitting the phrase describing the earth ("like lead melting in fire") has made γῆ ("the earth") as well as τὰ ἔργα ("the works") the subject of εὑρεθήσεται ("will be found"). No doubt he did this because he wished to move swiftly to the idea of judgment, and thought of the earth as the place where the deeds of the wicked were to be found, but when it is seen that he is abbreviating his source, then the slight awkwardness of his use of γῆ . . . as well as the grammatical incorrectness of the singular εὑρεθήσεται . . . become intelligible (cf. 2:11, 17, where his abbreviation of Jude has produced difficulties or infelicities) (1983, 320).

This source–critical analysis is an intriguing hypothesis but does it help locate 2 Peter? Allowing that von Allmen, Marín, and Bauckham have rightly recognized a Jewish (or Christian?) apocalyptic source, there is no assistance provided from this insight that assists with finding a time of composition or geographical locale.[68] At best a general observation can be made—this Jewish apocalyptic source was known to at least two documents thought to derive from Rome in the late first/early second century.

g) A parallel between *Barn.* 15:4 and 2 Peter can be noted. The former reads as follows:

> Notice, children, what is the meaning of "He made an end in six days"? He means this: that the Lord will make an end of everything in six thousand years, for a day with him means a thousand years . . . (Lake, LCL).

Second Peter 3:8 is quite close to this passage, and both must derive ultimately from Ps 90:4 (LXX 89:4). This biblical phrase was used widely and developed in different ways (e.g., Sir 18:9–11 may be inspired by the Psalm reference; *2 Bar.* 48:12–13; cf. Irenaeus, *Haer.* 5.28.3). On the basis of criteria 3.5.1 (possibility that both used an earlier source) and 3.5.2 (widely attested expressions), this parallel should not be cited as an instance of possible dependence.

---

[68]If Lightfoot's identification of this source as the Book of Eldad and Modat is correct, this would not help either. Little is known about this document beyond a few references such as that found in Herm. *Vis.* 2.3.4.

h) Another parallel with *Barnabas* is worth noting, but it presents both textual and interpretive challenges.

ποιεῖτε ἵνα εὑρεθῆτε ἐν ἡμέρᾳ κρίσεως (*Barn.* 21:6)

γῆ καὶ τὰ ἐν αὐτῇ ἔργα εὑρεθήσεται (2 Pet 3:10)

Wolters finds these passages so close "(the same absolute use of *heuriskesthai*, the same eschatological context, the same link with ethical exhortation) that it looks like an explicit verbal echo" (1987, 411). This passage is indeed close when Wolters' own reading of 2 Pet 3:10 is accepted, namely that εὑρεθήσεται is the preferred text (see discussion of the issues involved in this variant on p.76 n.51). But this is not certain,[69] and so 3.5.5 (parallels based on unresolved textual difficulties) must be considered. Also, the meaning of εὑρεθήσεται is disputed (see the different senses listed on p.76 n.51). If one of these alternative readings or senses is accepted, the parallel with *Barnabas* is not as striking (in which case 3.5.4 is pertinent, parallels based on suspect interpretation). Wolters may be right, but the evidence is not compelling, and so one cannot argue that *Barnabas* knew 2 Peter.

i) Both Polycarp's *Letter to the Philippians* and 2 Peter refer to the wisdom of Paul.

> For neither am I, nor is any other like me, able to follow the wisdom of the blessed and glorious Paul, who when he was among you in the presence of the men of that time taught accurately and stedfastly the word of truth, and also when he was absent wrote letters to you (Pol. *Phil* 3.2 [Lake, LCL]).

> just as also our beloved brother Paul, according to the wisdom given him, wrote to you (2 Pet 3:15).

It is not remarkable that different writers would describe Paul in this way and refer at the same time to his writings. Such a general parallel should be omitted from consideration (3.1.4).

j) The similarities between *Did.* 3:6–8 and the vocabulary of 2 Peter and Jude impressed Spitta (1885, 534 n.; γόγγυσος [cf. Jude 16]; βλασφημία, αὐθάδης, and τρέμων [2 Pet 2:10]). Chase points out that τρέμων is part of a phrase derived from Isa 66:2 (and so 3.5.1, earlier source). There is nothing in the wider context to suggest a connection (3.3.8; cf. 3.2.8). Chase writes: "When the whole chapter of the *Didaché* is read, the idea that we have here a literary link with 2 P vanishes"

---

[69]Some hold that εὑρεθήσεται is the best reading of the extant variants (i.e., it best explains the others), but that it is itself a corruption of an earlier reading (e.g., Metzger 1971, 705–06). Wolters is aware that some argue this way (1987, 406). He attempts to show that not only is εὑρεθήσεται the best of the extant readings but that it also originates with Peter and that its meaning makes sense in its context.

(1898–1904, 799–800).

k) Also worth noting is a close parallel between Justin Martyr (not among the Apostolic Fathers) and 2 Peter, perhaps suggesting the former's familiarity with 2 Pet 2:1. A case for this was put forward by Dillenseger (1907, 177–79) and developed further by Bauckham (1983, 237).

> And just as there were false prophets contemporaneous with your [the Jews'] holy prophets, so are there now many false teachers amongst us, of whom our Lord forewarned us to beware (*Dial.* 82.1; *ANF* 1:240).

A comparison of OT false prophets with false teachers in the early church appears to be unique to these two writings, and the term ψευδοδιδάσκαλοι is found in this form only in these passages in literature up to the time of Justin (cf. Pol. *Phil* 7:2; 237). The usual practice among early Christians was to refer to false prophets in predictions of the last days (e.g., Matt 24:11, 14; Mark 13:22; 1 John 4:1; *Did.* 16:3), and Justin normally did this himself (*Dial.* 35.3; 51.2; 82.2). Also, the passage in 2 Peter, Bauckham suggests, appears to be created for its context; it links the preceding and succeeding topics creating a chiastic structure. This fact argues against the mutual use of traditional material (237) and would suggest that the expression originated with Peter.

4.7 CONCLUSIONS

Scholarship is on solid ground in postulating a literary relationship between 2 Peter and Jude; the evidence is best explained by the hypothesis that 2 Peter was dependent on Jude. This relationship demonstrates how the author adapted existing material for his purposes. On the basis of this reworking of Jude, it seems reasonable to assume that, when other texts have influenced the writer, they too have been adapted to suit the new context. There is far less parallel material between 2 Peter and 1 Peter, the Gospels, and Paul, and conclusions therefore need to be more tentative (3.2.1 [length of parallel material]). There is no reason why the author could not have used these writings, but the parallels in each case are not extensive. The account of the transfiguration likely points to knowledge of the Gospels (perhaps Matthew). Though brief, dependence is the simplest explanation for the parallels.[70] Appealing to oral tradition is speculative, and text relationships are the more obvious explanation. With respect to the Pauline material, it is possible that the author would not want to imitate that apostle even if he were familiar with his writings (Peter himself was a pillar in the church so there is no reason to expect that he would borrow from Paul's letters). Occasional similarities with 1 Peter are understandable; the writer was familiar with it (2 Pet 3:1) and claimed to be writing a follow–up to it ("This is now . . . the second letter I am

---

[70]In the case of the transfiguration story, the burden of proof changes and would be on those arguing that 2 Peter does not depend on the written Gospel(s).

writing to you"). Here extensive parallels should not be expected—and indeed they do not appear—since the author had no reason to repeat what was already said in the first letter. As for texts reflecting awareness of 2 Peter, the case for the *Apocalypse of Peter* is not strong. With respect to the Apostolic Fathers, there are no probable cases of dependence on 2 Peter.

By applying the criteria outlined in chapter 3, it has been found that some of the text relationships suggested between 2 Peter and other early Christian literature are not as obvious as sometimes argued. In cases where similar material exists, other explanations can be put forward to explain the parallels. Still, it remains possible for historians to locate 2 Peter within a broad, religious milieu, grouped with other early Christian texts from the mid–first through the second century that interpret Scripture for the needs of the Christian community, respond to the problem of false prophets/teachers, and encourage godly living while waiting for the return of Christ. At times these shared interests are more precise, as for example an interest in (re)telling the story of Jesus' transfiguration (Matthew, 2 Peter, the *Apocalypse of Peter*). But with such observations little is gained in narrowing the location of the text to a more specific place or time.

CHAPTER 5
EVALUATION OF THE PARALLELS APPROACH
FOR LOCATING TEXTS

This thesis has argued that the final word about certain background matters related to 2 Peter cannot be given. Given the nature of the evidence, conclusions about such things as provenance, audience,[1] some literary relationships, and date, typically treated in introductions to the NT, must necessarily be tentative. More specifically, in the case of texts lacking sufficient information to determine such things (like 2 Peter), the value of parallels with other texts is limited; they do not provide a reliable basis to determine a specific context. This is not to despair over the potential for the exegete to understand the text or to diminish the value of reading one early Christian writing in the light of others. Second Peter can properly be located in a broad context, namely, early Greek–speaking Christianity of the first and second centuries. However, attempts to narrow this environment further are invariably frustrated by the existence of plausible, alternative models. The problem is that the claim for one environment cannot be shown to be stronger than claims for others.

In this concluding chapter, some implications of this state–of–affairs for 2 Peter studies are considered. First (5.1) the evaluation of 2 Peter as something of an anomaly in the NT is discussed. It is argued that the challenges facing historians who study this document do not justify relegating it to the margins of NT studies. As an illustration of this point, a comparison with other NT writings (the Pastoral Epistles) demonstrates that 2 Peter is in fact quite similar to at least three other epistles in the Christian canon. Second (5.2), some closing reflections attempt to put a positive light on the value of 2 Peter for the study of early Christianity.

---

[1]If 2 Peter is pseudonymous its vague address ("To those who have received a faith as precious as ours" [1:1]) can be explained. A pseudepigraphal letter with a specific address would run the risk of being exposed as a forgery. A vague destination/address, or a letter addressed to a person no longer living, would avoid this danger.

5.1 SECOND PETER AND THE PASTORAL EPISTLES

For historians interested in an analysis of the first hundred years of the Christian movement, the boundaries imposed on the relevant literature—canonical and noncanonical—may seem a little artificial, but this boundary will never be removed (cf. appendix 2, p.145).[2] Since this is the case, discussion about the unity of the NT writings as a whole are bound to occur. When 2 Peter is considered in such dialogue, it is often viewed as in some sense an anomaly among the group.[3]

> The second letter of Peter and the letter of Jude are marginalized in the NT canon, disliked when not disowned. Even those who find merit in them do not rank them among the important NT writings. They are seldom read and less often studied. Since there is almost surely a literary connection between them, they are also invariably joined together, so that even each one's distinctive witness to the Christian faith is obscured (Johnson 1999, 495).

Further, there is wide agreement that 2 Peter is likely the latest document of the NT (e.g., Elliott 1992, 287), and so the tendency to compare it with noncanonical documents, especially of the second century, is understandable. But what has emerged as a result is a frequently stated conclusion: Second Peter is a distant relative of other NT writings. With the near consensus that Peter was not the author of this epistle, it is often *distinguished from* other NT writings rather than *compared with* them.[4]

Studies on the similarities between 2 Peter and the Pauline corpus have usually had the goal of identifying the referent(s) of 2 Pet 3:15–16. Many of the letters in the Pauline corpus have been suggested (even theories of a lost letter [so Lenski; Spitta]), yet the Pastoral Epistles do not appear to have been considered in this regard. All attempts to identify a specific Pauline writing involve an implied assumption—Paul provided a source for the author of 2 Peter. It was argued in chapter 4 however that there is insufficient basis to assert *absolutely* that 2 Peter was dependent on any of the Pauline writings individually or even as a whole (4.4). The purpose of the comparison that follows is not source criticism. Rather, the

---

[2]Some may be concerned that scholars operating within a faith tradition that appreciates the NT as an inspired collection would treat its writings differently than they would other historical writings. Faith and objectivity are not mutually exclusive.

[3]Cf. Chester and Martin: "In the esteem of many readers 2 Peter stands on the fringe of the New Testament. Its claim to be heard as an authentic witness to Christ and his way is muffled and indistinct" (1994, 146; see 146–51 for a helpful survey of ancient and modern suspicion of the letter's authenticity and value). At the 1999 annual meeting of the Society of Biblical Literature in Boston, Professor J. Daryl Charles said that research focused on the General Epistles involves working "as it were, in the hinterlands of biblical studies. . . . this corpus is the Rodney Dangerfield of the NT; it can never get any respect" (1999, 1).

[4]Presently in scholarship, the burden of proof is put on those claiming it is similar to other writings in the canon. It is suggested here that this should be the other way around.

following pages will present similarities between 2 Peter and the Pastoral Epistles in order to make the point that 2 Peter is *not unlike* other NT literature. That the similarities that are presented below are not of the sort that naturally suggest a source may explain why the Pastorals have not been proposed as the Pauline writings referred to in 2 Pet 3:15–16.

5.1.1 THEMES COMMON TO 2 PETER AND THE PASTORAL EPISTLES

Occasionally the Pastoral Epistles and 2 Peter are spoken about in the same breath (e.g., Childs 1984, 470–71; Perrin and Duling 1982, 384–85; Brown 1997, 771 [especially 2 Timothy]), but there does not appear to be anything of a systematic comparison of these writings. Commenting generally on the similarities between them, Sidebottom writes: "The writer knows of a collection of Pauline epistles (3.15f.), but shows very little influence from them in his work—much less than Jude. . . . The Pastoral Epistles provide far more parallels. Here is, in fact, the *milieu* of this epistle" (1967, 97–98).[5] Many of the similarities that can be observed are the result of common use of literary conventions (letters, pseudepigraphy, testaments [2 Peter, 2 Timothy], polemics). A few examples follow.

First, the threats addressed in these writings can be compared. Unlike earlier NT writings, the Pastorals and 2 Peter, with Jude, picture enemies inside the church:

> . . . this teaching is envisaged as not coming from without. It is a teaching which was propagated *within* the community . . . . Jude, like the Pastorals, does not make any real attempt to answer the challenge of this teaching . . . . *the Christianity which Jude addressed was not a pure unadulterated faith* . . . . A similar conclusion would have to be drawn from II Peter since the key chapter (II Peter 2) is so heavily dependent on Jude (Dunn 1990, 281, 283; italics original).

This is made more emphatic in 2 Peter than in Jude (Jude 12–13 cf. 2 Pet 2:13b, 17; so Kahmann 1989, 109). Are the problems facing the intended readers in the Pastorals, 2 Peter, and Jude, like James, perversions of Pauline Christianity?

> II Peter and Jude are manifestly attacks on perversions of Christianity, perversions which had arisen, at least in part, through the kind of misappropriation of Pauline

---

[5]The data given is as follows: "The word 'godliness' (piety) appears in 2 Peter at 1.3,6,7; 3.11; and in the Pastorals at 1 Tim. 2.2; 3:16; 4.7,8; 6:3,5,6,11; 2 Tim. 3.5; Tit. 1.1 and nowhere else in the New Testament except Ac. 3.12 . . . . The use of the word 'faith' in 2 Peter of the Christian religion itself or a virtue is paralleled in the Pastorals, where it occurs thirty–three times. 'Myths' (of the kind spun by an incipient gnosticism) are referred to in 2 Pet. 1.16 and in 1 Tim. 1.4; 4.7; 2 Tim. 4.4; Tit. 1.14. 'Remind' (a word typical of an age of 'looking back') appears at 1.12; 3.1; and in 2 Tim. 2.14; Tit. 3.1 as well as Jude 5" (97–98). For other general observations on similarities, see Marxsen (1968, 244), Soards (1988, 3839), and J. A. T. Robinson (1976, 171).

doctrines which Paul himself attacks (e.g. in Rom. vi). The Pastoral Epistles are also concerned in part with correcting perversions of Pauline teaching, and it is notoriously possible that James may . . . have something of the sort in view in Chapter ii (Moule 1982, 268).

Second, polemics play a major role in 2 Peter and the Pastorals. The Pastoral Epistles, unlike the other Pauline writings, resort to name–calling and do not engage with the false teachings of the opponents to the same extent, which makes identifying them difficult (this resembles 2 Peter; though compare comments on 1 Tim 6:3–12 below). One study offers a possible direction for this area of investigation. Robert Karris has isolated what he calls a traditional schema in the polemic of philosophers against the sophists. He further observes that the Pastorals appear to make use of this schema and, by a type of redaction–critical analysis of how the schema was used and changed, he attempts to reconstruct the nature of the opponents addressed in the letters. The schema includes the following components: (1) greed; (2) deceivers; (3) not practicing what they preach; (4) verbal disputes; (5) catalogues of vices; (6) women (1973, 551–55). Not all these components are evident in 2 Peter (3, 4, 6 are not represented), but this direction of research, towards recognizing conventional language in picturing enemies, is a helpful step. More recently Luke Johnson has focused on anti–Jewish slander in the NT, which he compares with the slander tossed back and forth between the Greek philosophical schools. He makes the point that verbal abuse was common in the ancient world and that the NT examples are not all that exceptional by comparison (Johnson 1989, 419–41; see esp. 441). Generally 2 Peter resembles the Pastoral Epistles in its use of conventional polemics.

Despair of recovering the identity of the opponents in 2 Peter (e.g., Windisch 1951, 98–99) and a trend towards descriptive surveys of the opponents' views (e.g., Michl 1968, 185–87) as opposed to historical analogies, was observed by Neyrey in his 1977 Yale dissertation (5–6). Here and in subsequent publications, he has reversed this trend somewhat by calling attention to affinities between the offending teachings addressed by 2 Peter and Epicurean anti–providence polemic[6] such as that found in Plutarch's *De Sera Numinis Vindicta* (1977, 172–210).[7] Neyrey wisely withheld final judgment on whether Epicurean anti–providence polemic was a source for 2 Peter's opponents or, if they should be identified as Epicureans (1977,

---

[6]Esp. 1993. "It is the hypothesis of this commentary that the opponents were either Epicureans, who rejected traditional theodicy, or 'scoffers' (*Apikoros*) who espoused a similar deviant theology" (122; full discussion 122–28).

[7]One of his contributions was a methodological improvement on previous research. Instead of focusing on 2 Pet 2 for study of the opponents, which he recognized as "biased, stereotyped slander and, therefore, of little value in determining the issues of the controversy" (1977, 32), he placed most weight on more explicit information in chs. 1 and 3 (e.g., 3:4). For a critique of Neyrey's conclusions about the Epicurean characteristics of the opponents' teaching, see Charles 1997, 45–46 and throughout.

210; cf. 1993, 122).[8]

The interest here is simply to observe the similarity between research on the Pastoral Epistles and 2 Peter; a skepticism has emerged regarding the possibility of identifying the opponents. In addition to the study by Karris referred to above, many (e.g., Spicq 1966, 28; Windisch 1951, 91; Chaine 1939, 18–24; Johnson 1989, 419–41) have called attention to the stereotyped nature of the polemics in the Pastorals, but only to a lesser extent has this has been recognized in Jude (Wisse) and 2 Peter (Spicq 1966, 201).

Third, there is clearly a connection between 2 Peter and Pauline Christianity (2 Pet 3:15–16). At times, 2 Peter is closer to the Pastorals than the non–disputed letters. For example, 2 Pet 3:15 credits Paul with writing about the "patience of our Lord" as salvation. This thought is found in Rom 2:4:

> . . . do you despise the riches of his kindness and forebearance and patience? Do you not realize that God's kindness is meant to lead you to repentance? (cf. 3:25; 9:22; 11:22).

It is also found in a more biographical sense in 1 Tim 1:16.

> . . . I received mercy, so that in me, as the foremost [sinner], Jesus Christ might display the utmost patience, making me an example to those who would come to believe in him for eternal life.

A few indications suggest that 2 Peter is closer to the parallel in 1 Timothy. To begin with, (a) in Romans the subject is clearly God, who shows patience, whereas in 1 Timothy it is Jesus Christ. Though it is not certain, 2 Peter's "our Lord" likely

---

[8]It may prove fruitful to compare the threat of false teachers described in 2 Peter with the problem of false prophets frequently addressed in the OT (of course the writer himself does this very thing in 2:1). The prophetic descriptions of false prophets in the Scriptures (esp. Jeremiah) and early Jewish writings offered a wealth of material to portray the enemies of God. It was here that the primary influence on the author's polemical language is to be found, whether consciously or not.

Is it possible that the early Christians themselves were being called false prophets/teachers because their predictions that Christ would return had not been fulfilled (e.g., 2 Pet 3:4)? Prophets were after all vindicated as being true only when their messages came to pass (Deut 18:20–22; Jer 28:9). By implication, any delay in the fulfillment of their words would understandably be very uncomfortable. Even the true prophet would be open to ridicule or persecution as is illustrated frequently in the Scriptures (e.g., the preexilic prophets waiting for the fall of Jerusalem). It is not difficult to imagine a similar pressure with respect to early Christians. On one level, the delay of Christ's coming was a test of faith but it would also be, on another level, a test of their credibility—their legitimacy as messengers of God. The taunts referred to in 2 Pet 3:4 (cf. Ezek 12:22) were certainly not isolated to the setting of this epistle. How did the prophets (and early Christians) answer the problem of delay and the challenge to their legitimacy as spokesmen for God? For one thing, there was an appeal to past fulfillment as seen in Peter's use of the flood–judgment as a proof.

refers to Jesus Christ since "Lord" is most frequently applied to Jesus (1:2, 8, 11, 14, 16; 2:20; 3:2, 10[?], 18), and God is usually referred to more explicitly (though cf. 2:9, 11; 3:8–9, 10[?]). There is also (b) the common use of the rare βραδύνω in 1 Tim 3:15 and 2 Pet 3:9, found only here in the NT (in verb form). Since 2 Pet 3:9 and 15 are connected by the repeated use of μακροθυμ– (verb 3:9; noun 3:15; also in Rom 2:4 and 1 Tim 1:16) and by subject matter, the paralleled vocabulary lends support to the argument.

Fourth and finally, similar issues of interpretation face scholars. Frances Young's treatment of the theology of Pastoral Epistles calls attention to the exegetical challenges of passages speaking of the relation of Christ to God (specifically 1 Tim 2:5–6; 3:16; 6:13–16; 2 Tim 1:9–10; 2:11–13; Titus 3:4–7). Young finds in this language a significant distance from Paul's theology (1994, 63). With the agency Christology of these verses, the titles for Christ and God are almost interchangeable and this, along with other evidence, leads Young to find in the Pastorals "language that . . . intriguingly parallels the 'ruler–cult'" (65; see 59–68 for the full treatment of Christology). While these claims concerning the distance between the Pastorals and Paul may be overstated, it is interesting to find the suggestion that 2 Peter may be the nearest NT writing to the language and thought of the Pastorals (65 n.23).

Young illustrates the unique challenge presented by the Pastoral Epistles in the area of theology. The Pastorals are more often than not described in terms of their *differences from* Pauline (and deuteropauline) literature. Similarly, as noted above, 2 Peter is treated in terms of its *differences from* the rest of the NT (most emphatically in Käsemann). In this respect, similar challenges confront the exegete in studying the Pastorals and 2 Peter, but these problems extend beyond theology: difficulties in dating, distinctive vocabulary, common use of pseudepigraphy (though debated), and an inability to place these writings geographically are not likely to be resolved with any degree of certainty.[9]

5.1.2 MORE SPECIFIC DETAILS COMMON TO 2 PETER AND THE PASTORAL EPISTLES

The previous comments were quite general. The observations that follow present more detailed points for comparison.

a) With respect to the false teachers, there is a similar use of tense. Second Peter oscillates between the present and the future tense, as 1 Tim 4:1–3 and 2 Tim 3:1–5.

b) Among linguistic similarities that can be noted are the following (complete NT occurrences of the form of the word given): βραδύνω: 1 Tim 3:15; 2 Pet 3:9; εὐσέβεια: (Acts 3:12); 1 Tim 2:2; 3:16; 4:7, 8; 6:3, 5, 6, 11; 2 Tim 3:5; Titus 1:1;

---

[9]Other more general themes in common can be noted. For example, these letters all reflect a high view of Scripture. Also, there is a common desire that none perish which perhaps reflects a similar appeal to Ezek 18:23 in 1 Tim 2:4 and 2 Pet 3:9.

2 Pet 1:3, 6, 7; 3:11[10]; ἐμπλέκω: 2 Tim 2:4; 2 Pet 2:20; μακροθυμία (of God): (Rom 2:4; 9:22; 2 Cor 6:6; Gal 5:22; Eph 4:2; Col 3:12); 2 Tim 4:2; 1 Pet 3:20; (of Christ) 1 Tim 1:16; 2 Pet 3:15[11]; μῦθος: 1 Tim 1:4; 4:7; 2 Tim 4:4; Titus 1:14; 2 Pet 1:16; σοφίζω: 2 Tim 3:15; 2 Pet 1:16; ὑπόμνησις: 2 Tim 1:5; 2 Pet 1:13; 3:1; αὐθάδης: Titus 1:7; 2 Pet 2:10.

With respect to style and language, the Pastorals and 2 Peter are distinct among NT writings:

> The Pastorals speak in the lofty style used by the Greek world and occasionally even by Greek–speaking Judaism. Insofar as a lofty style of language can become commonplace, it has done so here. One should not be deceived by the fact that the language of the Pastoral Epistles (and, for example, that of the 2nd Epistle of Peter as well, which is related to it) seems relatively unique within the NT (Dibelius and Conzelmann 1972, 145).

This is of course a highly subjective evaluation but one that is based on the observation of general similarities shared by these writings.

c) A interesting pattern appears in 2 Peter. The points of contact noted above between this epistle and the Pastorals often occur in those places where 2 Peter is *not* dependent on Jude (particularly chs. 1 and 3). If this observation is correct, it is hard to determine how this should be understood. It may say more about Jude's individuality (unrelieved polemic) than it does about 2 Peter and the Pastorals. Similarities between the Pastorals and 2 Peter are even found at points where the latter is clearly interacting with Jude, suggesting that redaction of Jude by Peter brought the text into alignment with certain characteristics of the Pastorals. This is illustrated by comparing Jude 4, 2 Pet 2:1–3, and various phrases from the Pastorals.

Jude 4	2 Pet 2:1–3	The Pastorals Epistles
"certain intruders"	"false teachers"	
"have stolen in among you"	"will be . . . among you"	
"deny our only Master and Lord, Jesus Christ"	"[t]hey will even deny the Master who bought them"	

---

[10]The possibility of a source relationship is hinted at by Knight III: "if 2 Peter has been influenced by the [Pastoral Epistles] or at least by 1 Timothy (cf. especially 2 Pet 3:15), then the use of εὐσέβεια in Acts (Luke), the [Pastoral Epistles], and 2 Peter finds a most satisfactory solution" (1992, 118).

[11]"Peter may have had 1 Tim. 1:16 in mind in 2 Pet. 3:15, where he refers to Paul writing of the Lord's patience toward them" (Knight III 1992, 103).

	"[they] will secretly bring in destructive opinions" (αἱρέσεις ἀπωλείας)	
	"many will follow their licentious ways, and because of these teachers, the way of truth will be maligned" (cf. 2:17–21)	concern that the name of God and Christian teaching is not blasphemed because of inappropriate behaviour (e.g., 1 Tim 6:1); concern that the word of God may not be discredited because of behaviour (Titus 2:5)
	"in their greed they will exploit you with deceptive words"	"a bishop, as God's steward, must be blameless . . . [not] greedy for gain" (Titus 1:7); "rebellious people . . . are upsetting whole families by teaching for sordid gain what it is not right to teach" (Titus 1:10–11); "depraved in mind and bereft of truth, imagining that godliness is a means of gain" (1 Tim 6:5); "people will be . . . lovers of money" (2 Tim 3:2)

In this example, the general references in Jude become more specific in 2 Peter: first, "certain intruders" become "false teachers," and second, a general attribute, which could find expression in either behaviour or doctrine (denying God), is more carefully specified as erroneous teaching. There is no reference to the greed of the opponents anywhere in Jude, but it is introduced to 2 Peter. It is interesting that this description is used repeatedly in the Pastorals suggesting a common pattern in the polemic (note that greed was part of the schema identified by Karris, see above). Also in this 2 Peter passage is a similar concern about bringing the faith into disrepute, a theme also absent from Jude. Reviling the true way could refer to conduct or teaching in early Christian writings. Isaiah 52:5, which is applied to the scandal of heresy in 2 Peter and to low moral standards among Christians in the Pastorals, may also be a possible influence (Lindars 1961, 22–23).

A second illustration of this phenomenon relates to the use of villains as examples of inappropriate behaviour.

Jude 6–9	2 Pet 2:5–11
"And the angels who did not keep their own position, but left their proper dwelling, he has kept in eternal chains in deepest darkness for the judgment of the great Day" (6)	"For if God did not spare the angels when they sinned, but cast them into hell and committed them to chains of deepest darkness to be kept until the judgment . . . " (2:4)

	"and if he did not spare the ancient world, even though he saved Noah, a herald of righteousness, with seven others, when he brought a flood on a world of the ungodly" (2:5)
"Likewise, Sodom and Gomorrah and the surrounding cities, which, in the same manner as they, indulged in sexual immorality and pursued unnatural lust, serve as an example by undergoing a punishment of eternal fire" (7)	"and if by turning the cities of Sodom and Gomorrah to ashes he condemned them to extinction and made them an example of what is coming to the ungodly" (2:6)
	"and if he rescued Lot, a righteous man greatly distressed by the licentiousness of the lawless . . . *then the Lord knows how to rescue the godly from trial, and to keep the unrighteous under punishment until the day of judgment*" (2:7, 9)
"Yet in the same way these dreamers also defile the flesh, reject authority, and slander the glorious ones"(8)	"especially those who indulge their flesh in depraved lust, and who despise authority. Bold and willful, they are not afraid to slander the glorious ones" (2:10)

The point to be made here is most clearly seen in 2 Pet 2:9, which does not have a Jude parallel (the italicized portion). Two themes stand out in a comparison of the villains in Jude and 2 Peter. First, whereas Jude's primary concern is to demonstrate the judgment of the wicked, Peter goes beyond this in his redaction of Jude to highlight God's preservation of the righteous who live in the midst of a sinful world. Introducing the Lot and Noah narratives provides striking images of how God delivers his own people and presents the contrast between the righteous and the wicked more clearly than the imprisoned–angels story and the Sodom and Gomorrah story (the former does not deal with people; the latter does not provide an example of redemption).[12]

Second, and building on the first point, the presentation of the enemies of God in Jude (a commentary on the "certain intruders [who] have stolen in among you" [v.3]) is largely devoid of a positive counterpart (though cf. 7b). There is no ambiguity in Jude about who the characters in the drama are: believers are called and preserved (vv.1, 24) and the wicked face a pre–ordained judgment (v.4). In the Pastorals and 2 Peter, on the other hand, there is more ambiguity. There is a heightened sense of danger as Christians might be duped into following these villains and fall from the truth themselves (2 Pet 1:9; 2:2, 14, 18; 3:17; cf. 1 Tim 1:19; 3:6; 2 Tim 1:15 [?]; 2:14–18; 4:3–4, 9 [?]). Second Peter's incorporation of

---

[12]Jude does not mention Lot at this point. However, the Sodom and Gomorrah reference in Jude no doubt brought the related Lot narrative to mind as Peter was writing.

the Jude material therefore goes beyond what that earlier writer was doing. In Jude, the villain–types are used to make the point that those who challenge the church now (i.e., in the first readers' day) will be judged as the types were (i.e., the angels, Sodom and Gomorrah). But in 2 Peter (see esp. 2:9) the issue is two–fold: judgment is inevitable for the evil (eventually), and the faithful will be preserved (now and in the future).

Again, with respect to the function of villainous examples, the pattern that emerges in 2 Peter more closely resembles the Pastorals than does Jude. For Jude they are mentioned to prove the certainty of judgment (v.13) and to provide an example (δεῖγμα; cf. 2 Pet 2:6, ὑπόδειγμα). In Peter and Paul, they are illustrative of how the righteous are contrasted with the wicked. A few specific observations can be made.

First Timothy 1:3–20 suggests that "certain persons/some people" (vv.3, 6–7) may teach inappropriate things. A specific example is provided in vv.19–20 (Hymenaeus and Alexander). Instructive in this passage as a whole is the parallelism between these villains and the faithful (namely Paul and Timothy): the villains are delivered to Satan (v.20), Paul and Timothy receive mercy (vv.16, 3).

False teachers are described in 1 Tim 6:3–12 as bereft of truth and they imagine that "godliness is a means of gain" (v.5). Rather than simply calling them names in that passage (greedy), Paul takes time to explain their error ("there is a great gain in godliness combined with contentment," v.6) and presents their fault in contrast with proper behaviour: "if we have food and clothing, we will be content with these" (v.8).

In 2 Tim 3:1–17, Paul compares himself with his opponents. In the last days people will be lovers of themselves, unholy, and so on (vv.1–9). This lengthy description is then followed by a positive counterpart: "Now you have observed my teaching, my conduct, my aim in life, my faith, my patience, my love, my steadfastness" (v.10–11). Again, the villains are described in v.13 only to be followed by the example of Timothy himself, who is to "continue in what [he has] learned and firmly believed" (v.14). At each step, the Pastoral Epistles present positive alternatives to the negative behaviour of the errorists. Peter does the same as seen, for example, in his description of Noah as "a herald of righteousness" (2:5) and Lot as "a righteous man" (2:7). Jude is content simply to paint the opponents' portrait.

d) A final similarity to be presented between 2 Peter and the Pastorals is a mutual interest in the theme of knowledge. This is noticed by comparing the opening and closing of the letter: "in the knowledge of God" and "grow in the grace and knowledge of our Lord and Savior Jesus Christ" (1:2; 3:18). Both of these passages diverge from expected phrasing by the introduction of the term knowledge (Fornberg 1977, 14), and this interest in the subject is found throughout (1:3, 5–6, 9; 2:20–21, etc.). Such knowledge is redemptive (1:2–3), and through it one escapes the corrupt world (2:20). This emphasis is further illustrated by comparing Jude 10 with 2 Pet 2:12; in the former the adversaries are credited with knowing some things by instinct, but in the latter this is not the case—"the adversaries are denied all understanding" (48–49 and n.2). In 2 Pet 3:16 the opponents are ignorant and unstable.

This emphasis on knowledge/lack of knowledge is absent from Jude and therefore something introduced by the author of 2 Peter. Similarly, the Pastorals stress knowledge of the truth (1 Tim 2:4; 2 Tim 2:25; 3:7; Titus 1:1). This is expressed in various ways such as the warnings against false teachers, praise and instructions for true teachers, and reminders of the sources for knowledge and truth (Scripture, prophets, apostles, elders). A related theme is the call to believers to strive toward truth (note the shared interest in the word–group σπουδ– [make haste, be zealous, zeal]; 2 Tim 2:15; 4:9, 21; Titus 3:12, 13; 2 Pet 1:5, 10, 15; 3:14; cf. Jude 3).

It should not be taken for granted that the Pastoral Epistles represent a unified group, though they have been treated as such above. It is more appropriate to treat texts individually:

> Characterizations of "the Pastorals" are typically drawn from all three letters coalesced into a whole, while the individual characteristics of the respective letters are overlooked. The Pastorals are often said, for example, to contain an elaborate ecclesial structure. But 2 Timothy lacks any reference to order at all, and Titus contains only a trace. Reference is also made to "the opponents in the Pastorals," even though there is a distinct profile in each of the letters. Such generalizing dulls the perception of the individual letters, heightening a sense of their isolation from the rest of the Pauline corpus (Johnson 1999, 424).

Similarly: "There is . . . nothing to indicate that they were written at the same time or from the same place, or that the author intended them to be studied together" (Carson, Moo and Morris 1992, 359). This complicates attempts to speak of a shared milieu for the Pastorals and 2 Peter. A sensitivity to the distinctiveness of 1 Timothy, 2 Timothy, and Titus, when comparing them with 2 Peter, may show that one of them is closer to the latter than the others.[13] Or negatively, it may suggest that the apparent parallels are inconsequential when seen between the letters individually (coincidence, common vocabulary, the result of a shared genre, common Christian traditions, and so on). This limits the value of comments like that of Perrin and Duling who, on the basis of affinity of perspective between 2 Peter and the Pastorals, date them to the same period (1982, 385). When such an argument is made, it is assumed that the Pastorals are a unified group. However, claims of a shared location for the Pastorals and 2 Peter—whether geographical,

---

[13]Second Timothy is probably the closest to 2 Peter owing to the fact that they are similar in their intent (a farewell discourse from a renowned spiritual leader). In Brown's words: "In many ways II Pet resembles II Tim. Each is a last testament of a famous apostle; and each appeals to the witness of the apostle, respectively Peter and Paul. Each is concerned about the intrusion of false teachers upon whom opprobrium is heaped. For guidance each assumes a deposit of faith" (1997, 771).

theological, or chronological—may be assessed differently depending on how one views the letters to Timothy and Titus in relation to one another. The most that can be said is that 2 Peter shares various characteristics with the Pastoral Epistles as a whole. In spite of the need for caution, the common language, style and themes in the Pastorals is striking, and should be given its due. There is much to be said for taking them as a group.

To conclude, this brief illustration of shared characteristics with other NT writings makes the relegation of 2 Peter to the fringe of the NT a meaningless evaluation.

5.2 A TEXT WITHOUT A HOME: WHEN EXACT HISTORICAL LOCATION PROVES TO BE IMPOSSIBLE

Is the fact that questions remain regarding 2 Peter's historical location really a problem? Since so little is known about earliest Christianity, it would be very surprising to be able to specify the context of an anonymous or pseudepigraphal text. Historians must bring appropriate expectations to the extant literature, because the writings of the earliest Christians rarely supply the kind of evidence needed to identify specific historical contexts. Still, though scholarship remains unable to determine a precise location for 2 Peter, some positive insights can be gained.

a) Second Peter reminds historians that reconstructions of early Christianity should be considered tentative when the evidence is limited to texts alone. This is normal. Early Christian history is not extraordinary in this regard; historians attempting to locate literature in other periods face similar difficulties. Second Peter, with its stubborn refusal to be located within broad theoretical schemes of early church development, forces students to focus on the document on its own terms before placing it in broad categories (cf. appendix 2 where it is argued that historical reconstructions must begin with texts, not with theoretical models).

b) This may sound obvious, but the failure to locate 2 Peter satisfactorily because of limited knowledge about the early church should serve to increase the significance of the content of the text. Details about origin and audience, authorship and date are out of reach, but the voice of an early Christian pastor is heard in the text. It seems ironic that some NT scholars choose to downplay the value of one of the few voices from the early centuries, because there is insufficient evidence to determine its origin![14]

---

[14]That scholars have generally neglected 2 Peter is clear. Snyder called attention to this situation in 1979, 265. Supplements to his *JETS* bibliography were made by Hupper (1980) and Bauckham (1982; see also idem 1988a and Pearson 1989 for further surveys of scholarly study of 2 Peter). Since that time however there has been a significant shift in this state of affairs judging by the literature being produced. This statement is based on a literature search by the present writer following up on the earlier *JETS* bibliographies (Gilmour 1999c). With no attempt at being exhaustive well over one hundred studies (for the most part excluding commentaries, introductions, and encyclopaedia articles) are listed, primarily between 1982 and 1999.

c) Owing to the text's defeat of modern, scholarly ingenuity (a), and owing also to the value of this text as one of the precious few monuments of earliest Christianity (b), limited understanding of the historical setting of this document forces readers to let the author speak. Whether fiction or not, Peter intended his letter to be read as a letter, not as a source for the historian seeking to reconstruct the history of earliest Christianity (cf. pp.2 n.1 and 3). It stands to reason that interpretation is best served when the intended genre of the text (a letter, a last testament) is respected.

APPENDIX 1

In the following pages parallels are observed between a canonical Gospel and noncanonical literature. As a contribution to the overall argument of the dissertation, this study is intended to develop the idea outlined in section 3.3.4 in more detail by considering a specific example. There it was argued that parallels between texts (especially when removed by a considerable amount of time) may result from the earlier writing's influence (text A) on the genre in which a later author communicated (text B). In such cases, B is not necessarily directly influenced by A (the writer may not have even known that document), but text A was an indirect influence, as it contributed to the shape of the literary conventions known to and used by the author of B. This appendix illustrates the possibility that similarities between writings may be indirect. Specifically, it examines how Homer's significant influence in the ancient world may have contributed to the shape of stories about postmortem experiences. Since Luke himself was an educated Greek speaker who likely had at least some knowledge of Homer, and since he also included a postmortem story in his writing (Luke 16:19–31), the possibility of influence from one to the other is at least plausible.

HINTS OF HOMER IN LUKE 16:19–31?[1]

Luke 16:19–31 and *Odyssey* book 11 (cf. 24.1–204) both describe journeys to hades (ᾅδης) and share several common themes: the futility of worldly wealth in the afterlife, torment, a concern for living loved ones, and so on. Though literary descents to the underworld are by no means unique to these two examples,[2] some observations on these texts will explore the possibility of an indirect influence of

---

[1]The following study appeared in *Didaskalia* 10 (1999):23–33 and is included here in a slightly abbreviated and adapted form. It is reprinted with permission.

[2]For Greco–Roman examples see Bernstein 1993, 19–129; for Jewish and Christian examples see Himmelfarb 1983 and Bauckham 1998, 9–48.

the *Odyssey* on the Gospel of Luke. One possible connection between them is found in the rhetorical education Luke would have received, of which Homer's writings were a part.

1.1 EDUCATION IN THE ANCIENT WORLD

Familiarity with Homer's works was widespread in the ancient world, and it is generally accepted that even in Palestine educated children would have had exposure to the Greek epics.[3] Particularly in the area of rhetorical training, Homer was required reading. Quintilian for one placed a high value on reading both Homer and Virgil as a starting point for training young boys: "[their] intelligence needs to be further developed for the full appreciation of [these writers'] merits: but there is plenty of time for that since the boy will read them more than once" (*Inst.* 1.8.5 [Butler, LCL]). At the very least, such students would be familiar with words and sentences drawn from Homer, which were used in the learning process. Furthermore, the orator was enjoined to have at his disposal examples drawn from the poets of old, since they provided a storehouse of knowledge and experience "as Homer so frequently bears witness" (*Inst.* 12.4.1–2 [Butler, LCL]).

Can Luke be linked to this rhetorical tradition? At several points Luke 16:19–31 itself is consistent in employing principles and strategies outlined by the rhetoricians. For example, Aristotle suggests that, on occasion, fear (defined in *Rhet.* 2.5.1) may be the desired effect of oration. An audience may need to be reminded that, like greater people before them, they too could suffer (*Rhet.* 2.5.15). In Luke 16, the evils of wealth are addressed; since those who "were lovers of money" (v.14) comprised part of the audience, it is appropriate to present the judgment of an unjust rich man. Elsewhere Aristotle speaks of the value of a previous judgment with respect to a similar matter, "if possible when the judgement was unanimous or the same at all times" (*Rhet.* 2.23.12 [Freese, LCL]). Presumably, even the Pharisees in attendance would have agreed that the rich man was wrong for not showing mercy.[4] This parable provides precedent for a judgment on the wealthy.

According to Aristotle, "pity" is stirred when pain occurs in one not deserving it (as most would see Lazarus; *Rhet.* 2.8.2) and the opposite, "indignation," when prosperity is found in those not worthy of it (2.8.9). These emotions—pity and indignation—will be found in men of good character (possibly implied in Luke if the audience in Luke 16, "the disciples" [v.1], is placed in contrast to the

---

[3]On Homer's educational role in Hellenistic Judaism see Hengel 1974, 1:65–78 and Lieberman 1962, 112–13. On the more general influence of Greco–Roman culture see Bilezikian 1977, 48–49.

[4]Jews were required to have concern for the poor (e.g., Deut 15:7–11). Amos condemns those who "push aside the needy in the gate" (5:12; cf. Luke 16:20) and in Proverbs it is said that "[i]f you close your ear to the cry of the poor, you will cry out and not be heard" (21:13)—an appropriate passage in this context.

money–loving Pharisees who were listening in [v.14]).

These few points illustrate the potential of a rhetorical–critical analysis of the parable in question. However, the remainder of this paper will concentrate on the traditions behind this pericope. This is linked to the previous points of Luke's rhetorical strategy, in that rhetorical training was a means by which classical Greek compositions were circulated. Clearly Luke had some rhetorical training to his credit;[5] this presupposition lies behind the thesis outlined below.

1.2 THE INTERPRETATION OF LUKE 16:19–31

To discuss yet another possible source for the story of Lazarus and the rich man may seem a little taxing to students of Luke[6] who have encountered many such studies, especially since the work of Gressmann earlier in the century.[7] However, it is noteworthy that reference to the *Odyssey* does not appear to be among suggested parallels.[8]

This presentation does not challenge other theories of possible backgrounds but complements them. As said above, similar texts abound in both Greco–Roman, Jewish and Christian writings. The most likely connection between Luke and Homer—if one is to be found—is Homer's influence on the broader genre of afterlife/underworld literature, which Luke may have known in some form.

Two developments in the study of this parable make comparison inviting. The first involves concern about the weight placed on the Egyptian parallel. Jeremias is a frequently cited representative of this emphasis; he suggests that familiarity with this story is "essential" for a detailed understanding of the parable (Jeremias 1972, 183). However, concerns have been raised about the validity of this source (e.g., Bultmann 1963, 196–97, 204) including: (a) its similarities are limited to one section of the parable, and (b) the extent of its dissimilarities. A second (related) change of opinion recommends a wider search for the background(s). Hock has found scholarship implicitly arguing that the "comparative net" should not be cast beyond the Jewish milieu. As a result, sources from the larger Greco–Roman world "are seldom considered, never seriously." He continues:

But why not cast the comparative net wider? After all, the text of the parable is in

---

[5]For discussion of rhetorical education and evidence of this in the Gospels, see Mack and Robbins 1989, ch. 2.

[6]For a helpful summary of proposed parallels to this story, see Bauckham, 1998, 97–118.

[7]Gressmann (1918) proposed that the source of the Lazarus parable could be found in the Egyptian story of Setme and Si–Osiris and Jewish writings developed from it. This opinion has been perpetuated by influential studies such as Jeremias' *The Parables of Jesus* (1972, 182–87). For a summary of this story and its limitations as a possible source see Bauckham 1998, 97–103, Grobel 1963–64, 373–82, and Hock 1987, 448–53.

[8]There are occasional references to similarities in specific details (e.g., Fitzmyer 1985, 2:1576) but nothing of a sustained comparison of the two texts.

Greek, and it is part of a larger two–volume work that was intended for persons whose familiarity with Greco–Roman society is not in doubt (1987, 455–56).

Hock himself focuses on the Cynic Lucian's *Gallus* and *Cataplus*. Bauckham develops this methodological proposal further, noting that "the true significance of the parable emerges when attention is given to all available parallels," the differences as well as the similarities (1998, 118).

1.3 OD. 11 AND LUKE 16:19–31[9]

In *Odyssey* book 10, the goddess Circe promised to end Odysseus' wanderings and send him home (10.483–85), but he was first required to visit hades (10.491) with the main purpose of seeing the spirit of the Theban Teiresias. During this visit, the epic's hero met several "spirits of those that are dead" (11.37–38 [Murray, LCL]), and in the narrative of these encounters, some similarities with Luke 16:19–31 can be observed.

1.3.1 A CHASM OF SEPARATION

This terrifying aspect of Jesus' parable (Luke 16:26) has a counterpart in Odysseus' inability to embrace his mother in hades: "I was fain to clasp the spirit of my dead mother" (*Od.* 11.204–05 [Murray, LCL]; cf. the attempt by Agamemnon, 11.390–94). In despair the hero requested an explanation and she replied: "this is the appointed way with mortals when one dies. For the sinews no longer hold the flesh and the bones together, but the strong might of blazing fire [cf. Luke 16:24] destroys these" (11.218–20 [Murray, LCL]).

Background information to Luke's language here is scarce (see Fitzmyer 1985, 2:1133; Marshall 1978, 638), and exploring individual terms (e.g., χάσμα, διαβαίνω) does not contribute much. (For the notion of separation see *1 En.* 18:11–12; 22:8–14 as an earlier Jewish example). Of course the situation described between Odysseus and his mother on the one hand and Lazarus and the rich man on the other are extremely different, but the point is the same—the dead are separated (from the living [Homer]/from the righteous [Jesus]).

1.3.2 THIRST NOT SATISFIED

Dives' longing to have his tongue cooled (Luke 16:24; cf. 2 Esd 8:59) might suggest, to readers familiar with Homer's account of hades, the torments of

---

[9]Other traces of Homer have been noted in the writings of Luke. In particular, it has been observed that Luke's sea narrative of Acts 27:1–26 bears some resemblance to Greco–Roman texts, especially Homer. For examples of storms and sea wrecks, see *Od.* 5.291–332; 9.62–81; 12.201–303. See comments in Johnson 1992, 445–56 and Praeder 1984, 683–706.

Tantalus[10] who in violent torment (cf. Luke 16:24–25, 28) was "standing in a pool, and the water came nigh unto his chin. He seemed as one athirst, but could not take a drink; for as often as that old man stooped down, eager to drink, so often would the water be swallowed up and vanish away" (11.583–87 [Murray, LCL]). Likewise, the fruit of trees would be blown away by the wind as he would reach to take them. Part of the reversal–of–fortunes theme in the Lucan parable must certainly involve the subject of food which so distinguished Lazarus from Dives in life (Luke 16:19–21).

1.3.3 WEALTH IN LIFE NOT SATISFYING IN DEATH

This is certainly a theme in Luke 16:19–31[11] and also in Homer's epic. One intriguing example is found in the conversation between Odysseus and Achilles. There was no consolation in the former's words that he was blessed in life and ruled mightily in death:

> Nay, seek not to speak soothingly to me of death, glorious Odysseus. I should choose, so I might live on earth, to serve as the hireling of another, of some portionless man whose livelihood was but small, rather than be lord over all the dead that have perished (11.488–91 [Murray, LCL]).

This reversal, where the poor and powerless are viewed with greater esteem after death, is frequent in both secular and religious, Greek and Jewish writings.

1.3.4 CONCERN FOR LIVING LOVED ONES

Again there are similarities with other stories, both Greco–Roman and Jewish. Worth noting is the Jewish or Christian *Book* (or *Penitence*) *of Jannes and Jambres* described by Bauckham. He finds similarities between this text and Luke 16:27–28 but does not go so far as to say there is a specific link:

> . . . the resemblance is close enough to make the possibility suggested in Luke 16.27–28 [of a return to the living] one which could have been familiar to Jesus' hearers from a traditional Jewish story. We cannot be sure that the story in this form was available to them, and there can be no question of identifying the story as a source of the parable. But as a parallel to the parable, it confirms that the motif employed in Luke 16.27–28 could easily have been current in Jewish storytelling (1998, 114).

---

[10]See Himmelfarb's comments on *Od.* 11.582–92 and the theme of tantalization in Jewish parallels (1983, 92–94).

[11]Jeremias points to lessons in Luke 16:19–31 drawn from the two sections of the passage: (1) the reversal of fortune in the after–life (vv. 19–26) and (2) the petition of the rich man regarding his brothers (vv. 27–31) with an emphasis on the latter (1972, 186).

Attempts to find a Jewish background should not be pressed too hard to the exclusion of other possibilities, since the notion of a return from death is not unknown in Greek writings (e.g., Plato, *Resp.* 10.614–21; Ovid, *Metam.* 10). Could Jewish stories have developed themes from earlier Greco–Roman narratives? At the very least, the *Odyssey* should be considered because of its early date. On several occasions in *Od.* 11, concern for the living is expressed by the dead (see *Od.*11.370–76; 457–61; cf. Odysseus' request to the spirit of his mother, *Od.* 11.170–79): "And other spirits of those dead and gone stood sorrowing, and each asked of those dear to him" (11.541–42).

1.3.5 THE VALUE OF BURIAL

It is mentioned that Lazarus was "carried away by the angels," perhaps suggesting that he was left unburied by men (cf. Herm. *Vis.* 2.2,7; Herm. *Sim.* 9.27,3; *Od.* 24.186–90; see Fitzmyer 1985, 2:1132).[12] In contrast, there is specific reference to the rich man's burial (16:22). In *Od.* 11, Odysseus' first conversation (51–80) is with his comrade Elpenor who was killed at the house of Circe (*Od.* 10.552–60). A desperate plea (and accompanying warning!) is given by the spirit for a proper burial of his body. Elsewhere in Homer this theme is given similar attention. For example, in the *Illiad* Patroklos appears in a dream to Achilles and complains that he cannot enter hades until he receives proper burial (23.71–74).[13] Jesus' care in mentioning this detail may be a subtle twist; even a proper burial cannot afford peace in the afterlife.

1.3.6 A WISE MAN IN THE AFTERLIFE

Abraham's presence in the afterlife with Lazarus is not surprising. Jewish heroes frequently played a prominent role in such accounts.[14] In the case of Homer's narrative, the visit to the wise Teiresias was the primary reason for the journey to the underworld.

---

[12]Whereas this motif may be hinted at here it is a key part of the Egyptian/Jewish story mentioned above which is often proposed as a parallel. Bauckham notes that in a Jewish context it is unlikely that even a beggar would go unburied (1998, 100 n.7) however in a literary context some license should be allowed to the writer for effect.

[13]For an example of a proper burial see *Od.* 24.35–92. The most illuminating example of such concerns in Greco–Roman literature is found in Sophocles' *Antigone*.

[14]For examples of Jewish legends where key figures like Abraham and Moses visit heaven and hell, see Ginzberg 1909; on texts which "take the form of guided tours" of hell, see Himmelfarb 1985, 45–67.

1.4 THE LAZARUS STORY AS A REWORKED MYTH?

Saul Lieberman explored the frequently accepted view of a rabbinic ban on the study of Greek wisdom (1962, 100–14). While commenting on rabbinic attitudes toward pagan writings is outside the scope of this paper, it is helpful to note that the reading of Homeric texts would not have been forbidden by the Rabbis.[15] Furthermore, there are instances where both Jews (e.g., *t.Abod. Zar* 6.4; *b.Sanh* 63b) and Christians[16] mock the idols described in pagan writings, including Homer. *If* these later traditions reflect anything of the situation of first–century Israel, Lieberman may be correct to suggest "that the contents of Homer's books were well known in certain Jewish circles of Palestine" (1962, 113). Is it possible that Jesus used a familiar story, replete with pagan views of the afterlife, and demythologized its contents? By doing so, he maintained the form of the story but incorporated (true) theological content. Background parallels can then be understood as a vehicle for Jesus' message and the Lord's message itself as a subtle polemic against erroneous views of the afterlife.[17]

Two final considerations should be made. What was Jesus' purpose in appealing to a familiar story to present a warning to the rich, and what type of example is given in Luke 16:19–31? Aristotle defines paradigm (παράδειγμα; example, instance) as including both the historical (παραβολή, parable) and the fictitious (λόγος):

> There are two kinds of examples; namely, one which consists in relating things that have happened before, and another in inventing them oneself (*Rhet.* 2.20.2 [Freese, LCL]).

By things that have happened before the ancients did not think of specific events in actuality—this is paradigm—rather:

> The source of the παραβολή . . . was the generally available world of human observation and experience. They understood it as fiction, i.e., invented by the rhetor to illustrate the point to be made. It did not point to a specific and actual

---

[15]The challenge has been raised that Jews could not have read works with frequent references to the names of idols on the basis of Exod 23:13 (e.g., see Mek. [re. Exod 23:13]). This is also true of later Christian teaching. Tertullian for one followed a similar argument but notice that while he forbade its teachings, he did not forbid studying such texts. See Lieberman's explanation of such injunctions (1962, 111–13).

[16]For example, the Emperor Julian decreed that Christians should not teach classic literature: "Let them first really persuade their pupils that neither Homer nor Hesiod nor any of these writers whom they expounded, and have declared to be guilty of impiety, folly and error in regard to the gods . . ." (*Ep.* 36, 423b; taken from Lieberman 1962, 112–13).

[17]Cf. Bilezikian's study on Mark where he suggests that the structure of the gospel "imitated a compatible model available in contemporary forms of literature," namely the Greek tragedies (1977, 17 and throughout).

case, but generalized by casting its subjects as abstractions (e.g., "nature"), classes (e.g., "farmers"), or indefinite subjects (e.g., "a certain one") (Mack and Robbins 1989, 148; see full discussion, 144–51).

Luke 16:19 and 16:20 employ indefinite pronouns to introduce the protagonists: ἄνθρωπος/πτωχὸς δέ τις. Admittedly the use of a personal name is unique yet, despite claims that this precludes the classification parable (e.g., Summers 1972, 195), it seems just as likely that the name was a play on words.[18]

How is an afterlife experience part of the world of human observation and experience? Perhaps this glimpse into hades was observable in that it was part of a fluid, widespread, literary world. Jesus appealed to a general source—the body of afterlife–experience literature—which may well have been known through a number of different versions. Homer's *Odyssey* was the Greek example *par excellence* and on this basis deserves attention in considerations of the parable.

The intention of this short study has been twofold: to suggest that the background of Jesus' parable should not be limited to a single source by proposing yet another possible parallel to Luke 16:19–31. The parallels described are not so unique as to demand sole attention to the epic for exegesis of the passage. However two considerations must not be overlooked: (1) Homer had an exalted role in rhetorical education. Since this education influenced Luke, the claim that hints of Homeric verse appear in his writings seems like a reasonable conjecture. (2) Homer's influence on similar stories must also be recognized. It seems inappropriate to limit Luke exclusively to Jewish backgrounds given the similarities found in Homer and other Greco–Roman texts.[19]

---

[18]Lazarus was the Greek form of the Hebrew name Eliezar, which is shortened to Lazar in Palestinian usage, and means "the one whom God helps" (Lachs 1987, 314 and 315 n.6). Also, the name may be included simply to help facilitate dialogue.

[19]Cf. Hock (1987). The early church did not seem to make many connections between Scripture and the Homeric texts, perhaps the result of the suspicions described earlier. Lamberton writes: "Origen is the only early Christian author known to me who makes explicit the analogy between the reading of Homer and the reading of the Gospels. He considers it to be largely historically accurate, but to incorporate fantastic elements that are to be interpreted allegorically" (1986:81; see Origen *Cels.* 1.42; 4.38). Dennis R. MacDonald has argued that Homeric literature was imitated by some early Christian authors. In his study of the second Gospel he writes: "the key to Mark's composition has less to do with its genre than with its imitation of specific texts of a different genre: Mark wrote a prose epic modeled largely after the *Odyssey* and the ending of the *Iliad*" (2000:3; cf. his 1994 study of the *Acts of Andrew*).

APPENDIX 2

This appendix provides an illustration of some of the challenges facing historians with respect to the location of texts. It is deliberately less academic in terms of style (due in part to the nature of the subject matter). It is hoped that this section will provide readers with a fresh perspective on what is by now a familiar topic (locating texts). In particular, it examines two areas of concern raised above: first, the *process* of placing texts of unknown origin in a larger historical context, and second, the *evidence used* in that process (including parallels). Furthermore, it explores how various clues gathered in the study of texts can lead readers to very different conclusions.

HOW TO APPROACH A STRANGE MANUSCRIPT:
A NOVEL ('S) LOOK AT THE HISTORICAL TASK[1]

Many obstacles stand in the way of an objective reading of individual NT documents; I will mention just two. First, analyzing a document that is part of a larger collection can be like trying to appreciate the distinctive sound of a lone soprano singing in a mass choir—naturally that single voice blends in with the others. Students of the NT experience something like this the moment they attempt to specialize, to focus on a specific text on its own apart from its canonical roommates (and this would also be true for other religious traditions whose sacred writings incorporate a wide variety of documents by different authors, e.g., Tanak). And while attempts have been made to approach the history of early Christianity without attention to this arbitrary limitation on the evidence (cf. discussion in Räisänen 1990, 100–03), it remains that modern historians have inherited a canon and to divorce one work from this larger group is not so easily done. A second obstacle stems from the fact that scholars are part of a tradition of interpretation.

---

[1]The following appeared in *ARC* 27 (1999):97–107 and has been slightly edited for this context. It is reprinted with permission.

The many opinions about the NT writings that exist invariably influence students in their research. Not surprisingly, labels are often attached to texts on the basis of critical judgments, and so we here terms like deuteropauline, pseudepigraphal, early catholic, and so on. Whether or not such categories do justice to the writings assigned to them is not at issue here. The point is simply that there is a challenge facing the NT scholar who wants to analyze objectively a NT writing on its own merit.

My own research at the present time does not involve one of the stronger voices in the NT choir. If Paul is a lead tenor, if the Gospel writers get the audience to their feet, 2 Peter is among the supporting chorus members, and one that, some feel, occasionally goes out of tune. There are a few reasons why its distinctiveness among the NT writings has not been appreciated. To begin, many assume that it is not the work of the Apostle Peter. As well, it appears to make extensive use of another minor chorus member (i.e., Jude). Finally, not only is 2 Peter less prominent than Paul, some suggest it represents a falling away from those qualities that made Paul such a strong singer in the first place (e.g., Käsemann 1982a; see n.7 below).

This is not the place to discuss any of these issues. What follows is an analogy —one that illustrates the value of silencing the din of such background noises that distract us from the object of our attention. Sometimes that object of study is so closely associated with other documents, or characterized by previous assessments about that writing's merit (or lack thereof), that a new way of looking at the subject matter is needed. Of course, recognizing relationships to other writings is important as well: 2 Peter is part of the Christian canon; source criticism demonstrates a literary relationship to Jude; it can be contrasted in some ways with Paul and other NT texts. These all assist the scholarly analysis of 2 Peter. But before we can make profitable use of comparing and contrasting 2 Peter with other early Christian writings, it is necessary to hear its *distinctive voice*. And so, if only for a moment, it must be removed from these environments and allowed to speak on its own.

In what follows I present a way of imagining the objective, presuppositionless approach to ancient religious texts.[2] My goal is to draw insights from a little–known novel by Canadian author James De Mille (1833–1880), who, in addition to teaching classics, rhetoric, history, and literature at Acadia and Dalhousie Universities, was a prolific writer, with as many as thirty novels to his credit. It is his best known work, *A Strange Manuscript Found in a Copper Cylinder* (published posthumously in 1888), in which we are interested here.[3] It tells the story of four friends aboard a yacht who happen upon a container floating

---

[2]Of course such a thing does not exist but in the realm of imagination we can justify some reflection on an ideal situation (cf. opening comments on p.1 of this book).

[3]According to Parks, writing over twenty years ago, this novel "is at last becoming recognized as a minor classic of Canadian fiction" (1976, 61).

on the water. Inside is found a letter by one Adam More, an Englishman "carried by a series of incredible events to a land from which escape is as impossible as from the grave," and a remarkable narrative telling his story.[4] Intrigued by the discovery, the sailors take turns reading the story out loud to one another—this comprises the bulk of the novel—pausing at various points to provide commentary and speculation with regards to the origin, intention, and meaning of Adam More's tale.

I am by no means a literary critic, and certainly no expert on De Mille's work. My comments do not even address the novel in its entirety, but only those sections where those who found the strange manuscript evaluate its contents, share views on what type of literature it is, and develop theories regarding its origin. And herein lies my interest: the process by which they approach a document of unknown background is not unlike that of the NT scholar (or the student of any ancient text for that matter), who is often confronted with writings providing precious little information regarding date, provenance, and authorship. For this reason, a few notes on De Mille's book may be of interest for those concerned with historical methodology. De Mille's expertise in a variety of areas (languages, history, literature), coupled with his skill as a story teller, provides an interesting vehicle for reflection on this subject.

Since many individual writings in the NT resemble Adam More's story (unknown origin, unknown age), and since the interpretation of this writing by those in the boat has parallels with the speculations of the academic community (is it a hoax? is it true? etc.), I will try to point out how their efforts to understand a strange manuscript provide a heuristic model for imagining the task of the biblical scholar. What is most intriguing of all is that the sailors' analysis of the manuscript lacked preconceived judgments—it literally floated to them while they were adrift at sea (De Mille 1986, 5). Though of course we cannot recreate this in our own analysis of strange manuscripts, we do ourselves a service at times by accepting the objects of our scholarly focus as appearing, as it were, out of nowhere. Before looking at the sailors' strange manuscript, a few more words about those in the NT.

After 'hearing' the voice of an individual writing—i.e., separating it from other voices—there is then a need to locate it within a historical context to the extent that the available data allows and as best we can. Not all NT texts are entirely unknown from the historian's perspective. Paul's writings, for example, can be placed by–and–large in a particular time and context with a fair degree of certainty. But many individual writings are anonymous (e.g., Hebrews) or perhaps even pseudonymous (e.g., 2 Peter). Furthermore, there is not sufficient information about the earliest years of the Christian movement to know precisely where to locate such writings. As a result, when attention turns to individual texts, there is

---

[4]De Mille 1986, 8 (this edition is referred to throughout). A fine biography of De Mille and discussion of his work is available in Monk 1991. See also R. E. Watters' introduction to the McClelland and Stewart edition (1969), and Parks (1976 and his introduction to De Mille 1986 [xvii–lix]).

a need to rely on the very subjective, though still necessary enterprise of reconstructing the context of the work in question. Possible clues are assembled as various questions are asked: What historical events were known to the author? What events, had they been known, would likely have been included by the author? What indications are there of a geographical provenance? What writings did the author know and use? What other writings appear to have been familiar with this document? How does this writing resemble, differ from, show development from, other writings of approximately the same period and subject matter? And so on. Here again I circle back to De Mille's fascinating book. The men in the boat illustrate the process of historical inquiry. In what follows, I will briefly describe various steps they take when they happen upon Adam More's story, and comment on their methodology.

In this story Lord Featherstone, owner of the yacht called the *Falcon*, takes a few of his friends on a cruise to the southern latitudes as he had grown "weary of life in England" (1). In discussing the strange manuscript, their individual areas of expertise are brought to light: Dr. Congreve is well–learned in such diverse areas as geography, palaeontology, and botany; Noel Oxenden, "late of Trinity College, Cambridge," is a linguist; Otto Melick, the most sceptical of the bunch, is a *littérateur* from London. Featherstone himself, we are told, had "plenty of brain if he chose to make use of it" (60) though he seems content to listen to good stories and usually remains neutral in his conclusions (e.g., 155).[5] In their conversations about the discovery,[6] these wide–ranging talents are employed in the analysis of the strange manuscript.

1) The first step can be stated briefly. Naturally, as with the study of other manuscripts, the sailors have to consider the *physical evidence*. In doing so, some clues are found that assisted their inquiry. As the copper cylinder which preserved Adam More's writings was pulled from the sea, it is observed that it "must have been floating for ages" (5). Later, it is concluded that the successive layers of barnacles on the cylinder "show a submersion of at least three years, perhaps more" (62). Also, it proves to be significant that the manuscript was written on papyrus, not regular paper. From this, the case for the narrative being an account of actual events is bolstered. As the doctor argues, "You can find but little [papyrus] in existence at the present day. . . . Now, I hold that a sensation novelist would never have thought of papyrus. If he didn't wish to use paper, he could have found a dozen other things" (62–63; cf. 7–9).

The primary physical evidence in the study of the NT and Christian origins is obviously the text. In the case of the NT, however, we are not dealing with the original autographs but with later copies of them. Still, numerous manuscripts

---

[5]Featherstone is the picture of contentment as the story opens: "Suspended between the two masts, in an Indian hammock, lay Featherstone, with a cigar in his mouth and a novel in his hand, which he was pretending to read" (1–2).

[6]The sections with which we are concerned, namely, the analysis of the manuscript, are found on pp. 1–9, 60–71, 143–55, 226–39, and 269.

(many of them fragmentary) have to be reconstructed in order to determine what Paul, or John, or Jude actually said. Only after we have given attention to the physical evidence can we take steps towards interpretation.

2) When first turning to the manuscript itself, the sailors (with the exception of Melick) *take the story at face value*. More's letter of introduction states his reason for writing: "Oh, unknown friend! whoever you are. I entreat you to let this message be made known in some way to my father" (8). For the most part, this motivation is accepted as is the narrative itself (cf. 229). Though some details pose "difficult questions," the doctor remained content to say "I see no reason why it should not be as More says" (69) and again (regarding a point of geography) "I see no reason to disbelieve it" (70).

NT scholars should also show respect to the authors of the primary sources. To automatically assume that Luke's portrait of the church must have been entirely without basis, or to say Paul or Jesus could not have said this or that, casts a shadow of uncertainty on the texts even before they are allowed to speak. With respect to 2 Peter, there has been a tendency to assume that its theological contribution is not significant.[7] However, such a judgment obviously reads the letter in contrast to other writings before listening to 2 Peter on its own. Though the seafarers make comparisons of the strange manuscript with other known writings (see point 3 below), these had no specific connection to Adam More's work and remained only a comparison. In the case of those scholars who measure 2 Peter's worth against Paul (e.g., Käsemann), there is the assumption that Paul represents a legitimate standard. If we let 2 Peter speak for itself, as the sailors were forced to let Adam More speak for himself, we are in a better position to make objective, unbiased assessments.

3) In the opening dialogue, entitled "Scientific Theories and Scepticism" (60–71), Dr. Congreve is unimpressed by Melick's claim that the manuscript is merely a hoax. As part of his response, he moves towards an analysis of *internal evidence*. This involves both the observation that More's geography is accurate and that the presence of some fantastic elements in the story does not imply that the tale is a fiction.[8] In support of the author's accuracy, the doctor employs a tool frequently used in the historical task, namely, the observation of parallels. He points out that Adam More's description of the geography (Antarctica) resembles that of Captain James Clarke Ross, which (conveniently!) the doctor had just read. He begins: "mark the coincidence between Ross's report and More's manuscript" (64–65). By referring to the description of a known explorer, some confirmation of the accuracy of More's presentation is provided.[9] The ensuing discussion allows

---

[7]E.g., Käsemann's well known essay on 2 Peter speaks of it as doing "discredit to its object" (i.e., a defence of the primitive hope of Christ's return; 1982a, 169; cf. 2.2.2).

[8]E.g., regarding a reference to sea–serpents the doctor says: "Some of these so–called fossil animals may have their representatives still living in the remoter parts of the world" (67).

[9]E.g., "I can prove that the statements here are corroborated by those of Captain Ross in his account of that great voyage from which he returned not very long ago" (63). For background

for a few methodological considerations about what can be learned on the basis of parallels between authors.

a) First, Melick proposes that the story may have been written by one of Ross's men who was thrown overboard (65). This would explain the similarities/accuracy More shares with Ross, and supports Melick's theory that the author of the manuscript was a sensation–novelist (61–62, 65).[10] In effect then, Melick proposes that the descriptions of More and Ross were derived from a common situation. His theory was sharply challenged however because it was too difficult to support (65 and throughout).

b) Rather than a shared context, the doctor proves that More's tale must have been independent of Captain Ross. Based on their prior evaluation of the physical evidence (62), he feels confident that "This [the strange manuscript] must have been written at least three years ago, and [therefore] the writer could not have known anything about Ross's discoveries" (65). Independence of the separate accounts is therefore confirmed; Ross and More were describing the same thing without reference to one another.

c) A further parallel is proposed, namely, between More and an American expedition headed by Charles Wilkes. In this case, the parallel is shown to be unfounded as Wilkes was inaccurate. "I believe Wilkes's antarctic continent will some day be penetrated by ships, which will sail for hundreds of miles farther south" (64). In other words, Wilkes did not find a continent as More had done, and therefore the parallel is not legitimate.

De Mille reminds readers that caution in the use of parallels is necessary. One needs to be aware of chronological factors (could this writer have known that one?) before claiming a specific relationship, and to acknowledge that similarities can turn out to be superficial (and therefore prove, or disprove, nothing). As this dissertation has shown, NT studies are marked by frequent appeal to literary parallels. We are reminded that pitfalls exist, and that there is always a need to be aware of alternative explanations for similarities found between one author and another.

4) While respecting the author of the strange manuscript (cf. point 2 above), the doctor also recognized *the limitations of the primary source*. At one point, when asked a certain question about More's narrative, he responds: "Unfortunately, More is not at all close or accurate in his descriptions; he has a decidedly unscientific mind, and so one cannot feel sure" (144). Again later he says that More "is too general in his descriptions. He has not a scientific mind, and he gives but few data" (148). On another occasion, Dr. Congreve simply admits that an

---

information on Ross's expedition, as well as Wilkes' voyage (referred to below), see Malcolm Parks' (ed.) explanatory notes in De Mille 1986, 276–77.

[10]Melick was quick to say: "If I'd been on that expedition I should probably have written it to beguile the time," and again, "The fact is . . . it's not a sailor's yarn at all. No sailor would ever express himself in that way. That's what struck me from the first. It has the ring of a confounded sensation–monger all through" (65).

answer to a question asked is not possible on the basis of the evidence: "It is difficult to make it out accurately . . . . More gives no data" (65).

NT scholarship on the other hand has not been so willing to admit that at times conclusions must be reserved. Speculation in the form of elaborate hypotheses has become a common way of making the evidence say more than is there. The reserve of the sailors with respect to speculation is a splendid model for NT scholars who possess so little in the way of evidence.[11] We also find in the sailors' analysis of internal evidence the initial assumption that the simplest explanation is probably the best one (as in the previous note).[12]

5) The good historian knows how to *ask good questions*. While one must respect the evidence, it is still entirely appropriate to raise questions based on this evidence. In contrast to the optimistic tenor of much of the discussion regarding the manuscript, Melick's reservations stand out—in Featherstone's words, he is "a professional cynic, sceptic, and scoffer" (145). He is the first to voice an opinion ("it's a transparent hoax," 61), and throughout the novel De Mille uses him as a foil to set–up further reasons in support of authenticity. We see this in the doctor's response to the view just mentioned: "you've a very vivid imagination [Melick]; but come, let us discuss this for a little while in a common–sense way" (61). So even though Melick's negative stance is regularly dismissed, it serves an important role in the structure of the novel, and indeed allows the narrative to move forward (meaning the narrative of the sailors' conversations, not the novel as a whole). But scepticism can be taken too far, and De Mille seems to cast Melick in a negative light in this regard. He becomes the odd man out when "the others evidently sympathized with the doctor's view, and regarded Melick as carrying his scepticism to an absurd excess" (70).

There is no shortage of examples that could be cited from NT research of scepticism carried to an "absurd excess."[13] But it remains, nonetheless, that constant questioning forces the discipline to fine–tune its methods, and to move forward only with great caution toward larger reconstructions of the early church. There is such a thing as a healthy scepticism even if, like those interrupted by Melick, some may find repeated challenges to surface–level readings of the data a little wearying.

6) Touching on all the previous comments is the issue of *genre*, and at this point the disagreements between Oxenden and Congreve, on the one hand, and Melick, on the other, surface most clearly. Being confident that the manuscript

---

[11]Commenting on the climate described, we see the doctor's reluctance to venture into the realm of theory: "In answer to that we must leave ascertained facts and trust to theories, unless, indeed, we accept as valid the statements of this remarkable manuscript. For my own part, I see no reason why it should not be as More says" (69).

[12]On the need to avoid excessive historical speculation, see Wisse 1992.

[13]A dramatic illustration is found in those occasional scholars who question whether Jesus ever actually existed (e.g., Arthur Drews [1865–1935] and William Benjamin Smith [1850–1934]).

describes actual events, the former two tend to focus on arguments justifying individual details: geographical accuracy, scientific explanations, proposals explaining the existence of a civilization at the south pole, and so on. But Melick takes the story as a whole and calls attention to similarities with other literature. At one point he offers the following objection: "I simply criticise from a literary point of view, and I don't like his underground cavern with the stream running through it. It sounds like one of the voyages of Sinbad the Sailor. Nor do I like his description; he evidently is writing for effect" (66).

In taking this route toward an explanation, Melick looks for the author's motive (to write a sensation–novel)[14] and his means of achieving this end (imitating conventions of such writings). This is developed throughout the debate. While criticizing the literary skills of the author, Melick again refers to the author's intentions:

> His plan is one thing and his execution quite another. His plan is not bad, but he fails utterly in his execution. The style is detestable.[15] If he had written in the style of a plain seaman, and told a simple unvarnished tale, it would have been all right. In order to carry out properly such a plan as this the writer should take Defoe as his model, or, still better, Dean Swift. *Gulliver's Travels* and *Robinson Crusoe* show what can be done in this way, and form a standard by which all other attempts must be judged. But this writer is tawdry; he has the worst vices of the sensational school—he shows everywhere marks of haste, gross carelessness, and universal feebleness (228).

By placing this writing in a literary tradition or genre, the case for authenticity is, by Melick's reasoning, sharply undermined.[16]

Melick also finds in the story "a good deal of quiet satire" (226) and a "perpetual undercurrent of meaning and innuendo . . . found in every line" (227), which implies the deliberate, creative work of the author, not the simple presentation of facts Oxenden suggests in the same conversation.

7) Needless to say, a group of people looking at the same evidence will often reach *different conclusions*. This is seen in a delightful exchange between two of the sailors.

> "Do you mean to say that you still accept all this as *bona fide*?" "Do you mean to say," retorted Oxenden, "that you still have any doubt about the authenticity of this remarkable manuscript?" At this each looked at the other; Melick elevated his

---

[14]Once the story was discovered and gained attention, the author would then come forward and take credit for his creation—so argues Melick. "Some fellow wanted to get up a sensation novel and introduce it to the world with a great flourish of trumpets, and so he has taken this way of going about it . . . . he has counted on its being picked up, and perhaps published" (61).

[15]A playful self–critique by De Mille?

[16]The influence of these and other writers on De Mille is discussed by Parks (1976, 64–66, 74, 77 n.11 and [as ed.] De Mille 1986, 301) and Woodcock (1973).

eyebrows, and Oxenden shrugged his shoulders; but each seemed unable to find words to express his amazement at the other's stupidity, and so they took refuge in silence (229).

But are their conclusions (and ours) reached on the basis of the evidence, or on the basis of presuppositions brought to the historical task? R. E. Watters (1969, xvii) summarizes the various views held by the sailors as follows: "The four men who find the manuscript disagree about how to classify it: a sensational novel, a satirical romance, a scientific romance, a satire on humanity, a plain narrative of facts, are all suggested in turn." This being the case, it becomes imperative that the historian be aware of presuppositions and prejudices being brought to the evidence. "Every reader," continues Watters, "like the four who retrieved the manuscript, may readily discover his [or her] own interests and values reflected in the *Copper Cylinder*." Of course, what is true of sailors is equally true of NT scholars.

In what has been considered, De Mille's novel reminds us that the historian's encounter with a manuscript of uncertain origin represents an adventure. In Featherstone's words, "By Jove! . . . this is really getting to be something tremendous" (1986, 25). De Mille also reminds us that while some steps in the quest for answers are profitable, others are less constructive. But the key point I would like to make is this: our questioning, our analysis, our exploration of origins, must begin with the text itself, not (often theoretical) contexts. Some might question this, but it remains that we lack certain evidence of a specific context for many early Christian writings (such as 2 Peter). What is usually offered instead are hypothetical scenarios. Good as some of these may be, they are still just hypotheses. If we allow them to shape our conclusions before we listen to the text itself, we are already listening to the choir, not the individual singer we want to hear.

Historians also resemble sailors on other levels. No final conclusions are reached by the four friends, a state of affairs students of the NT often have to accept. As seen, limitations on the historical task are imposed by scant evidence, but human nature being what it is imposes others as well: "That's enough for to–day," says Featherstone, in the closing words of this story, "I'm tired and can't read any more. It's time for supper" (269).

APPENDIX 3[17]

WHAT CONSTITUTES A PARALLEL?	
3.1.1	Quotations or summary of or reference to a writing where use of a source is acknowledged by the author (and known to the modern reader)
3.1.2	Unidentified but precise borrowing: Use of a source is not acknowledged by the author but recognized by modern readers
3.1.3	Imprecise borrowing where the identification of sources is relatively certain to modern readers but not acknowledged by the ancient author
3.1.4	Incidental similarities between texts that are too imprecise to posit borrowing

---

[17]Appendices 3–7 are intended to summarize briefly the arguments made in ch. 3. Each list touches on issues related to the use of parallels in historical study.

APPENDIX 4

	FACTORS THAT LEND WEIGHT TO ARGUMENTS CLAIMING THAT PARALLELS ARE DUE TO LITERARY DEPENDENCE	
3.2.1	Length of parallel sections
3.2.2	Clustering of parallels
3.2.3	Parallels appearing in the same order
3.2.4	Striking parallels
3.2.5	An author strays from usual patterns of writing
3.2.6	Awkward editing may signal use of a source
3.2.7	Editorial habits evident in one text appear in another
3.2.8	Similarities in the wider context of the two texts in addition to the parallel(s) in question (cf. 3.3.8)
3.2.9	Scholarly consensus

APPENDIX 5

COMPLICATIONS WITH SOURCE THEORIES: FACTORS THAT WEAKEN CLAIMS OF LITERARY DEPENDENCE, LEAD TO MISTAKEN CLAIMS OF LITERARY DEPENDENCE, OR OBSCURE REAL DEPENDENCE	
3.3.1	The suspected source could not have been available to the proposed borrower
3.3.2	An author may have deliberately obscured use of a source for a variety of reasons
3.3.3	The parallel may be explained by an intermediary source
3.3.4	A parallel may represent the influence of an early text on the wider genre in which a later author is writing
3.3.5	Authorial creativity may mean that an author's work is unlike other literature in his or her environment
3.3.6	The modern reader may be guided by presuppositions that make the discovery of parallels desirable or undesirable
3.3.7	Appeal to similarity in atmosphere runs the risk of oversimplification
3.3.8	Claims of text dependence are weakened if there is little similarity in the content of the two writings being compared
3.3.9	The absence of parallels

APPENDIX 6

CONCLUSIONS POSSIBLE ON THE BASIS OF PARALLELS	
3.4.1	Direct dependence
3.4.2	Common authorship
3.4.3	Use of a common source
3.4.4	Deliberate imitation
3.4.5	Origin in a school
3.4.6	A shared milieu

APPENDIX 7

	PARALLELS THAT ARE NOT RELIABLE FOR REACHING CONCLUSIONS ABOUT DEPENDENCY	
3.5.1	Parallels between texts possibly resulting from common use of an earlier source
3.5.2	Widely attested parallels
3.5.3	Arguments based on style or typical writing/thought patterns
3.5.4	Parallels based on suspect translation, or interpretation of difficult passages, or on what appears to be extensive redaction
3.5.5	Parallels based on texts where there are unresolved textual difficulties

APPENDIX 8

RICHARD HAYS' CRITERIA FOR DETERMINING THE PRESENCE OF AN INTERTEXTUAL ECHO (1989, 29–32)

1. Availability	Was the proposed source of the echo available to the author and original readers?
2. Volume	How distinctive or prominent is the precursor text within Scripture (i.e., the source material)?
3. Recurrence	How often does the borrower elsewhere cite or allude to the same Scriptural passage (i.e., the source material)?
4. Thematic Coherence	How well does the alleged echo fit into the line of argument that the borrowing author is developing?
5. Historical Plausibility	Could the borrowing author have intended the alleged meaning effect? Could the readers have understood it?[18]
6. History of Interpretation	Have other interpreters heard the same echoes?
7. Satisfaction	Does the proposed reading make sense? Does it illuminate the surrounding discourse? Does it produce for the reader a satisfying account of the effect of the intertextual relation?

---

[18]Hays adds that it is possible that Paul wrote things that were not understood by his readers (1989, 30).

WORKS CONSULTED

Abbott, Edwin A. 1882. On the Second Epistle of St. Peter: I. Had the Author Read Josephus? *Expositor* 2:49–63.

Abrams, M. H. et al. eds. 1987. *The Norton Anthology of English Literature.* 5th ed. New York: W.W. Norton & Company.

Albertz, Rainer. 1994. *From the Exile to the Maccabees.* Vol. 2 of *A History of Israelite Religion in the Old Testament Period.* Translated by John Bowden. Louisville: Westminster.

Alexander, Loveday C. A. 1992. Schools, Hellenistic. Pages 1005–11 in vol. 5 of *Anchor Bible Dictionary.* Edited by David Noel Freedman et al. 6 vols. New York: Doubleday.

Alexander, Patrick H. et al. eds. 1999. *The SBL Handbook of Style: For Ancient Near Eastern, Biblical, and Early Christian Studies.* Peabody, Mass.:Hendrickson.

Apostolic Fathers. 1952. *The Apostolic Fathers.* LCL. Translated by Kirsopp Lake. Cambridge: Harvard University Press.

Aristotle. 1926. *Ars Rhetorica.* LCL. Translated by John Henry Freese. Cambridge: Harvard University Press.

Balz, Horst, and Wolfgang Schrage. 1973. *Die "Katholischen" Briefe.* DNTD. Göttingen: Vandenhoeck and Ruprecht.

Barker, Glenn W., William L. Lane, and J. Ramsey Michaels. 1969. *The New Testament Speaks.* New York: Harper & Row.

Barnett, Albert E. 1941. *Paul Becomes a Literary Influence.* Chicago: University of Chicago Press.

Bauckham, Richard J. 1983. *Jude, 2 Peter.* WBC 50. Waco, Texas: Word Books.

———. 1997. 2 Peter. Pages 923–27 in *Dictionary of the Later New Testament & Its Developments.* Edited by Ralph P. Martin and Peter H. Davids. Downers Grove, Ill.: InterVarsity.

———. 1982. 2 Peter: A Supplementary Bibliography. *JETS* 25:91–93.

———. 1988a. 2 Peter: An Account of Research. *ANRW* 2.25.5:3713–52.

———. 1994. The Apocalypse of Peter: A Jewish Christian Apocalypse from the Time of Bar Kokhba. *Apocrypha* 5:7–111.

———. 1988b. The Apocalypse of Peter: An Account of Research. *ANRW* 2.25.6:4712–50.

———. 1998. *The Fate of the Dead: Studies on the Jewish and Christian Apocalypses.* NovTSup 93. Leiden: Brill.

Bauer, Walter. 1971. *Orthodoxy and Heresy in Earliest Christianity.* Edited by Robert A. Kraft and Gerhard Krodel. Translated by a team from the Philadelphia Seminar on Christian Origins. Philadelphia: Fortress.

162 THE SIGNIFICANCE OF PARALLELS

Baur, F. C. 1831. Die Christuspartei in der korinthischen Gemeinde, der Gegensatz des petrinischen und paulinischen Christenthums in der ältesten Kirche, der Apostel Petrus in Rom. *Tübinger Zeitschrift für Theologie* 4:61–206.

Berger, Klaus. 1994. *Theologiegeschichte des Urchristentums: Theologie des Neuen Testaments.* Tübingen–Basel: Francke.

Bernstein, Alan E. 1993. *The Formation of Hell: Death and Retribution in the Ancient and Early Christian Worlds.* Ithaca and London: Cornell.

Best, Ernest. 1971. *1 Peter.* NCB. London: Marshall, Morgan & Scott.

Bettenson, Henry, ed. 1943. *Documents of the Christian Church.* London: Oxford University Press.

Bigg, Charles. 1901. *A Critical and Exegetical Commentary on the Epistles of St. Peter and St. Jude.* ICC. Edinburgh: T & T Clark.

Bilezikian, Gilbert C. 1977. *The Liberated Gospel: A Comparison of the Gospel of Mark and Greek Tragedy.* Grand Rapids: Baker.

Blum, Edwin A. 1981. 2 Peter. Pages 25–89 in vol. 12 of *The Expositor's Bible Commentary.* Edited by Frank E. Gaebelein et al. 12 vols. Grand Rapids: Zondervan.

Boobyer, G. H. 1959. The Indebtedness of 2 Peter to 1 Peter. Pages 34–53 in *New Testament Essays: Studies in Memory of Thomas Walter Manson.* Edited by A. J. B. Higgins. Manchester: University of Manchester Press.

Boring, M. Eugene, Klause Berger, and Carsten Colpe, eds. 1995. *Hellenistic Commentary to the New Testament.* Translated by M. Eugene Boring. Nashville: Abingdon.

Boswell, James. 1965. *Life of Johnson.* London: Oxford University Press.

Bouchat, Robert Alan. 1992. Dating the Second Epistle of Peter. Ph.D. dissertation, Baylor University.

Bousset, Wilhelm. 1926. *Die Religion des Judentums im späthellenistischen Zeitalter.* Edited by H. Gressmann. 3d ed. Tübingen: Mohr.

Brawley, Robert L. 1995. *Text to Text Pours Forth Speech: Voices of Scripture in Luke–Acts.* Bloomington and Indianapolis: Indiana University Press.

Brown, Raymond E. 1997. *An Introduction to the New Testament.* ABRL. New York: Doubleday.

Bultmann, Rudolf. 1963. *The History of the Synoptic Tradition.* Translated by John Marsh. New York: Harper & Row.

Caffin, B. C. 1983. The Second Epistle General of Peter. Pages i(–xvi)–91 in vol. 22 of *The Pulpit Commentary.* Edited by H. D. M. Spence and Joseph S. Exell. 23 vols. Repr., Grand Rapids: Eerdmans.

Carson, D. A., Douglas J. Moo and Leon Morris. 1992. *An Introduction to the New Testament.* Grand Rapids: Zondervan.

Carter, Jeffrey R. 1998. Description is not Explanation: A Methodology of Comparison. *MTSR* 10:133–48.

Cavallin, H. C. C. 1979. The False Teachers of 2 Pt as Pseudo–Prophets. *NovT* 21:263–70.

Chaine, Joseph. 1939. *Les épîtres catholiques: La seconde épître de saint Pierre, les épîtres de saint Jean, l'épître de saint Jude.* Ebib. 2d ed. Paris: J. Gabalda.

Chance, J. Bradley and Milton P. Horne. 2000. *Rereading the Bible: An Introduction to the Biblical Story.* Upper Saddle River: Prentice Hall.

Charles, J. Daryl. 1999. The Function of Moral Typology in 2 Peter. Paper presented at the annual meeting of the SBL. Boston Nov. 20.

———. 1998. The Language and Logic of Virtue in 2 Peter 1:5–7. *BBR* 8:55–73.

———. 1997. *Virtue amidst Vice: The Catalog of Virtues in 2 Peter 1.* JSNTSup 150. Sheffield: Sheffield Academic Press.

Charlesworth, James Hamilton. 1985. *The Old Testament Pseudepigrapha and the New*

Testament: Prolegomena for the Study of Christian Origins. Cambridge: Cambridge University Press.

Chase, F. H. 1898–1904. Peter, Second Epistle of. Pages 796–818 in vol. 3 of *A Dictionary of the Bible*. Edited by J. Hastings. 5 vols. Edinburgh: T & T Clark.

Chester, Andrew and Ralph P. Martin. 1994. *The Theology of the Letters of James, Peter, and Jude*. New Testament Theology. Edited by James D. G. Dunn. Cambridge: Cambridge University Press.

Childs, Brevard S. 1984. *The New Testament Canon: An Introduction*. Philadelphia: Fortress.

Crehan, J. 1982. New Light on 2 Peter from the Bodmer Papyrus. *SE* 7:145–49.

Crossan, John Dominic. 1998. *The Birth of Christianity: Discovering What Happened in the Years Immediately After the Execution of Jesus*. New York: HarperSanFrancisco.

———. 1991. *The Historical Jesus: The Life of a Mediterranean Jewish Peasant*. New York: HarperSanFrancisco.

Culpepper, R. Alan. 1975. *The Johannine School: An Evaluation of the Johannine–School Hypothesis Based on an Investigation of the Nature of Ancient Schools*. SBLDS 26. Missoula, Montana: Scholars Press.

Dalton, William J. 1979. The Interpretation of 1 Peter 3,19 and 4,6: Light from 2 Peter. *Bib* 60:547–55.

Danker, Frederick W. 1962. II Peter 3:10 and Psalm of Solomon 17:10. *ZNW* 53:82–86.

Davids, Peter H. 1993. The Pseudepigrapha in the Catholic Epistles. Pages 228–45 in *The Pseudepigrapha and Early Biblical Interpretation*. JSPSup 14. Edited by James H. Charlesworth and Craig A. Evans. Sheffield: JSOT Press.

Deissmann, Adolph. 1988. *Bible Studies: Contributions Chiefly from Papyri and Inscriptions to the History of the Language, the Literature, and the Religion of Hellenistic Judaism and Primitive Christianity*. Translated by Alexander Grieve. Repr., Peabody, Mass.: Hendrickson.

———. 1995. *Light From the Ancient Near East: The New Testament Illustrated by Recently Discovered Texts of the Graeco–Roman World*. Translated by Lionel R. M. Strachan. Repr., Peabody, Mass: Hedrickson.

De Mille, James. 1986. *A Strange Manuscript Found in a Copper Cylinder*. Edited by Malcolm Parks. Ottawa: Carleton University Press.

Denaux, Adelbert. 1996. Review of Leif E. Vaage, *Galilean Upstarts: Jesus' First Followers According to Q*. *JBL* 115:136–38.

Dibelius, Martin and Hans Conzelmann. 1972. *The Pastoral Epistles*. Hermeneia. Translated by Philip Buttolph and Adela Yarbro. Philadelphia: Fortress.

Dillenseger, P. J. 1907. L'authenticité de la IIᵃ Petri. *Mélanges de la faculté orientale de l'université Saint Joseph, Beyrouth* 2:173–212.

Donaldson, T. L. 1983. Parallels: Use, Misuse and Limitations. *EvQ* 55:193–210.

Donfried, Karl P. 1974. *The Setting of Second Clement in Early Christianity*. NovTSup 38. Leiden: Brill.

Dowd, Sharyn. 1992. 2 Peter. Page 373 in *The Women's Bible Commentary*. Edited by Carol A. Newsom and Sharon H. Ringe. London: SPCK.

Dunn, James D. G. 1997. Pseudepigraphy. Pages 977–84 in *Dictionary of the Later New Testament & Its Development*. Edited by Ralph P. Martin and Peter H. Davids. Downers Grove, Ill.: InterVarsity.

———. 1990. *Unity and Diversity in the New Testament: An Enquiry into the Character of Earliest Christianity*. 2d ed. London: SCM.

Dunnett, Walter M. 1988. The Hermeneutics of Jude and 2 Peter: The Use of Ancient Jewish Traditions. *JETS* 31:287–92.

Dylan, Bob. 1985. *Lyrics: 1962–1985*. New York: Alfred A. Knopf.

Ebright, Homer Kingsley. 1917. *The Petrine Epistles: A Critical Study of Authorship*. Cincinnati: Methodist Book Concern.

Ehrman, Bart D. 1997. *The New Testament: A Historical Introduction to the Early Christian Writings*. New York: Oxford University Press.

Elliott, John H. 1969. A Catholic Gospel: Reflections on 'Early Catholicism' in the New Testament. *CBQ* 31:213–23.

———. 1992. Peter, Second Epistle of. Pages 282–87 in vol. 5 of *Anchor Bible Dictionary*. Edited by David Noel Freedman et al. 6 vols. New York: Doubleday.

Ellis, E. Earle. 1992. Pseudonymity and Canonicity of New Testament Documents. Pages 212–24 in *Worship, Theology and Ministry in the Early Church: Essays in Honor of Ralph P. Martin*. Edited by Michael J. Wilkins and Terence Paige. Sheffield: Sheffield Academic Press.

Evans, Craig A., Robert L. Webb, and Richard A. Wiebe, eds. 1993. *Nag Hammadi Texts and the Bible*. Leiden: Brill.

Falconer, R. A. 1902. Is 2 Peter a Genuine Epistle to the Christians of Samaria? *Expositor* 6.5:459–72; 6.6: 47–56, 117–27, 218–27.

Farkasfalvy, Denis. 1985. The Ecclesial Setting of Pseudepigraphy in Second Peter and its Role in the Formation of the Canon. *SecCent* 5:3–29.

Farrar, F. W. 1888. Dr. Abbott on the Second Epistle of St. Peter and Josephus. *Expositor* 3:58–69.

Ferguson, Everett. 1993. *Backgrounds of Early Christianity*. 2d ed. Grand Rapids: Eerdmans.

Fitzmyer, J. A. 1985. *The Gospel According to Luke (X–XXIV)*. AB. New York: Doubleday.

Fornberg, Tord. 1977. *An Early Church in a Pluralistic Society: A Study of 2 Peter*. ConBNT 9. Lund: C. W. K. Gleerup.

Fuchs, E. and P. Reymond. 1980. *La deuxième épître de Saint Pierre – L'épître de Saint Jude*. CNT 13b. 2ème série. Paris/Neuchâtel: Delachaux and Niestle.

Garnet, Paul. 1973. O'Callaghan's Fragments: Our Earliest New Testament Texts? *EvQ* 45:6–12.

Gilmour, Michael J. 1999a. Hints of Homer in Luke 16:19–31? *Didaskalia* 10:23–33.

———. 1999b. How to Approach a Strange Manuscript: A Novel('s) Look at the Historical Task. *ARC* 27:97–107.

———. 1999c. 2 Peter in Recent Research: A Bibliography. *JETS* 42:673–78.

———. 2001. Reflections on the Authorship of 2 Peter. *EvQ* 73:291–309.

Ginzberg, L. 1909. *The Legends of the Jews*. Philadelphia: Jewish Publication Society.

Green, Michael. 1987. *2 Peter and Jude*. Rev. ed. Tyndale. Leicester, England: InterVarsity.

———. 1960. *2 Peter Reconsidered*. London: Tyndale.

Gressmann, H. 1918. *Vom reichen Mann und armen Lazarus: eine literargeschichtliche Studie*. Abhandlungen der königlich preussischen Akademie der Wissenschaften: Philosophisch–historische Klasse 7. Berlin: Verlag der königlich Akademie der Wissenschaft.

Grobel, K. 1963–64. '. . . Whose Name Was Neves'. *NTS* 10:373–382.

Gunkel, Hermann. 1903. *Zum religionsgeschichtlichen Verständnis des Neuen Testament*. Göttingen: Vandenhoeck & Ruprecht.

Guthrie, Donald. 1990. *New Testament Introduction*. 4th ed. rev. Downers Grove, Ill.: InterVarsity Press.

Harnack, A. von. 1897. *Die Chronologie der altchristlichen Litteratur bis Eusebius*. Vol. 2 of *Geschichte der altchristlichen Litteratur bis Eusebius*. Leipzig: J. C. Hinrichs.

———. 1958. *What is Christianity?* Translated by Thomas Bailey Saunders. London: Ernest Benn.

Harrington, Daniel J. 1973. Review of Martin McNamara, *Targum and Testament*. *CBQ*

35:253–54.

Harvey, A. E. 1990. The Testament of Simeon Peter. Pages 339–54 in *A Tribute to Geza Vermes: Essays on Jewish and Christian Literature and History*. JSOTSup 100. Edited by Philip R. Davies and Richard T. White. Sheffield: Sheffield Academic Press.

Hauer, Christian E. and William A. Young. 2001. *An Introduction to the Bible: A Journey into Three Worlds*. 5th ed. Upper Saddle River, N.J.: Prentice Hall.

Haulotte, Edgar. 1974. Review of James M. Robinson and Helmut Koester, *Trajectories through Early Christianity*. *Bib* 55:112–17.

Hays, Richard B. 1989. *Echoes of Scripture in the Letters of Paul*. New Haven and London: Yale University Press.

Henderson, Ian H. 1995. Style–Switching in the Didache: Fingerprint or Argument? Pages 177–209 in *The Didache in Context: Essays on Its Text, History, and Transmission*. NovTSup 77. Edited by Clayton N. Jefford. Leiden: Brill.

Hengel, Martin. 1974. *Judaism and Hellenism*. Translated by John Bowden. London: SCM.

Hennecke, Edgar, and Wilhelm Schneemelcher, eds. 1965. *New Testament Apocrypha*. Translated by R. McL. Wilson. 2 vols. Philadelphia: Westminster.

Henry, Patrick. 1979. *New Directions in New Testament Study*. Philadelphia: Westminster.

Hiebert, D. Edmond. 1989. *Second Peter and Jude: An Expositional Commentary*. Greenville, S.C.: Unusual Publications.

Hills, Julian V. 1991. Parables, Pretenders and Prophecies: Translation and Interpretation in the Apocalypse of Peter 2. *RB* 4:560–73.

Hillyer, Norman. 1992. *1 and 2 Peter, Jude*. NIBCNT 16. Peabody, Mass.: Hendrickson.

Himmelfarb, Martha. 1983. *Tours of Hell: An Apocalyptic Form in Jewish and Christian Literature*. Ithaca and London: Cornell.

Hock, R. F. 1987. Lazarus and Micyllus: Greco–Roman Backgrounds to Luke 16:19–31. *JBL* 106:448–55.

Homer. 1919. *The Odyssey*. LCL. Translated by A. T. Murray. London: Heinemann.

Hübner, Hans. Review of Klaus Berger, *Theologiegeschichte des Urchristentums: Theologie des Neuen Testaments*. *Review of Theological Literature* 1:36–46.

Hupper, W. G. 1980. Additions to 'A 2 Peter Bibliography.' *JETS* 23:65–66.

Hurtado, Larry W. 1988. *One God, One Lord: Early Christian Devotion and Ancient Jewish Monotheism*. Philadelphia: Fortress.

James, M. R. 1911. A New Text of the Apocalypse of Peter. *JTS* 12:36–54, 157, 362–83, 73–83.

———. 1924. *The Apocryphal New Testament*. Oxford: Oxford University Press.

Jeremias, Joachim. 1972. *The Parables of Jesus*. Translated by S. H. Hooke. 2d rev. ed. New York: Scribners.

Johnson, Luke Timothy. 1992. *The Acts of the Apostles*. Sacra Pagina Series 5. Edited by Daniel J. Harrington. Collegeville, Minn.: Liturgical Press.

———. 1989. The New Testament's Anti–Jewish Slander and the Conventions of Ancient Polemic. *JBL* 108:419–41.

———. 1999. *The Writings of the New Testament: An Interpretation*. Rev. ed. Minneapolis: Fortress.

Justin Martyr. 1994. *The Ante–Nicene Fathers*. Edited by Alexander Roberts and James Donaldson. 1885–1887. 10 vols. Repr., Peabody, Mass.: Hendrickson.

Kahmann, Johannes. 1989. The Second Letter of Peter and the Letter of Jude: Their Mutual Relationship. Pages 105–21 in *The New Testament in Early Christianity: La réception des écrits néotestamentaires dans le christianisme primitif*. Edited by Jean–Marie Sevrin. Translated by Peter Judge. Leuven: Leuven University Press.

Karris, Robert J. 1973. The Background and Significance of the Polemic of the Pastoral

Epistles. *JBL* 92:549–64.

Käsemann, Ernst. 1982a. An Apologia for Primitive Christian Eschatology. Pages 165–95 in *Essays on New Testament Themes*. Translated by W. J. Montague. Philadelphia: Fortress.

———. 1982b. The Canon of the New Testament and the Unity of the Church. Pages 95–107 in *Essays on New Testament Themes*. Translated by W. J. Montague. Philadelphia: Fortress.

Kelly, J. N. D. 1969. *A Commentary on The Epistles of Peter and of Jude*. BNTC. Reprint, Peabody, Mass.: Hendrickson.

King, Marchant A. 1964. Jude and 1 and 2 Peter: Notes on the Bodmer Manuscript. *Bsac* 121:54–57.

Kistemaker, Simon. 1973. Review of James M. Robinson and Helmut Koester, *Trajectories through Early Christianity*. *WTJ* 35:338–40.

———. 1987. *Exposition of the Epistles of Peter and of the Epistle of Jude*. NTC. Grand Rapids: Baker.

Klinger, Jerzy. 1973. The Second Epistle of Peter: An Essay in Understanding. Translated Paul Garrett. *St. Vladimir's Theological Quarterly* 17:152–69.

Knight III, George W. 1992. *The Pastoral Epistles*. NIGTC. Grand Rapids: Eerdmans.

Knight, Jonathan. 1995. *2 Peter and Jude*. NTG. Sheffield: Sheffield Academic Press.

Koester, Helmut. 1957. *Synoptische Überlieferung bei den apostolischen Vätern*. TU 65. Berlin: Akademie–Verlag.

———. 1988. Introduction to *The Gospel of Thomas*. Pages 124–26 in *The Nag Hammadi Library*. Edited by James M. Robinson. Leiden: Brill.

Kruger, Michael J. 1999. The Authenticity of 2 Peter. *JETS* 42:645–71.

Kümmel, Werner Georg. 1972. *The New Testament: The History of the Investigation of Its Problems*. Translated by S. McLean Gilmour and Howard C. Kee. London: Abingdon.

———. 1975. *Introduction to the New Testament*. Translated by Howard Clark Kee. Rev. ed. Nashville: Abingdon.

Lachs, Samuel Tobias. 1987. *A Rabbinic Commentary on the New Testament: The Gospel of Matthew, Mark, and Luke*. Hoboken, New Jersey: Ktav.

Lamberton, Robert. 1986. *Homer the Theologian: Neoplatonist Allegorical Reading and the Growth of the Epic Tradition*. Berkeley: University of California Press.

Légasse, Simon. 1996. Review of Klaus Berger, *Theologiegeschichte des Urchristentums*. *Bib* 77:278–81.

Lenhard, Von Hellmut. 1961. Ein Beitrag zur Übersetzung von II Ptr 3 10 d. *ZNW* 52:128–29.

Lenski, R. C. H. 1945. *The Interpretation of the Epistles of St. Peter, St. John and St. Jude*. Columbus, Ohio: Wartburg Press.

Lias, J. J. 1913. The Genuineness of the Second Epistle of St. Peter. *BSac* 70:599–606.

Lieberman, Saul. 1962. *Hellenism in Jewish Palestine*. New York: Jewish Theological Seminary of America.

Lightfoot, J. B. 1989. *The Apostolic Fathers*. Edited and revised by Michael W. Holmes. Translated by J. R. Harmer. 2d ed. Grand Rapids: Baker.

Lindars, Barnabas. 1961. *New Testament Apolegetic: The Doctrinal Significance of the Old Testament Quotations*. London: SCM.

Lindemann, Andreas. 1979. *Paulus im ältesten Christentum: Das Bild des Apostels und die Rezeption der paulinischen Theologie in der frühchristlichen Literatur bis Marcion*. BHT 58. Tübingen: Mohr.

Longenecker, Richard N. 1974. Ancient Amanuenses and the Pauline Epistles. Pages 281–97 in *New Dimensions in New Testament Study*. Edited by Richard N. Longenecker and Merrill C. Tenney. Grand Rapids: Zondervan.

MacDonald, Dennis R. 1994. *Christianizing Homer: "The Odyssey," Plato, and "The Acts of Andrew."* New York: Oxford University Press.

———. 2000. *The Homeric Epics and the Gospel of Mark.* New Haven and London: Yale University Press.

Mack, Burton L. and Vernon K. Robbins. 1989. *Patterns of Persuasion in the Gospels.* Sonoma, California: Polebridge.

MacKenzie, Robert K. 1987. Revelation: A Jewish/Christian Book? *ARC* 15:51–60.

———. 1997. *The Author of the Apocalypse: A Review of the Prevailing Hypothesis of Jewish–Christian Authorship.* Mellen Biblical Press Series 51. Lewiston: Mellen Biblical Press.

Marshall, I. Howard. 1974. 'Early Catholicism' in the New Testament. Pages 217–31 in *New Dimensions in New Testament Study.* Edited by Richard N. Longenecker and Merrill C. Tenney. Grand Rapids: Zondervan.

———. 1978. *Commentary on Luke: A Commentary on the Greek Text.* NIGTC. Grand Rapids: Eerdmans.

———. 1985. Review of Richard J. Bauckham, *Jude, 2 Peter. EvQ* 57:78.

Martin, R. A., and John H. Elliott. 1982. *James, I–II Peter, Jude.* ACNT. Minneapolis: Augsburg.

Martin, R. P. 1993a. Early Catholicism. Pages 223–25 in *Dictionary of Paul and His Letters.* Edited by Gerald F. Hawthorne and Ralph P. Martin. Downers Grove, Ill.: InterVarsity Press.

———. 1993b. Hymns, Hymn Fragments, Songs, Spiritual Songs. Pages 419–23 in *Dictionary of Paul and His Letters.* Edited by Gerald F. Hawthorne and Ralph P. Martin. Downers Grove, Ill.: InterVarsity Press.

Marxsen, W. 1968. *Introduction to the New Testament.* Philadelphia: Fortress.

Maurer, C. 1965. Apocalypse of Peter. Pages 663–68 in vol. 2 of *New Testament Apocrypha.* Edited by Edgar Hennecke and Wilhelm Schneemelcher. Translated by R. McL. Wilson. 2 vols. Philadelphia: Westminster.

Mayor, Joseph B. 1907. *The Epistle of St. Jude and the Second Epistle of St. Peter.* London: Macmillan.

McNamara, M. 1960. The Unity of Second Peter: A Reconsideration. *Scr* 12:13–19.

Meade, David G. 1986. *Pseudonymity and Canon: An Investigation into the Relationship of Authorship and Authority in Jewish and Earliest Christian Tradition.* Grand Rapids: Eerdmans / Tübingen: J. C. B. Mohr (Paul Siebeck).

Meeks, Wayne A. 1983. *The First Urban Christians: The Social World of the Apostle Paul.* New Haven and London: Yale University Press.

Metzger, Bruce M. 1971. *A Textual Commentary on the Greek New Testament.* London: United Bible Society.

———. 1968. Methodology in the Study of the Mystery Religions and Early Christianity. Pages 1–24 in *Historical and Literary Studies: Pagan, Jewish and Christian.* Leiden: Brill.

———. 1992. *The Text of the New Testament: Its Transmission, Corruption, and Restoration.* 3d ed. New York: Oxford University Press.

Meyer, Ben F. 1986. *The Early Christians: Their World Mission and Self–Discovery.* Good News Studies 16. Wilmington, Delaware: Michael Glazier.

Michl, Johann. 1968. *Die Katholischen Briefe.* Regensburg: Pustet.

Miller, Robert J. 1996. Is There Independent Attestation for the Transfiguration in 2 Peter? *NTS* 42:620–25.

Moffatt, James. 1911. *An Introduction to the Literature of the New Testament.* International Theological Library. New York: Charles Scribner's Sons.

Monk, Patricia. 1991. *The Gilded Beaver: An Introduction to the Life and Work of James De Mille.* Toronto: ECW Press.

Moo, Douglas J. 1996. *2 Peter and Jude*. The NIV Application Commentary. Grand Rapids: Zondervan.

Moore, G. F. 1921. Christian Writers on Judaism. *HTR* 14:227–54.

Moule, C. F. D. 1977. *The Origin of Christology*. Cambridge: Cambridge University Press.

———. 1982. *The Birth of the New Testament*. 3d rev. ed. San Francisco: Harper & Row.

Mounce, Robert H. 1982. *A Living Hope: A Commentary on 1 and 2 Peter*. Grand Rapids: Eerdmans.

Neufeld, K. H. 1972. 'Frühkatholizismus'–Idee und Begriff. *ZKT* 94:1–28.

Neyrey, Jerome H. 1977. The Form and Background of the Polemic in 2 Peter. Ph.D. dissertation, Yale University.

———. 1980a. The Apologetic Use of the Transfiguration in 2 Peter 1:16–21. *CBQ* 42:505–19.

———. 1980b. The Form and Background of the Polemic in 2 Peter. *JBL* 99:407–31.

———. 1993. *2 Peter, Jude: A New Translation with Introduction and Commentary*. AB 37. New York: Doubleday.

Oberforcher, Robert. 1996. Review of Klaus Berger, *Theologiegeschichte des Urchristentums*. *ZKT* 118:265–67.

Osburn, Carroll D. 1992. Discourse Analysis and Jewish Apocalyptic in the Epistle of Jude. Pages 287–319 in *Linguistics and New Testament Interpretation: Essays on Discourse Analysis*. Edited by David Alan Black. Nashville: Broadman.

Packer, J. I. 1958. *'Fundamentalism' and the Word of God*. InterVarsity Press.

Palmer, Spencer J., Roger R. Keller, Dong Sull Choi, and James A. Toronto. 1997. *Religions of the World: A Latter–day Saint View*. Rev. and enl. ed. Provo, Utah: Brigham Young University.

Parks, M. G. 1976. Strange to Strangers Only. *Canadian Literature* 70:61–78.

Pearson, Birger A. 1969. A Reminiscence of Classical Myth at II Peter 2.4. *GRBS* 10:71–80.

———. 1989. James, 1–2 Peter, Jude. Pages 371–406 in *The New Testament and its Modern Interpreters*. Edited by Eldon Jay Epp and George W. MacRae. Philadelphia: Fortress / Atlanta: Scholars Press.

———. 1990. The Apocalypse of Peter and Canonical 2 Peter. Pages 67–74 in *Gnosticism and the Early Christian World: In Honor of James M. Robinson*. Edited by J. E. Goehring et al. Sonoma: Polebridge.

Perkins, Pheme. 1995. *First and Second Peter, James, and Jude*. Interpretation. Louisville: John Knox.

Perrin, Norman and Dennis C. Duling. 1982. *The New Testament: An Introduction: Proclamation and Parenesis, Myth and History*. 2d. ed. New York: HBJ.

Pettem, Michael. 1987. Matthew: Jewish Christian or Gentile Christian? *ARC* 15:30–37.

Picirilli, Robert E. 1988. Allusions to 2 Peter in the Apostolic Fathers. *JSNT* 33:57–83.

Plumptre, E. H. 1892. *The General Epistles of St Peter and St Jude*. CGTSC. Cambridge: Cambridge University Press.

Porter, Stanley E. 1995. Pauline Authorship and the Pastoral Epistles: Implications for Canon. *BBR* 5:105–23.

Praeder S. M. 1984. Acts 27:1–28:16: Sea Voyages in Ancient Literature and the Theology of Luke–Acts. *CBQ* 46:683–706.

Prümm, K. 1929. De genuino Apocalypsis Petri textu, Examen testium iam notorum et novi fragmenti Raineriani. *Bib* 10:62–80.

Quintilian. 1920. *Institutio Oratoria*. LCL. Translated by H. E. Butler. Cambridge: Harvard University Press.

Räisänen, Heikki. 1990. *Beyond New Testament Theology*. London: SCM Press.

Reicke, Bo. 1964. *The Epistles of James, Peter, and Jude*. AB. Garden City, N.Y.: Doubleday.

Riesner, R. 1984. Der zweite Petrus–Brief und die Eschatologie. Pages 124–43 in *Zukünftserwartung in biblischer Sicht: Beiträge zur Eschatologie*. Edited by G. Maier. Wuppertal: Brockhaus.

Robinson, James M., gen. ed. 1988. *The Nag Hammadi Library*. Rev. ed. Leiden: Brill.

Robinson, James M. and Helmut Koester. 1971. *Trajectories through Early Christianity*. Philadelphia: Fortress.

Robinson, John A. T. 1976. *Redating the New Testament*. London: SCM Press.

Robinson, Tom. 1990. From the Apostolate to the Episcopate: Reflections on Development. Pages 225–50 in *Self–Definition and Self–Discovery in Early Christianity: A Study in Changing Horizons: Essays in Appreciation of Ben F. Meyer from Former Students*. Edited by David J. Hawkins and Tom Robinson. Lewiston: Edwin Mellen.

Robson, E. I. 1915. *Studies in the Second Epistle of St Peter*. Cambridge: Cambridge University Press.

Rosenblatt, Marie–Eloise. 1994. 2 Peter. Pages 399–405 in vol. 2 of *Searching the Scriptures: A Feminist Introduction/Commentary*. Edited by Elisabeth Schüssler Fiorenza. New York: Crossroad.

Rowston, Douglas J. 1974–1975. The Most Neglected Book in the New Testament. *NTS* 21:554–63.

Russell, D. S. 1964. *The Method and Message of Jewish Apocalyptic*. Philadelphia: Westminster.

Sanders, E. P., and Margaret Davies. 1989. *Studying the Synoptic Gospels*. London: SCM / Valley Forge, PA: Trinity.

Sandmel, Samuel. 1962. Parallelomania. *JBL* 81:1–13.

Schelkle, K. H. 1961. *Die Petrusbriefe, der Judasbrief*. HTKNT 13. Freiburg: Herder.

Schmidt, David Henry. 1972. The Peter Writings: Their Redactors and Their Relationships. Ph.D. dissertation, Northwestern University.

Schulz, S. 1976. *Die Mitte der Schrift: der Frühkatholizismus im Neuen Testament als Herausforderung an den Protestantismus*. Stuttgart: Kreuz Verlag.

Selvidge, Marla J. 1999. *The New Testament: A Timeless Book for all Peoples*. Upper Saddle River, N.J.: Prentice Hall.

Selwyn, Edward Gordon. 1952. *The First Epistle of St. Peter*. London: Macmillan.

Sidebottom, E. M. 1967. *James, Jude, 2 Peter*. NCBC. Grand Rapids: Eerdman / London: Marshall, Morgan & Scott.

Smith, Terence V. 1985. *Petrine Controversies in Early Christianity: Attitudes Towards Peter in Christian Writings of the First Two Centuries*. WUNT 15. Tübingen: Mohr.

Snyder, J. A. 1979. A 2 Peter Bibliography. *JETS* 22:265–67.

Soards, Marion L. 1988. 1 Peter, 2 Peter and Jude as Evidence for a Petrine School. *ANRW* 2.25.5:3828–44.

Spicq, C. 1966. *Les Epîtres de Saint Pierre*. SB. Paris: Gabalda.

Spitta, F. 1885. *Der zweite Brief des Petrus und der Brief des Judas*. Halle a. S.: Verlag der Buchhandlung des Waisenhauses.

Stendahl, Krister. 1976. *Paul Among Jews and Gentiles: And Other Essays*. Philadelphia: Fortress.

Stoutenburg, Dennis. 1996. *With One Voice / B'Qol Echad: The Sermon on the Mount and Rabbinic Literature*. San Francisco / London / Bethesda: International Scholars Press.

Summers, R. 1972. *Commentary on Luke*. Waco, Texas: Word Books.

The Church of Jesus Christ of Latter–day Saints. 1996. *Our Heritage: A Brief History of The Church of Jesus Christ of Latter–day Saints*. Salt Lake City, Utah: The Church of Jesus Christ of Latter–day Saints.

The Watch Tower Bible and Tract Society. 1988. *Revelation: Its Grand Climax At Hand!*. Brooklyn: Watchtower Bible and Tract Society of New York.

————. 1990. *"All Scripture Is Inspired of God and Beneficial."* Brooklyn: Watchtower Bible and Tract Society of New York.

Thiede, C. P. 1986. A Pagan Reader of 2 Peter: Cosmic Conflagration in 2 Peter 3 and the OCTAVIUS of Minucius Felix. *JSNT* 26:79–96.

Thurén, Lauri. 1997. Hey Jude! Asking for the Original Situation and Message of a Catholic Epistle. *NTS* 43:451–65.

————. 1996. Style Never Goes Out of Fashion: 2 Peter Re–Evaluated. Pages 329–47 in *Rhetoric, Scripture and Theology: Essays from the 1994 Pretoria Conference.* JSNTSup 131. Edited by Stanley E. Porter and Thomas H. Olbricht. Sheffield: Sheffield Academic Press.

Tuckett, C. M. 1983. 1 Corinthians and Q. *JBL* 102:607–19.

————. 1987. *Reading the New Testament: Methods of Interpretation.* Philadelphia: Fortress.

————. 1989. Synoptic Tradition in the Didache. Pages 197–230 in *The New Testament in Early Christianity / La réception des écrits néo–testamentaires dans le christianisme primitif.* BETL 86. Edited by J. –M. Sevrin. Louvain: Louvain University Press.

Vielhauer, P. 1975. *Geschichte der urchristlichen Literatur: Einleitung in das Neue Testament, die Apokryphen und die Apostolischen Väter.* Berlin–New York: Walter de Gruyter.

Wall, Robert W. 1995. Pauline Authorship and the Pastoral Epistles: A Response to S. E. Porter. *BBR* 5:125–28.

Wilson, Stephen G. "Gentile Judaizers." *NTS* 38 (1992): 605–16.

Von Allmen, D. 1966. L'apocalyptique juive et le retard de la parousie en II Pierre 3:1–13. *RTP* 16:255–74.

Waltner, Erland and J. Daryl Charles. 1999. *1–2 Peter, Jude.* Believers Church Bible Commentary. Edited by Elmer A. Martens and Willard M. Swartley. Scottdale, Pa.: Herald Press.

Ward, Vanessa Oliver. 1988. Addenda [to Marion Soards' 1 & 2 Peter, Jude: Evidence for a Petrine School]. *ANRW* 2.25.5:3844–49.

Watson, Duane F. 1988. *Invention, Arrangement, and Style: Rhetorical Criticism of Jude and 2 Peter.* SBLDS 104. Atlanta: Scholars Press.

Watters, R. E. 1969. Introduction to *A Strange Manuscript Found in a Copper Cylinder.* Toronto: McClelland and Stewart.

Wenham, David. 1987. Being 'Found' on the Last Day: New Light on 2 Peter 3.10 and 2 Corinthians 5.3. *NTS* 33:477–79.

Werdermann, H. 1913. *Die Irrlehrer des Judas–und 2. Petrusbriefes.* BFCT 17. Gütersloh: C. Bertelsmann.

White, L. Michael. 1985–1986. Adolf Harnack and the 'Expansion' of Early Christianity: A Reappraisal of Social History. *SecCent* 5:97–127.

Wilson, R. McL. 1972. Review of James M. Robinson and Helmut Koester, *Trajectories through Early Christianity. JTS* 23:475–77.

Windisch, Hans. 1951. *Die katholischen Briefe.* HNT 15. Edited by H. Preisker. 3d ed. Tübingen: Mohr.

Wisse, Frederik. 1972. The Epistle of Jude in the History of Heresiology. Pages 133–43 in *Essays on the Nag Hammadi Texts in Honour of Alexander Böhlig.* Nag Hammadi Studies III. Edited by Martin Krause. Leiden: Brill.

————. 1992. Historical Method and the Johannine Community. *ARC* 20:35–42.

Wolff, Richard. 1960. *A Commentary on the Epistle of Jude.* Grand Rapids: Zondervan.

Wolters, Al. 1987. Worldview and Textual Criticism in 2 Peter 3:10. *WTJ* 49:405–13.

————. 1990. 'Partners of the Deity': A Covenantal Reading of 2 Peter 1:4. *CTJ* 25:28–44.

Woodcock, George. 1973. De Mille and the Utopian Vision. *Journal of Canadian Fiction* 2:174–79.

Wright, N. T. 1996. *Jesus and the Victory of God*. Vol. 2 of *Christian Origins and the Question of God*. Minneapolis: Fortress.

Young, Frances. 1994. *The Theology of the Pastoral Letters*. New Testament Theology. Edited by James D. G. Dunn. Cambridge: Cambridge University Press.

Zahl, Paul F. M. 1998. A Tribute to Ernst Käsemann and a Theological Testament. *Anglican Theological Review* 80:382–94.

Zahn, Theodor. 1953. *Introduction to the New Testament*. Translated by John Moore Trout, et al. 3 vols. Grand Rapids: Kregal.

INDEX OF MODERN AUTHORS